ISBN: 9781290904988

Published by:
HardPress Publishing
8345 NW 66TH ST #2561
MIAMI FL 33166-2626

Email: info@hardpress.net
Web: http://www.hardpress.net

HISTORY

OF THE

INDUCTIVE SCIENCES,

FROM THE

EARLIEST TO THE PRESENT TIME.

BY WILLIAM WHEWELL, D.D.,

MASTER OF TRINITY COLLEGE, CAMBRIDGE.

A NEW EDITION, REVISED AND CONTINUED.

IN THREE VOLUMES.

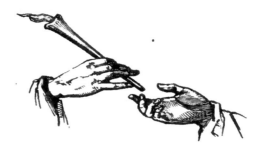

Λαμπάδια ἔχοντες διαδώσουσιν ἀλλήλοις.

VOLUME THE FIRST.

LONDON:

JOHN W. PARKER, WEST STRAND.

M.DCCC.XLVII.

TO

SIR JOHN FREDERICK WILLIAM HERSCHEL,

K. G. H.

My DEAR HERSCHEL,

It is with no common pleasure that I take up my pen to dedicate these volumes to you. They are the result of trains of thought which have often been the subject of our conversation, and of which the origin goes back to the period of our early companionship at the University. And if I had ever wavered in my purpose of combining such reflections and researches into a whole, I should have derived a renewed impulse and increased animation from your delightful Discourse on a kindred subject. For I could not have read it without finding this portion of philosophy invested with a fresh charm; and though I might be well aware that I could not aspire to that large share of popularity which your work so justly gained, I should still have reflected, that something was due to the subject itself, and should have hoped that my own aim was so far similar to yours, that the present work might have a chance of exciting an interest in some of your readers. That it will interest you, I do not at all hesitate to believe.

If you were now in England I should stop here: but when a friend is removed for years to a far distant land,

a 2

we seem to acquire a right to speak openly of his good qualities. I cannot, therefore, prevail upon myself to lay down my pen without alluding to the affectionate admiration of your moral and social, as well as intellectual excellencies, which springs up in the hearts of your friends, whenever you are thought of. They are much delighted to look upon the halo of deserved fame which plays round your head; but still more, to recollect, as one of them said, that your head is far from being the best part about you.

May your sojourn in the southern hemisphere be as happy and successful as its object is noble and worthy of you; and may your return home be speedy and prosperous, as soon as your purpose is attained.

Ever, my dear Herschel, Yours,

22 *March*, 1837.   W. WHEWELL.

P. S. So I wrote nearly ten years ago, when you were at the Cape of Good Hope, employed in your great task of making a complete standard survey of the nebulæ and double stars visible to man. Now that you are, as I trust, in a few weeks about to put the crowning stone upon your edifice by the publication of your " Observations in the Southern Hemisphere," I cannot refrain from congratulating you upon having had your life ennobled by the conception and happy execution of so great a design, and once more offering you my wishes that you may long enjoy the glory you have so well won.

W. W.

TRINITY COLLEGE,
Nov. 22, 1846.

PREFACE

THE demand for a new edition of my *History of the Inductive Sciences* imposes upon me the welcome duty of correcting the mistakes and supplying some of the deficiencies of the former edition. In doing this, I have for the most part made only slight changes in the text, and such as were required to rectify absolutely erroneous assertions. I have not even altered the references to the time and circumstances which were present when I formerly wrote, but have reserved for Notes the notices of subsequent events, and the other additions which I thought necessary. I have followed this plan, as the best, both for the reader and the subject.

Those who already know the work, if they wish again to refer to it, will naturally think of it such as it is, and not such as I might make it by writing it afresh. To attempt to incorporate with the former narrative of the progress of each science, a view of its most recent advance, would really be to write each portion of the history from a new

point of view, and thus, to write a new work, not
to publish a new edition.

I have, however, in Notes at the end of each
Book, given an account of some of the most important recent advances in each subject, considered as
an Inductive Science. I introduce this limitation,
because it is my justification, as well in the present
as in the former edition, for the omission of many
topics which are of great interest, both in a practical and in a scientific view, but which are applications of discoveries already made, not steps towards
discovery ;—deductive results of laws of nature, not
inductions of such laws from observation. This was
my reason for passing over such inventions as
printing and porcelain, glass and gunpowder, steam-
boats and rail-roads, gas-lighting and chemical
bleaching, in the former edition ; this is my excuse
for saying nothing now of photography, the electric
telegraph, and other striking recent inventions. I
have omitted, for like reasons, many remarkable
inventions, still more directly bearing upon the
progress of science, as Daniel's galvanic battery,
and the very ingenious battery of Mr. Grove. Even
implements of scientific research, if we are not able
to bring into view the points to which they lead,
cannot be put in their place in the history of

science; just as in a history of a present war, those military operations of which the aim and effect are yet unknown, cannot be rightly narrated.

From this cause, it can hardly happen but that such a work as this must fail to give to some distinguished contemporary labourers in the field of science the pre-eminence and lustre which their activity and intelligence merit; because their labour is not yet crowned by its result. For such cases, my office is like writing the story of Columbus while he was still sailing westwards. So far as I have ventured to deal with lines of scientific research at present incomplete, what I have to offer is rather a discussion of principles than a narrative of facts; and accordingly, such discussions, on several points now in question, will be found in the *Philosophy of the Inductive Sciences;*—sufficient, I hope, to show that I have stopped where I have, out of no want of sympathy with the ulterior progress of knowledge.

In correcting the errours of the work, I have availed myself of all the critiques of the former edition which have come under my notice, without regard to the spirit in which they were written, whether hostile or friendly. I have not noticed such criticism in any other way than by thus using it. A series of controversial Notes would have been of little value to the reader; and I trust my critics will be content without further acknowledgment of the assistance which I have derived from them. Those who wrote kindly will, I am sure, willingly bestow upon me this additional kindness; and if any have criticized me in another temper, I hope they will not be sorry to see that I have no wish to perpetuate our hostilities.

But it is only justice to the work to say that the errours which required correction were neither numerous (considering its extent,) nor fundamental. And there is one circumstance which gives me a hope that this essay may have some permanent value. The attempt to throw the histories of all the Sciences into Inductive Epochs, each Epoch having its Prelude and its Sequel, and thus to combine the persons and the events which fill these histories into intelligible groups, was, so far as I know, new. To these Epochs, as they are selected and presented in this work, I have seen no objection made; and it would seem, therefore, to be generally allowed that the Epochs here marked out, are the cardinal points of scientific history. Nor have I seen any complaint (with one exception, of slight importance, but fully noticed in this edition,) that the principal figures in each Epoch are not properly chosen. I have had, therefore, little to alter, either in the general outline or in the detail of the work.

The German translator of this History, the late Director of the Imperial Observatory at Vienna, M. Littrow, has added to his translation, besides other valuable notes, a biographical notice of each of the persons mentioned in the work. But though these additions are very interesting, they did not belong to the plan of the work as I had conceived it, and would have greatly augmented its bulk. I have, therefore, with a few exceptions, omitted them.

I have not introduced any new branches of science into this edition, and on this account, among others, I have said nothing of the recent progress of Organic Chemistry. The discoveries which are alleged to have been made in that department will require to have many intermediate steps clearly marked and fairly established, before they can stand by the side of Historical Chemistry as examples of Inductive Science. Still less have I attempted to introduce any notice of recent steps in the sciences which I have more especially termed *Organic*, as Zoology and Physiology. I am aware that the study of the nervous system, for instance, has been prosecuted with highly interesting results. But I never pretended to do more than give some examples of the historical progress of this subject, and shall not presume to carry the account further than I have already done.

I do not deviate from my original plan in thus limiting my narrative. For, as was formerly stated, the main object of the work was to present such a survey of the advances already made in physical knowledge, and of the mode in which they have been made, as might serve as a real and firm basis for our speculations concerning the progress of human knowledge, and the processes by which sciences are formed. And an attempt to frame such speculations on this basis was made in the *Philosophy of the Inductive Sciences*, which was published shortly after this History. To that work I must refer, for a further explanation of any views respecting the nature and progress of science which may here appear defective or obscure. It is my intention to prepare for the press a new edition of the work, as soon as I shall have finished the preparation of the present publication.

I add a Postscript, containing a notice of a few points in the history of science which have come into view during the printing of the following pages.

POSTSCRIPT TO THE SECOND EDITION.

(1). The planet exterior to Uranus, of which the existence was inferred by M. Le Verrier and Mr. Adams from the motions of Uranus (vol. II. Note (L)), has since been discovered. This confirmation of calculations founded upon the doctrine of universal gravitation, may be looked upon as the most remarkable event of the kind since the return of Halley's comet in 1757; and in some respects, as a more striking event even than that; inasmuch as the new planet had never been seen at all, and was discovered by mathematicians entirely by their feeling of its influence, which they perceived through the organ of mathematical calculation.

There can be no doubt that to M. Le Verrier belongs the glory of having first published a prediction of the place and appearance of the new planet, and of having thus occasioned its discovery by astronomical observers. M. Le Verrier's first prediction was published in the *Comptes Rendus de l'Acad. des Sciences*, for *June* 1, 1846, (not *Jan.* 1, as erroneously printed in my Note.) A subsequent paper on the subject was read Aug. 31. The planet was seen by M. Le Galle, at the Observatory of Berlin, on September 23, on which day he had received an

express application from M. Le Verrier, recommending him to endeavour to recognize the stranger by
its having a visible disk.   Professor Challis, at the
Observatory of Cambridge, was looking out for the
new planet from July 29, and saw it on Aug. 4, and
again on Aug. 12, but without recognizing it, in
consequence of his plan of not comparing his observations till he had accumulated a greater number
of them.   On Sept. 29, having read for the first time
M. Le Verrier's second paper, he altered his plan,
and paid attention to the physical appearance rather
than the position of the star.   On that very evening,
not having then heard of M. Le Galle's discovery, he
singled out the star by its seeming to have a disk.

M. Le Verrier's mode of discussing the circumstances of Uranus's motion, and inferring the new
planet from these circumstances, is in the highest
degree sagacious and masterly.   Justice to him
cannot require that the contemporaneous, though
unpublished, labours of Mr. Adams of St. John's
College, Cambridge, should not also be recorded.
Mr. Adams made his first calculations to account
for the anomalies in the motion of Uranus, on the
hypothesis of a more distant planet, in 1843[1].   At

---

[1] Mr. Adams informs me that as early as 1841 he conjectured
the existence of a planet exterior to Uranus, and recorded in a

first he had not taken into account the earlier Greenwich observations; but these were supplied to him by the Astronomer Royal, in 1844. In September, 1845, Mr. Adams communicated to Prof. Challis values of the elements of the supposed disturbing body; namely, its mean distance, mean longitude at a given epoch, longitude of perihelion, eccentricity of orbit, and mass. In the next month, he communicated to the Astronomer Royal values of the same elements, somewhat corrected. The note, p. 306, vol. II., of the present work, in which the names of MM. Le Verrier and Adams are mentioned in conjunction, was in the press in August, 1846, a month before the planet was seen. As I have stated in the text, Mr. Adams and M. Le Verrier assigned to the unseen planet nearly the same position; they also assigned to it nearly the same mass; namely, $2\frac{1}{2}$ times the mass of Uranus. And hence, supposing the density to be not greater than that of Uranus, it followed that the visible diameter

memorandum his design of examining its effect: but deferred the calculation till he had completed his preparation for his examintion in January 1843. He was the *Senior Wrangler* on that occasion. The *conjecture* of an exterior planet was not quite new. It had occurred to Mr. Hussey, M. Alexis Bouvard, and and M. Hansen, as early as 1834. See Mr. Airy's *Account* read to the Royal Astronomical Society, Nov. 13, 1846.

would be about 3″, an apparent magnitude not much smaller than Uranus himself.

M. Le Verrier has mentioned for the new planet the name *Neptunus;* and probably, deference to his authority as its discoverer will obtain general currency for this name.

(2). To the account of Tables of the Sun, Moon, and Planets, given vol. II. p. 304, I may add a notice of an important volume recently published; *Reductions of the Observations of Planets made at the Royal Observatory, Greenwich, from* 1750 *to* 1830, (1845). These Reductions were made under the superintendence of the Astronomer Royal, the computations being executed by order of the Lords of the Treasury, and published by order of the Lords of the Admiralty. The volume contains the observations reduced and compared with Lindenau's Tables of Mercury, Venus, and Mars, and with Bouvard's Tables of Jupiter, Saturn, and Uranus. The object of the work is stated to be (*Introd.* p. xxx.) "the comparison of a long series of observed places with theoretical places, computed by means of the same fundamental elements (duly corrected for perturbation) throughout." The ultimate end contemplated by such a work is the correction of the fundamental elements of the planetary motions.

(3). Upon a reconsideration of Mr. Airy's Treatise *On Tides and Waves*, I am no longer disposed to say, as I have said vol. ii. p. 311, that for the actual case of the distribution of land and water, nothing has been done to bring the hydrodynamical theory of oceanic tides into agreement with observation. In this admirable work, Mr. Airy has, by peculiar artifices, solved problems which come so near the actual cases that they may represent them. He has, in this way, deduced the laws of the semi-diurnal and the diurnal tide, and the other features of the tides which the equilibrium theory in some degree imitates; but he has also, taking into account the effect of friction, shown that the actual tide may be represented as the tide of an earlier epoch;—that the relative mass of the moon and sun, as inferred from the tides, would depend upon the depth of the ocean (Art. 455);—with many other results remarkably explaining the observed phenomena. He has also shown that the relation of the cotidal lines to the tide waves really propagated is, in complex cases, very obscure, because different waves of different magnitudes, travelling in different directions, may coexist, and the cotidal line is the compound result of all these.

(4). Page 509. Mr. Airy's explanation of the phenomena termed by Sir D. Brewster a *new property of light*, is completed in the *Philosophical Magazine* for Nov. 1846. It is there shown that a dependence of the breadth of the bands upon the aperture of the pupil, which had been supposed to result from the theory, and which does not appear in the experiment, did really result from certain limited conditions of the hypothesis, which conditions do not belong to the experiment; and that when the problem is solved without those limitations, the discrepance of theory and observation vanishes: so that, as Mr. Airy says, "this very remarkable experiment, which long appeared inexplicable, seems destined to give one of the strongest confirmations to the Undulatory Theory."

TRINITY COLLEGE, CAMBRIDGE,
November 7, 1846.

PREFACE TO THE FIRST EDITION.

At the present day, any endeavour to improve and extend the Philosophy of Science may hope to excite some interest. All persons of cultivated minds will agree, that a very important advantage would be gained, if any light could be thrown upon the modes of discovering truth, the powers that we possess for this end, and the points to which these may most profitably be applied. Most men, too, will allow, that in these respects much remains to be done. The attempts of this kind, made from time to time, are far from rendering future efforts superfluous. For example, the Great Reform of Philosophy and Method, in which Bacon so eloquently called upon men to unite their exertions in his day, has, even in ours, been very imperfectly carried into effect. And, even if his plan had been fully executed, it would now require to be pursued and extended. If Bacon had weighed well all that Science had achieved in his time, and⁻ had laid down a complete scheme of rules for scientific research, so far as they could be collected from the lights of that age, it would still be incumbent upon the philosophical world to augment as well as preserve the inheritance which he left; by combining with his doctrines such new views as the advances of later times cannot fail to produce or suggest; and by endeavouring to provide, for every kind of truth, methods of research as effective

as those to which we owe the clearest and surest
portions of our knowledge.   Such a renovation and
extension of the reform of philosophy appears to
belong peculiarly to our own time.   We may discern
no few or doubtful presages of its approach ; and an
attempt to give form and connexion to the elements
of such a scheme cannot now be considered pre-
mature.

The *Novum Organon* of Bacon was suitably
ushered into the world by his *Advancement of Learning ;* and any attempt to continue and extend his
Reform of the Methods and Philosophy of Science
may, like his, be most fitly preceded by, and founded
upon, a comprehensive Survey of the existing state
of human knowledge.   The wish to contribute something, however little it may be, to such a Reform,
gave rise to that study of the History of Science of
which the present Work is the fruit.   And the effect
of these researches has been, a persuasion, that we
need not despair of seeing, even in our own time,
a renovation of sound philosophy, directed by the
light which the History of Science sheds.   Such a
reform, when its Epoch shall arrive, will not be the
work of any single writer, but the result of the intellectual tendencies of the age.   He who is most forward in the work will wisely repeat the confession
of his sagacious predecessor : Ipse certè (ut ingenue
fatear) soleo æstimare hoc opus magis pro partu Tem-
poris quàm Ingenii.

To such a work, whensoever and by whomsoever
executed, I venture to hope that the present Volumes
may be usefully subservient.   But I trust, also, that

in its independent character, as a History, this book may be found not altogether unworthy of the aim which its title implies.

It is impossible not to see that the writer of such a history imposes upon himself a task of no ordinary difficulty and delicacy ; since it is necessary for him to pronounce a judgment upon the characters and achievements of all the great physical philosophers of all ages, and in all sciences. But the assumption of this judicial position is so inevitably involved in the functions of the historian (whatever be his subject), that he cannot justly be deemed presumptuous on that account. It is true, that the historian of the progress of science is required by his undertaking to judge of the merits of men, in reference to subjects which demand a far intenser and more methodical study than the historian of practical life gives to the actions of which he treats ; and the general voice of mankind,—which may often serve as a guide, because it rarely errs widely or permanently in its estimate of those who are prominent in public life,—is of little value when it speaks of things belonging to the region of exact science. But to balance these disadvantages, and to enable us to judge of the characters who must figure in our history, we may recollect that we have before us, not the record only of their actions, but the actions themselves ; for the acts of a philosopher are his writings. We do not receive his exploits on tradition, but by sight ; we do not read of him, we read him. And if I may speak of my own grounds of trust and encouragement in venturing on such a task, I knew that my life had

been principally spent in those studies which were
most requisite to enable me to understand what had
thus been done; and I had been in habits of intercourse with several of the most eminent men of science
of our time, both in our own and in other countries.
Having thus lived with some of the great intellects of
the past and the present, I had found myself capable
of rejoicing in their beauties, of admiring their endowments, and, I trusted, also, of understanding their
discoveries and views, their hopes and aims. I did
not, therefore, turn aside from the responsibility
which the character of the Historian of Science imposed upon me. I have not even shrunk from it
when it led me into the circle of those who are now
alive, and among whom we move. For it seemed to
me that to omit such portions of the history as I
must have omitted to avoid thus speaking of my
contemporaries, would have left my work mutilated
and incomplete; and would have prevented its forming a platform on which we might stand and look
forward into the future. I trusted, moreover, that
my study of the philosophers of former times had
enabled me to appreciate the discoveries of the present, and that I should be able to speak of persons
now alive, with the same impartiality and in the same
spirit as if they were already numbered with the great
men of the past. Seeking encouragement in these
reflections, and in the labour and thought which I was
conscious of having bestowed upon my task, I have
conducted my history from the earliest ages of the
speculative world up to our own days.

To some persons it may appear that I am not

justified in calling *that* a History of *the* Inductive Sciences, which contains an account of the progress of the *physical* sciences only. But it would have conveyed a false impression of my purpose, had I described my history in any manner which implied that the sciences which it embraces are partially selected or arbitrarily limited. Those of which the progress is exhibited in the present volumes, appear to me to form a connected and systematic body of knowledge. And if there be branches of knowledge which regard Morals, or Politics, or the Fine Arts, and which may properly be called Inductive (an opinion which I by no means gainsay) ; still it must be allowed, I think, that the processes of collecting general truths from assemblages of special facts, and of ascending from propositions of a limited to those of a larger generality, which the term *Induction* peculiarly implies, have hitherto been far more clearly exhibited in the physical sciences which form the subject of the present work, than in those hyperphysical sciences to which I have not extended my history. I will further add, that if I should be enabled hereafter to lay before the world a view of the Philosophy of Inductive Science in its general bearings, it will be requisite, in order to exhibit, in its due light the state of the philosophy of morals, or art, or any similar subject, to give a view of the steps by which it has reached its present position ; and thus such a work will supply that which some may judge wanting to fill up the outline of this historical undertaking.

As will easily be supposed, I have borrowed

largely from other writers. both of the histories of special sciences and of philosophy in general *. I have done this without scruple, since the novelty of my work was intended to consist, not in its superiority as a collection of facts, but in the point of view in which the facts were placed I have, however, in all cases, given references to my authorities, and there are very few instances in which I have not verified the references of previous historians, and studied the original authors. According to the plan which I have pursued, the history of each science forms a whole in itself, divided into distinct but connected members, by the *Epochs* of its successive advances. If I have satisfied the competent judges in each science by my selection of such epochs, the scheme of the work must be of permanent value, however imperfect may be the execution of any of its portions.

With all these grounds of hope, it is still impossible not to see that such an undertaking is, in no small degree, arduous, and its event obscure. But all who venture upon such tasks must gather trust

---

¹ Among these, I may mention as works to which I have peculiar obligations, Tennemann's Geschichte der Philosophie, Degerando's Histoire Comparée des Systèmes de Philosophie, Montucla's Histoire des Mathématiques, with Delalande's continuation of it, Delambre's Astronomie Ancienne, Astronomie du Moyen Age, Astronomie Moderne, and Astronomie du Dixhuitième Siécle; Bailly's Histoire d'Astronomie Ancienne, and Histoire d'Astronomie Moderne, Voiron's Histoire d'Astronomie (published as a continuation of Bailly), Fischer's Geschichte der Physik, Gmelin's Geschichte der Chemie, Thomson's History of Chemistry, Sprengel's History of Medicine, his History of Botany, and in all branches of Natural History and Physiology, Cuvier's works, in their historical, as in all other portions, most admirable and instructive.

and encouragement from reflections like those by which their great forerunner prepared himself for his endeavours ;—by recollecting that they are aiming to advance the best interests and privileges of man ; and that they may expect all the best and wisest of men to join them in their aspirations and to aid them in their labours.

" Concerning ourselves we speak not ; but as touching the matter which we have in hand, this we ask ;—that men deem it not to be the setting up of an Opinion, but the performing of a Work ; and that they receive this as a certainty ; that we are not laying the foundations of any sect or doctrine, but of the profit and dignity of mankind :—Furthermore, that being well disposed to what shall advantage themselves, and putting off factions and prejudices, they take common counsel with us, to the end that being by these our aids and appliances freed and defended from wanderings and impediments, they may lend their hands also to the labours which remain to be performed :—And yet, further, that they be of good hope ; neither feign and imagine to themselves this our Reform as something of infinite dimension and beyond the grasp of mortal man, when, in truth, it is, of infinite errour, the end and true limit ; and is by no means unmindful of the condition of mortality and humanity, not confiding that such a thing can be carried to its perfect close in the space of one single age, but assigning it as a task to a succession of generations."

Instaur. Mag. Præf. ad fin.

CONTENTS

OF

THE FIRST VOLUME.

CORRECTIONS.

Vol. I. p. 158, note [45], for *Acronical* read *Acronycal* (ἀκρονυκίος, happening at the extremity of the night).

    p. 315, line 24, *add*, the late Mr. Henderson of the Edinburgh Observatory, also determined the parallax of this star to be 1″.

Vol. II. p. 319, line 16, *for* 1835, *read* 1833.

    p. 500, line 17, *for* Lobeck *read* Seebeck.

INDEX OF PROPER NAMES.

The letters *a*, *b*, *c*, indicate vol. I., vol. II., vol. III., respectively.

INDEX OF TECHNICAL TERMS.

A LETTER

TO THE

AUTHOR OF *PROLEGOMENA LOGICA,*

BY THE

AUTHOR OF THE HISTORY AND PHILOSOPHY OF THE INDUCTIVE SCIENCES.

TRINITY COLLEGE,
Cambridge, Sept. 20, 1852.

DEAR SIR,

The following remarks were principally written a few months ago, when I had first the pleasure of receiving and reading your *Prolegomena Logica*. It appears to me that you, and others who are interested in the subjects which you have discussed in your book, may be willing to attend to the explanations which I have there offered; and I have therefore printed a few copies of the remarks.

I am, dear Sir,

Your obedient humble servant,

W. WHEWELL.

The Rev. H. L. Mansel.

THERE has been something curious in the reception which the philosophy of the German metaphysician Kant has met with in England. One class of persons have their minds fully made up that all "German metaphysics" is mystical and unintelligible, extravagant and absurd; and that Kant is eminently marked with those characteristics. As a representative of this opinion we may take a gentleman who has published "A History of Moral Science" in two volumes, and who writes thus :

"I must confess myself completely ignorant of the *Critical or Transcendental Philosophy* of Emanuel Kant. I have made several attempts to get a glimpse of his system, but have been obliged to give up the undertaking in despair. Talk of scholastic jargon and barbarism ! Why, if it were possible to extract all the verbal jargon of the schools, from the Christian era down to the fifteenth century, into one book, it would come far short of the obscurity of the *Critical Philosophy*. No English reader can form the most distant conception of Kant's writings without he saw them. [*sic*]. But let the reader suppose that every sentence of this book were cut separately out of it, all put into a bag, and well shaken, and then promiscuously taken out one by one, and placed in the form of a book again ; he might then have some faint idea of the *transcendental* opinions of this German writer."

Another author who must be considered as representing a very different degree of culture and thoughtfulness from the one just quoted, still speaks in a manner hardly less disparaging. The temperate and critical Dugald Stewart, in his

Dissertation on the Progress of the Moral Sciences, repeatedly mentions Kant's speculations, and always unfavourably. In note I to Part I. of the Dissertation he says, " In our own times, Kant and his followers seem to have thought that they had thrown a strong light on the nature of *space* and also of *time*, when they introduced the word *form* (*form of the intellect*) as a common term applicable to both. Is not this to revert to the scholastic folly of verbal generalization?" And in Part II. he gives a long and laborious criticism of a portion of Kant's speculations; of which the spirit may be collected from his describing them as resulting in "the metaphysical *conundrum*, that the human mind (considered as a *noumenon* and not as a *phenomenon*) neither exists in space nor time." And after mentioning Meiners and Herder along with Kant, he adds, " I am ashamed to say that in Great Britain the only one of these names which has been much talked of is Kant." And again in Note EE, he translates some portion of the German philosopher, adding, that to the expressions so employed he can attach no meaning.

But notwithstanding the unfavourable judgments of the Kantian doctrines which have thus prevailed both among cultured and uncultured men in this country, there have been other persons who have thought more highly of those doctrines. This estimation, on the part of some of our countrymen, has probably been produced in a great measure by the enduring reputation of Kant in Germany, and the importance which continues to be there ascribed to his views. And the course taken by several English writers, thus favourably disposed to the philosophy of Kant, has been to praise the philosophy in general terms, but to disparage the doctrines of Kant when presented by English writers, in an English dress. For instance, when the *Philosophy of the Inductive Sciences* was published (in 1840), the arguments which Kant employed to shew that space and time are *forms* of our perceptive power (p. 84 and 122) were given, although without adopting that phrase as essential to the doctrine. The arguments thus adopted were stated by translating, almost literally, Kant's own words; yet the author was charged by a Reviewer at the time, with explaining these doctrines "in a manner incompatible with the clear views of Emanuel Kant." It appeared to be assumed by the English admirers of the Kantian philosophy, that Kant's views were true and clear in Germany, but became untenable when adopted in England.

Stewart, in his criticism of Kant's doctrines, remarked that, in asserting that the human mind possesses, in its own ideas, an element of necessary and universal truth, not derived from experience, Kant had been anticipated by Price, by Cudworth, and even by Plato; to whose "Theætetus" both Price and Cudworth refer, as containing views similar to their own. And undoubtedly this doctrine of ideas, as indispensable sources of necessary truths, was promulgated and supported by weighty arguments in the Theætetus; and has ever since been held by many philosophers, in opposition to the contrary doctrine, also extensively held, that all truth is derived from experience. But, in pointing out this circumstance as diminishing the importance of Kant's speculations, Stewart did not sufficiently consider that doctrines, fundamentally the same, may discharge a very different office at different periods of the history of philosophy. Plato's Dialogues did not destroy, nor even diminish, the value of Cudworth's "Immutable Morality." Notwithstanding Cudworth's publications, Price's doctrines came out a little afterwards with the air and with the effect of novelties. Cudworth's assertion of ideas did not prevent the rise of Hume's skepticism; and it was Hume's skepticism which gave occasion to Kant's new assertion of necessary and universal truth, and to his examination into the grounds of the possibility and reality of such truth. To maintain such doctrine *after* the appearance of intermediate speculations, and with reference to them, was very different from maintaining it before; and this is the merit which Kant's admirers claim for him. Nor can it be denied that his writings produced an immense effect upon the mode of treating such questions in Germany; and have had, even in this country, an influence far beyond what Mr Stewart would have deemed their due.

But as injustice has thus been done to Kant by confounding his case with that of his predecessors of like opinions, so on the other hand, injustice has also been done, both to him and those who have followed him in the assertion of ideas, by confounding *their* case with his. This injustice seems to me to be committed by a writer on the History of Philosophy, who has given an account of the successive schools of philosophy up to our own time;—has assigned to Kant an important and prominent place in the recent history of metaphysics;—but has still maintained that Kant's philosophy, and indeed every philosophy, is and must be a failure. In order to prove this thesis, the author naturally has to examine Kant's doctrines and the reasons assigned for them, and to point out what he conceives to be the fallacy of these arguments. This accordingly he professes to do; but as soon as he has entered upon the argument, he substitutes, as his opponent, for the philosopher of Königsberg, a writer of our own time and country, who does not profess himself a Kantian, who has been repeatedly accused, with whatever justice, of misrepresenting what he has borrowed from Kant, and whose main views are, in the opinion of the writer himself, very different from Kant's. Mr Lewes *, in the chapter entitled " Examination of Kant's Fundamental Principles," after a preliminary statement of the points he intends to consider, says " Now to the question. As Kant confessedly was led to his own system by the speculations of Hume," and so on; and forthwith he introduces the name of *Dr Whewell,*

* *Biographical History of Philosophy,* 1846.

as the writer whose views he has to criticize, without stating how he connects him with Kant, and goes on arguing against *him* for a dozen pages to the end of the Chapter.

On the other hand, a still more recent writer has revived the censure of Dr Whewell's speculations as not doing justice to the Kantian philosophy. " It is much to be regretted," he says *, " that Dr Whewell, who has made good use of Kantian principles in many parts of his Philosophy of the Inductive Sciences," has not more accurately observed Kant's distinction between the necessary laws under which all men think, and the contingent laws under which certain men think of certain things. And further on, Mr Mansel, after giving great praise to the general spirit of the *Philosophy of the Inductive Sciences*, says " It is to be regretted that the accuracy of his theory has been in so many instances vitiated by a stumble at the threshold of the Critical Philosophy." Mr Mansel is, indeed, by much the most zealous English Kantian whose writings I have seen ;—among those, I mean, who have brought original powers of philosophical thought to bear upon such subjects; and have not been, as some have been, enslaved by an admiration of German systems, just as bigotted as the contempt of them which I noticed at the beginning of these remarks. And as Mr Mansel has stated distinctly some of the points in which he conceives that I have erred in deviating from the doctrines of Kant, I should wish to make a few remarks on those points. Such speculations will probably not have many readers ; yet the criticisms to which I have already referred show that they have some, and other criticisms of the same kind remain to be noticed as I proceed. Those who attach any importance to the views which have been recently promulgated on these subjects, the author may hope, will be willing that he should explain points in which he conceives himself to have been misunderstood.

* *Prolegomena Logica,* by H. L. Mansel, M.A. 1851.

Kant considers that Space and Time are conditions of perception, and hence, sources of necessary and universal truth. Dr Whewell agrees with Kant in placing in the mind certain sources of necessary truth; he calls these Fundamental Ideas, and reckons, besides Space and Time, others, as Cause, Likeness, Substance, and several more. Mr Mill, the most recent and able expounder of the opposite doctrine, derives all truths from Observation, and denies that there is such a separate source of truth as Ideas. Mr Mansel does not agree either with Mr Mill or Dr Whewell; he adheres to the original Kantian thesis, that Space and Time are sources of necessary truths, but denies the office to the other Fundamental Ideas of Dr Whewell. In reading what has been said by Mr Mill, Mr Mansel, and other critics, on the subject of what I have called *Fundamental Ideas*, I am led to perceive that I have expressed myself incautiously, with regard to the identity of character between the first two of these Fundamental Ideas, namely, Space and Time, and the others, as Force, Composition, and the like. And I am desirous of explaining, to those who take an interest in these speculations, how far I claim for the other Fundamental Ideas the same character and attributes as for Space and Time.

The special and characteristic property of all the Fundamental Ideas is what I have already mentioned, that they are the mental sources of necessary and universal scientific truths. I call them *Ideas*, as being something not derived from sensation, but governing sensation, and consequently, giving form to our experience;—*Fundamental*, as being the foundation of knowledge, or at least of Science. And the way in which those Ideas become the foundations of Science is, that when they are clearly and distinctly entertained in the mind, they give rise to inevitable convictions or intuitions, which may be expressed as *Axioms;* and these Axioms are the foundations of Sciences respective of each Idea. The Idea of

Space, when clearly possessed, gives rise to geometrical Axioms, and is thus the foundation of the Science of Geometry. The Idea of Mechanical Force, (a modification of the Idea of Cause,) when clearly developed in the mind, gives birth to Axioms which are the foundation of the Science of Mechanics. The Idea of Substance gives rise to the Axiom which is universally accepted,—that we cannot, by any process, (for instance, by chemical processes,) create or destroy matter, but can only combine and separate elements;—and thus gives rise to the Science of Chemistry.

Now it may be observed, that in giving this account of the foundation of Science, I lay stress on the condition that the Ideas must be *clearly and distinctly possessed.* The Idea of Space must be quite clear in the mind, or else the Axioms of Geometry will not be seen to be true: there will be no *intuition* of their truth ; and for a mind in such a state, there can be no Science of Geometry. A man may have a confused and perplexed, or a vacant and inert state of mind, in which it is not clearly apparent to him, that two straight lines cannot inclose a space. But this is not a frequent case. The Idea of Space is much more commonly clear in the minds of men than the other Ideas on which science depends, as Force, or Substance. It is much more common to find minds in which these latter Ideas are not so clear and distinct as to make the Axioms of Mechanics or of Chemistry self-evident. Indeed the examples of a state of mind in which the Ideas of Force or of Substance are so clear as to be made the basis of science, are comparatively few. They are the examples of minds scientifically cultivated, at least to some extent. Hence, though the Axioms of Mechanics or of Chemistry may be, in their own nature, as evident as those of Geometry, they are not evident to so many persons, nor at so early a period of intellectual or scientific culture. And this being the case, it is not surprising that some persons should doubt whether these Axioms are evident at all ;—should think that it is an error to assert that there exist, in such sciences as Mechanics or Chemistry, Fundamental Ideas, fit to be classed with Space, as being, like it, the origin of Axioms.

In speaking of all the Fundamental Ideas as being alike the source of Axioms when clearly possessed, without dwelling sufficiently upon the amount of mental discipline which is requisite to give the mind this clear possession of most of them; and in not keeping before the reader the different degrees of evidence which, in most minds, the Axioms of different sciences naturally have, I have, as I have said, given occasion to my readers to misunderstand me. I will point out one or two passages which show that this misunderstanding has occurred, and will try to remove it.

The character of axiomatic truths seen by intuition is, that they are not only seen to be true, but to be necessary ; —that the contrary of them is not only false, but inconceivable.' But this inconceivableness depends entirely upon the clearness of the Ideas which the axioms involve. So long as those Ideas are vague and indistinct, the contrary of an Axiom may be assented to, though it cannot be distinctly conceived. It may be assented to, not because it is possible, but because *we* do not see clearly what *is* possible. To a person who is only beginning to think geometrically, there may appear nothing absurd in the assertion, that two straight lines may inclose a space. And in the same manner, to a person who is only beginning to think of mechanical truths, it may not appear to be absurd, that in mechanical processes, Reaction should be greater or less than Action ; and so, again, to a person who has not thought steadily about Substance, it may not appear inconceivable, that by chemical operations, we should generate new matter, or destroy matter which already exists.

Here then we have a difficulty:——the test of axioms is that the contrary of them is inconceivable; and yet persons, till they have in some measure studied the subject, do not see this inconceivableness. Hence our Axioms must be evident only to a small number of thinkers; and seem not to deserve the name of self-evident or necessary truths.

This difficulty has been strongly urged by Mr Mill, as supporting his view, that all knowledge of truth is derived from experience. And in order that the opposite doctrine, which I have advocated, may not labour under any disadvantages which really do not belong to it, I must explain, that I do not by any means assert that those truths which I regard as necessary, are all equally evident to common thinkers, or evident to persons in all stages of intellectual developement. I may even say, that some of those truths which I regard as necessary, and the necessity of which I believe the human mind to be capable of seeing, by due preparation and thought, are still such, that this amount of preparation and thought is rare and peculiar; and I will willingly grant, that to attain to and preserve such a clearness and subtlety of mind as this intuition requires, is a task of no ordinary difficulty and labour.

This doctrine,——that some truths may be seen by intuition, but yet that the intuition of them may be a rare and difficult attainment,——I have not, it would seem, conveyed with sufficient clearness to obviate misapprehension. Mr Mill has noticed a passage of my Philosophy on this subject, which he has understood in a sense different from that which I intended. Speaking of the two Principles of Chemical Science, ——that combinations are definite in kind,——and in quantity,—— I had tried to elevate myself to the point of view in which these Principles are seen, not only to be true, but to be necessary. I was aware that even the profoundest chemists had not ventured to do this; yet it appeared to me that there were considerations which seemed to show that any other rule would imply that the world was a world on which the human mind could not employ itself in scientific speculation at all. These considerations I ventured to put forwards, not as views which could at present be generally accepted, but as views to which chemical philosophy appeared to me to tend. Mr Mill, not unnaturally I must admit, supposed me to mean that the two Principles of Chemistry just stated, are self-evident, in the same way and in the same degree as the Axioms of Geometry are so. I afterwards explained that what I meant to do was, to throw out an opinion, that *if* we could conceive the composition of bodies *distinctly*, we might be able to see that it is necessary that the modes of this composition should be definite. This Mr Mill does not object to: (*Logic*, I. p. 273. 3rd Ed.) but he calls it a great attenuation of my former opinion; which he understood to be that we, (that is, men in general,) already see, or may, or ought to see, this necessity. Such a general apprehension of the necessity of definite chemical composition I certainly never reckoned upon; and even in my own mind, the thought of such a necessity was rather an anticipation of what the intuitions of philosophical chemists in another generation would be, than an assertion of what they now are or ought to be; much less did I expect that persons, neither chemists nor philosophers, would already, or perhaps ever, see that a proposition, so recently discovered to be true, is not only true, but necessary.

Of the bearing of this view on the question at issue between Mr Mill and me, I may hereafter speak; but I will now notice other persons who have misunderstood me in the same way.

An able writer in the *Edinburgh Review* (No. 193, p. 29) has, in like manner, said, "Dr Whewell seems to us to have gone much too far in reducing to necessary truths what assuredly the generality of mankind will not feel to be so." It is a fact which I do not at all contest, that the *generality of mankind* will not feel the Axioms of Chemistry, or even of Mechanics, to be necessary truths. But I had said, not that the generality of mankind would feel this necessity, but (in a passage just before quoted by the Reviewer) that the mind under certain circumstances *attains a point of view* from which it can pronounce mechanical (and other) fundamental truths to be necessary in their nature, though disclosed to us by experience and observation.

Both the Edinburgh Reviewer and Mr Mansel appear to hold a distinction between the fundamental truths of Geometry, and those of the other subjects which I have classed with them. The latter says, that perhaps metaphysicians may hereafter establish the existence of other subjective conditions of intuitions (or, as I should call them, Fundamental Ideas,) besides Space and Time, but that in asserting such to exist in the science of Mechanics, I certainly go too far : and he gives as an instance, an Essay which I added to the Second Edition of the *Philosophy*, containing "a Demonstration that all matter is heavy." I certainly did not expect that the Principles asserted in that Essay would be assented to as readily or as generally as the Axioms of Geometry; but I conceive that I have there proved that Chemical Science, using the balance as one of its implements, cannot admit "imponderable bodies" among its elements. This impossibility will, I think, not only be found to exist in fact, but seen to exist necessarily, by chemists, in proportion as they advance towards general propositions of Chemical Science in which the so-called "imponderable fluids" enter. But even if I be right in this opinion, to how few will this necessity be made apparent, and how slowly will the intuition spread ! I am as well aware as my critics, that the necessity will probably never be apparent to ordinary thinkers.

Though Mr Mansel does not acknowledge any subjective conditions of intuition besides Space and Time, he does recognize other *kinds of necessity*, which, I should equally refer to Fundamental Ideas ; because they are, no less than Space and Time, the foundations of universal and necessary truths in science. Such are (*Prol. Log.* p. 123) the Principle of Substance ;——All Qualities exist in some subject : and the Principle of Causality ;——Every Event has its Cause. To these Principles he ascribes a " metaphysical necessity," the nature and grounds of which he analyses with great acuteness. But what I have to observe is, that whatever *differences* may be pointed out between the *grounds* of the necessity, in this case of *metaphysical* necessity, and in that which Mr M. calls *mathematical* necessity which belongs to the Conditions or Ideas of Space and of Time ; still, it is not the less true that the Ideas of Substance and of Cause, *do* afford a foundation for necessary truths, and that on these truths are built Sciences. That every Change must have a Cause, with the corresponding Axioms,——that the Cause is known by the Effect, and Measured by it,——is the basis of the Science of Mechanics. That there is a Substance to which qualities, belong, with the corresponding Axiom,——that we cannot create or destroy Substance, though we may alter Qualities by combining and separating Substances,——is the basis of the Science of Chemistry. And that this doctrine of the Indestructibility of Substance is a primary axiomatic truth, is certain ; both because it has been universally taken for granted by men seeking for general truths ; and because it is not and cannot be proved by experience. (See *Phil. Ind. Sc.* B. vi. chap. 3). So that I have here, even according to Mr Mansel's own statement, other grounds besides Space and Time, for necessary truths in Science.

Besides mathematical and metaphysical necessity, Mr Mansel recognizes also a *logical necessity*. I will not pretend to say that this kind of necessity is exactly represented by any of those Fundamental Ideas which are the basis of Science; but yet I think it will be found that this logical necessity mainly operates through the attribution of Names to things; and that a large portion of its cogency arises from these maxims,—that Names must be so imposed that General Propositions shall be possible,—and so that Reasoning shall be possible. Now these maxims are really the basis of Natural History, and are so stated in the *Philosophy of the Inductive Sciences.* The former maxim is the principle of all Classification; and though we have no syllogisms in Natural History, the apparatus of *genus, species, differentia,* and the like, which was introduced in the analysis of syllogistic reasoning, is really more constantly applied in Natural History than in any other science.

Besides the different kinds of necessity which Mr Mansel thus acknowledges, I do not see why he should not, on his own principles, recognize others; as indeed he appears to me to do. He acknowledges, I think, the distinction of Primary and Secondary qualities; and this must involve him in the doctrine that Secondary Qualities are necessarily perceived by means of a *Medium.* Again: he would, I think, acknowledge that in organized bodies, the parts exist for a *Purpose;* and Purpose is an Idea which cannot be inferred by reasoning from facts, without being possessed and applied as an Idea. So that there would, I conceive, exist, in his philosophy, all the grounds of necessary truth which I have termed Fundamental Ideas; only that he would further subdivide, classify, and analyse, the kinds and grounds of this necessity.

In this he would do well; and some of his distinctions and analyses of this kind are, in my judgment, very instructive. But I do not see what objection there can be to my putting together all these kinds of necessity, when my purpose requires it; and, inasmuch as they all are the bases of Science,

I may call them by a general name; for instance, Grounds of Scientific Necessity; and these are precisely what I mean by *Fundamental Ideas.*

That some steady thought, and even some progress in the construction of Science, is needed in order to see the necessity of the Axioms thus introduced, is true, and is repeatedly asserted and illustrated in the History of the Sciences. The necessity of such Axioms is seen, but it is not seen at first. It becomes clearer and clearer to each person, and clear to one person after another, as the human mind dwells more and more steadily on the several subjects of speculation. *There are scientific truths which are seen by intuition, but this intuition is progressive.* This is the remark which I wish to make in answer to those of my critics who have objected that truths which I have propounded as Axioms, are not evident to all.

That the Axioms of Science are not evident to all, is true enough, and too true. Take the Axiom of Substance:—that we may change the condition of a substance in various ways, but cannot destroy it. This has been assumed as evident by philosophers in all ages; but if we ask an ordinary person whether a body can be destroyed by fire, or diminished, will he unhesitatingly reply, that it cannot? It requires some thought to say, as the philosopher said, that the weight of the smoke is to be found by subtracting the weight of the ashes from that of the fuel; nay, even when this is said, it appears at, first, rather an epigram than a scientific truth. Yet it is by thinking only, not by an experiment, that, from a happy guess it becomes a scientific truth. And the thought is the basis, not the result, of experimental truths; for which reason I ascribe it to a Fundamental Idea. And so, such truths are the genuine growth of the human mind; not innate, as if they needed not to grow; still less, dead twigs plucked from experience and stuck in from without;

not universal, as if they grew up everywhere; but not the less, under favourable circumstances, the genuine growth of the scientific intellect.

Not only do I hold that the Axioms, on which the truths of science rest, grow from guesses into Axioms in various ways, and often gradually, and at different periods in different minds, and partially, even in the end; but I conceive that this may be shown by the history of science, as having really happened, with regard to all the most conspicuous of such principles. The scientific insight which enabled discoverers to achieve their exploits, implied that they were among the first to acquire an intuitive conviction of the Axioms of their Science: the controversies which form so large a portion of the history of science, arise from the struggles between the clearsighted and ، the dimsighted, between those who were forwards and those who were backwards in the progress of ideas; and these controversies have very often ended in diffusing generally a clearness of thought, on the controverted subject, which at first, the few only, or perhaps not even they, possessed. The History of Science consists of the History of Ideas, as well as of the History of Experience and Observation. The latter portion of the subject formed the principal matter of my *History* of the Inductive Sciences; the former occupied a large portion of the *Philosophy* of the Inductive Sciences; which, I may perhaps be allowed to explain, is, for the most part, a Historical Work no less than the other; and was written, in a great measure, at the same time, and from the same survey of the works of scientific writers.

I am aware that the explanation which I have given, may naturally provoke the opponents of the doctrine of scientific necessity to repeat their ordinary fundamental objections, in a form adapted to the expressions which I have used. They may say, the fact, that these so called Axioms thus become evident only during the progress of experience, proves that they are derived from experience: they may, in reply to our image, say, that truths are stuck into the mind by experience, as seeds are stuck into the ground; and that to maintain that they can grow under any other conditions, is to hold the ·doctrine of spontaneous generation, which is equally untenable in the intellectual and in the physical world. I shall not however here resume the general discussion; but shall only say briefly in reply, that Axioms,— for instance, this Axiom, that material substances cannot be created or annihilated by any process which we can apply, —though it becomes evident in the progress of experience, cannot be derived from experience; for it is a proposition which never has been nor can be proved by experience; but which, nevertheless, has been always assumed by men, seeking for general truths, as necessarily true, and as controlling and correcting all possible experience. And with regard to the image of vegetable developement, I may say, that as such developement implies both inherent forms in the living seed, and nutritive powers in earth and air; so the developement of our scientific ideas implies both a formative power, and materials acted on; and that, though the analogy must be very defective, we conceive that we best follow it by placing the formative power in the living mind, and in the external world the materials acted on: while the doctrine, that all truth is derived from experience only, appears to reject altogether one of these elements, or to assert the two to be one.

A

HISTORY

OF THE

INDUCTIVE SCIENCES.

INTRODUCTION.

" A JUST story of learning, containing the antiquities and originals of KNOWLEDGES, and their sects; their inventions, their diverse administrations and managings; their flourishings, their oppositions, decays, depressions, oblivions, removes; with the causes and occasions of them, and all other events concerning learning, throughout all ages of the world; I may truly affirm to be wanting.

" The use and end of which work I do not so much design for curiosity, or satisfaction of those that are the lovers of learning: but chiefly for a more serious and grave purpose; which is this, in few words, that it will make learned men more wise in the use and administration of learning."

BACON, *Advancement of Learning*, book ii.

INTRODUCTION.

IT is my purpose to write the History of some of the most important of the Physical Sciences, from the earliest to the most recent periods. I shall thus have to trace some of the most remarkable branches of human knowledge, from their first germ to their growth into a vast and varied assemblage of undisputed truths; from the acute, but fruitless, essays of the early Greek Philosophy, to the comprehensive systems, and demonstrated generalizations, which compose such sciences as the Mechanics, Astronomy, and Chemistry, of modern times.

The completeness of historical view which belongs to such a design, consists, not in accumulating all the details of the cultivation of each science, but in marking clearly the larger features of its formation. The historian must endeavour to point out how each of the important advances was made, by which the sciences have reached their present position; and when and by whom each of the valuable truths was obtained, of which the aggregate now constitutes a costly treasure.

Such a task, if fitly executed, must have a well-founded interest for all those who look at the existing condition of human knowledge with complacency and admiration. The present generation finds itself the heir of a vast patrimony of science; and it must needs concern us to know the steps by which these possessions were acquired, and the documents by which they are secured to us and our heirs for ever. Our species, from the time of its creation, has been travelling onwards in pursuit of truth; and now that we have reached a lofty and commanding position, with the broad light of day around us, it must be grateful to look back on the line of our past progress;—to review the journey, begun in early twilight amid primeval wilds; for a long time continued with slow advance and obscure prospects; and gradually and in later days followed along more open and lightsome paths, in a wide and fertile region. The historian of science, from early periods to the present times, may hope for favour on the score of the mere subject of his narrative, and in virtue of the curiosity which the men of the present day may naturally feel respecting the events and persons of his story.

But such a survey may possess also an interest of another kind; it may be instructive as well as agreeable; it may bring before the reader the present form and extent, the future hopes and prospects of science, as well as its past progress. The eminence on which we stand may enable us to see the land of promise, as well as the wilderness through which we have passed. The examination of the steps by which our ancestors acquired our intellectual estate, may make us acquainted with our expectations as well as our possessions ;—may not only remind us of what we have, but may teach us how to improve and increase our store. It will be universally expected that a History of Inductive Science should point out to us a philosophical distribution of the existing body of knowledge, and afford us some indication of the most promising mode of directing our future efforts to add to its extent and completeness.

To deduce such lessons from the past history of human knowledge, was the intention which originally gave rise to the present work. Nor is this portion of the design in any measure abandoned ; but its execution, if it take place, must be attempted in a separate and future treatise, *On the Philosophy of the Inductive Sciences*. An essay of this kind may, I trust, from the progress already made in it, be laid before the public at no long interval after the present history.

Though, therefore, many of the principles and maxims of such a work will disclose themselves with more or less of distinctness in the course of the history on which we are about to enter, the systematic and complete exposition of such principles must be reserved for this other treatise. My attempts and reflections have led me to the opinion that justice cannot be done to the subject without such a division of it.

To this future work, then, I must refer the reader who is disposed to require, at the outset, a precise explanation of the terms which occur in my title.   It is not possible, without entering into this philosophy, to explain adequately how science which is INDUCTIVE differs from that which is not so ; or why some portions of *knowledge* may properly be selected from the general mass and termed SCIENCE. It will be sufficient at present to say, that the sciences of which we have here to treat, are those which are commonly known as the *Physical Sciences;* and that by *Induction* is to be understood that process of collecting general truths from the examination of particular facts, by which such sciences have been formed.

There are, however, two or three remarks, of which the application will occur so frequently, and will tend so much to give us a clearer view of some of the subjects which occur in our history, that I will state them now in a brief and general manner (A).

Facts and Ideas.—In the first place, then, I remark, that, to the formation of science, two things are requisite ;—Facts and Ideas ; observation of Things without, and an inward effort of Thought ; or, in other words, Sense and Reason.   Neither of these elements, by itself, can constitute substantial general knowledge.   The impressions of sense, un-

connected by some rational and speculative principle, can only end in a practical acquaintance with
individual objects; the operations of the rational
faculties, on the other hand, if allowed to go on
without a constant reference to external things, can
lead only to empty abstraction and barren ingenuity. Real speculative knowledge demands the
combination of the two ingredients;—right reason,
and facts to reason upon. It has been well said,
that true knowledge is the interpretation of nature;
and thus it requires both the interpreting mind, and
nature for its subject; both the document, and the
ingenuity to read it aright. Thus invention, acuteness, and connexion of thought, are necessary on the
one hand, for the progress of philosophical knowledge; and on the other hand, the precise and
steady application of these faculties to facts well
known and clearly conceived. It is easy to point
out instances in which science has failed to advance,
in consequence of the absence of one or other of
these requisites; indeed, by far the greater part of
the course of the world, the history of most times
and most countries, exhibits a condition thus stationary with respect to knowledge. The facts, the
impressions on the senses, on which the first successful attempts at physical knowledge proceeded,
were as well known long before the time when they
were thus turned to account, as at that period. The
motions of the stars, and the effects of weight, were
familiar to man before the rise of the Greek astro-

nomy and mechanics: but the "diviner mind" was
still absent; the act of thought had not been exerted, by which these facts were bound together
under the form of laws and principles.   And even
at this day, the tribes of uncivilized and half-civilized
man over the whole face of the earth, have before
their eyes a vast body of facts, of exactly the same
nature as those with which Europe has built the
stately fabric of her physical philosophy; but, in
almost every other part of the earth, the process of
the intellect by which these facts become science, is
unknown.   The scientific faculty does not work.
The scattered stones are there, but the builder's
hand is wanting.   And again, we have no lack of
proof that mere activity of thought is equally ineffi-
cient in producing real knowledge.   Almost the
whole of the career of the Greek schools of philosophy; of the schoolmen of Europe in the middle
ages; of the Arabian and Indian philosophers;
shows us that we may have extreme ingenuity and
subtlety, invention and connexion, demonstration
and method; and yet that out of these germs, no
physical science may be developed.   We may obtain, by such means, logic and metaphysics, and
even geometry and algebra; but out of such materials we shall never form mechanics and optics,
chemistry and physiology.   How impossible the
formation of these sciences is without a constant
and careful reference to observation and experiment;—how rapid and prosperous their progress

may be when they draw from such sources the materials on which the mind of the philosopher employs itself;—the history of those branches of knowledge for the last three hundred years abundantly teaches us.

Accordingly, the existence of clear Ideas applied to distinct Facts will be discernible in the History of Science, whenever any marked advance takes place. And, in tracing the progress of the various provinces of knowledge which come under our survey, it will be important for us to see, that, at all such epochs, such a combination has occurred; that whenever any material step in general knowledge has been made,—whenever any philosophical discovery arrests our attention;—some man or men come before us, who have possessed, in an eminent degree, a clearness of the ideas which belong to the subject in question, and who have applied such ideas in a vigorous and distinct manner to ascertained facts and exact observations. We shall never proceed through any considerable range of our narrative, without having occasion to remind the reader of this reflection.

Successive Steps in Science.—But there is another remark which we must also make. Such sciences as we have here to do with, are, commonly, not formed by a single act;—they are not completed by the discovery of one great principle. On the contrary, they consist in a long-continued advance; a series of changes; a repeated

progress from one principle to another, different
and often apparently contradictory. Now, it is important to remember that this contradiction is apparent only. The principles which constituted the
triumph of the preceding stages of the science, may
appear to be subverted and ejected by the later
discoveries, but in fact they are, (so far as they
were true,) taken up into the subsequent doctrines
and included in them. They continue to be an
essential part of the science. The earlier truths
are not expelled but absorbed, not contradicted but
extended; and the history of each science, which
may thus appear like a succession of revolutions, is,
in reality, a series of developements. In the intellectual, as in the material world,—

> Omnia mutantur nil interit . . . . .
> Nec manet ut fuerat nec formas servat easdem,
> Sed tamen ipsa eadem est.

> All changes, nought is lost; the forms are changed,
> And that which has been is not what it was,
> Yet that which has been is.

Nothing which was done was useless or unessential,
though it ceases to be conspicuous and primary.

Thus the final form of each science contains the
substance of each of its preceding modifications;
and all that was at any antecedent period discovered and established, ministers to the ultimate
developement of its proper branch of knowledge.
Such previous doctrines may require to be made
precise and definite, to have their superfluous and

arbitrary portions expunged, to be expressed in new language, to be taken up into the body of science by various processes;—but they do not on such accounts cease to be true doctrines, or to form a portion of the essential constituents of our knowledge.

Terms record Discoveries.—The modes in which the earlier truths of science are preserved in its later forms, are indeed various. From being asserted at first as strange discoveries, such truths come at last to be implied as almost self-evident axioms. They are recorded by some familiar maxim, or perhaps by some new word or phrase, which becomes part of the current language of the philosophical world; and thus asserts a principle, while it appears merely to indicate a transient notion;—preserves as well as expresses a truth;—and, like a medal of gold, is a treasure as well as a token. We shall frequently have to notice the manner in which great discoveries thus stamp their impress upon the terms of a science; and, like great political revolutions, are recorded by the change of the current coin which has accompanied them.

Generalization.—The great changes which thus take place in the history of science, the revolutions of the intellectual world, have, as a usual and leading character, this, that they are steps of *generalization*;—transitions from particular truths to others of a wider extent, in which the former are included. This progress of knowledge, from individual facts

to universal laws,—from particular propositions to
general ones,—and from these to others still more
general, with reference to which the former generalizations are particular,—is so far familiar to men's
minds, that without here entering into further explanation, its nature will be understood sufficiently
to prepare the reader to recognise the exemplifi-
cations of such a process, which he will find at
every step of our advance.

Inductive Epochs; Preludes; Sequels.—In our
history, it is the *progress* of knowledge only which
we have to attend to.   This is the main action of
our drama; and all the events which do not bear
upon this, though they may relate to the cultivation and the cultivators of philosophy, are not a
necessary part of our theme.   Our narrative will
therefore consist mainly of successive steps of generalization, such as have just been mentioned.   But
among these, we shall find some of eminent and
decisive importance, which have more peculiarly
influenced the fortunes of physical philosophy, and
to which we may consider the rest as subordinate
and auxiliary.   These primary movements, when
the Inductive process, by which science is formed,
has been exercised in a more energetic and powerful manner, may be distinguished as the *Inductive
Epochs* of scientific history; and they deserve our
more express and pointed notice.   They are, for the
most part, marked by the great discoveries and the
great philosophical names which all civilized na-

tions have agreed in admiring. But, when we examine more clearly the history of such discoveries, we find that these epochs have not occurred suddenly and without preparation. They have been preceded by a period, which we may call their *Prelude*, during which the ideas and facts on which they turned were called into action;—were gradually evolved into clearness and connexion, permanency and certainty; till at last the discovery which marks the Epoch, seized and fixed for ever the truth which had till then been obscurely and doubtfully discerned. And again, when this step has been made by the principal discoverers, there may generally be observed another period, which we may call the *Sequel* of the Epoch, during which the discovery has acquired a more perfect certainty and a more complete developement among the leaders of the advance; has been diffused to the wider throng of the secondary cultivators of such knowledge, and traced into its distant consequences. This is a work, always of time and labour, often of difficulty and conflict. To distribute the History of science into such Epochs, with their Preludes and Sequels, if successfully attempted, must needs make the series and connexion of its occurrences more distinct and intelligible. Such periods form resting-places, where we pause till the dust of the confused march is laid, and the prospect of the path is clear.

Inductive Charts.—Since the advance of science

consists in collecting by induction true general laws
from particular facts, and in combining several such
laws into one higher generalization, in which they
still retain their truth ; we might form a Chart, or
Table, of the progress of each science, by setting
down the particular facts which have thus been combined, so as to form general truths, and by marking
the further union of these general truths into others
more comprehensive.   The Table of the progress of
any science would thus resemble the Map of a River,
in which the waters from separate sources unite
and make rivulets, which again meet with rivulets
from other fountains, and thus go on forming by
their junction trunks of a higher and higher order.
The representation of the state of a science in this
form, would necessarily exhibit all the principal
doctrines of the science; for each general truth contains the particular truths from which it was derived, and may be followed backwards till we have
these before us in their separate state.   And the
last and most advanced generalization would have,
in such a scheme, its proper place and the evidence
of its validity.   Hence such an *Inductive Table* of
each science would afford a criterion of the correctness of our distribution of the inductive Epochs, by
its coincidence with the views of the best judges, as
to the substantial contents of the science in question.   By forming, therefore, such Inductive Tables
of the principal sciences of which I have here to
speak, and by regulating by these tables, my views

of the history of the sciences, I conceive that I have secured the distribution of my history from material error; for no merely arbitrary division of the events could satisfy such conditions. But though I have constructed such charts to direct the course of the present history, I shall not insert them in the work, reserving them for the illustration of the philosophy of the subject; for to this they more properly belong, being a part of the *Logic of Induction.*

Stationary Periods.—By the lines of such maps the real advance of science is depicted, and nothing else. But there are several occurrences of other kinds, too interesting and too instructive to be altogether omitted. In order to understand the conditions of the progress of knowledge, we must attend, in some measure, to the failures as well as the successes by which such attempts have been attended. When we reflect during how small a portion of the whole history of human speculations, science has really been, in any marked degree, progressive, we must needs feel some curiosity to know what was doing in these *stationary* periods; what field could be found which admitted of so wide a deviation, or at least so protracted a wandering. It is highly necessary to our purpose, to describe the baffled enterprises as well as the achievements of human speculation.

Deduction.—During a great part of such stationary periods, we shall find that the process which we have spoken of as essential to the formation of

real science, the conjunction of clear ideas with distinct facts, was interrupted; and, in such cases, men
dealt with ideas alone.   They employed themselves
in reasoning from principles, and they arranged,
and classified, and analyzed their ideas, so as to
make their reasonings satisfy the requisitions of
our rational faculties.   This process of drawing
conclusions from our principles, by rigorous and
unimpeachable trains of demonstration, is termed
Deduction.   In its due place, it is a highly important part of every science ; but it has no value when
the fundamental principles, on which the whole of
the demonstration rests, have not first been obtained by the induction of facts, so as to supply the
materials of substantial truth.   Without such materials, a series of demonstrations resembles physical science only as a shadow resembles a real object.
To give a real significance to our propositions, Induction must provide what Deduction cannot supply.   From a pictured hook we can hang only a
pictured chain.

*Distinction of common Notions and Scientific
Ideas.*—When the notions with which men are
conversant in the common course of practical life;
which give meaning to their familiar language, and
employment to their hourly thoughts, are compared
with the Ideas on which exact science is founded,
we find that the two classes of intellectual operations have much that is common and much that is
different.   Without here attempting fully to explain

this relation, (which, indeed, is one of the hardest problems of our philosophy,) we may observe that they have this in common, that both are acquired by acts of the mind exercised in connecting external impressions, and may be employed in conducting a train of reasoning; or, speaking loosely, (for we cannot here pursue the subject so as to arrive at philosophical exactness,) we may say, that all notions and ideas are obtained by an *inductive*, and may be used in a *deductive* process. But scientific Ideas and common Notions differ in this, that the former are precise and stable, the latter vague and variable; the former are possessed with clear insight, and employed in a sense rigorously limited, and always identically the same; the latter have grown up in the mind from a thousand dim and diverse suggestions, and the obscurity and incongruity which belongs to their origin hangs about all their applications. Scientific Ideas can often be adequately exhibited for all the purposes of reasoning, by means of Definitions and Axioms; all attempts to reason by means of Definitions from common Notions, lead to empty forms or entire confusion.

Such common Notions are sufficient for the common practical conduct of human life; but man is not a practical creature merely; he has within him a *speculative* tendency, a pleasure in the contemplation of ideal relations, a love of knowledge *as* knowledge. It is this speculative tendency which brings to light the difference of common Notions and scientific Ideas, of which we have spoken. The mind analyzes such Notions, reasons upon them, combines and connects them; for it feels assured that intellectual things ought to be able to bear such handling. Even practical knowledge, we see clearly, is not possible without the use of the reason; and the speculative reason is only the reason satisfying itself of its own consistency. This speculative faculty cannot be controlled from acting. The mind cannot but claim a right to speculate concerning all its own acts and creations; yet, when it exercises this right upon its common practical notions, we find that it runs into barren abstractions and ever-recurring cycles of subtlety. Such Notions are like waters naturally stagnant; however much we urge and agitate them, they only revolve in stationary whirlpools. But the mind is capable of acquiring scientific Ideas, which are fitted to undergo this discussion and impulsion. When our speculations are duly fed from the spring-heads of observation, and frequently drawn off into the region of applied science, we may have a living stream of consistent and progressive knowledge. That science may be both real as to its import, and logical as to its form, the examples of many existing sciences sufficiently prove.

School Philosophy.—So long, however, as attempts are made to form sciences, without such a verification and realization of their fundamental ideas, there is, in the natural series of speculation, no self-correcting principle. A philosophy constructed on notions obscure, vague, and unsubstantial, and held in spite of the want of correspondence between its doctrines and the actual train of physical events, may long subsist, and occupy men's minds. Such a philosophy must depend for its permanence upon the pleasure which men feel in tracing the operations of their own and other men's minds, and in reducing them to logical consistency and systematical arrangement.

In these cases the main subjects of attention are not external objects, but speculations previously delivered; the object is not to interpret nature, but man's mind. The opinions of the masters are the facts which the disciples endeavour to reduce to unity, or to follow into consequences. A series of speculators who pursue such a course, may properly be termed a *School*, and their philosophy a *School Philosophy*; whether their agreement in such a mode of seeking knowledge arise from personal communication and tradition, or be merely the result of a community of intellectual character and propensity. The two great periods of School Philosophy (it will be recollected that we are here directing our attention mainly to physical science), were that of the Greeks and that of the Middle Ages;—the period of the first waking of science, and that of its mid-day slumber.

What has been said thus briefly and imperfectly, would require great detail and much explanation, to give it its full significance and authority.   But it seemed proper to state so much in this place, in order to render more intelligible and more instructive at the first aspect, the view of the attempted or effected progress of science.

It is, perhaps, a disadvantage inevitably attending an undertaking like the present, that it must set out with statements so abstract; and must present them without their adequate developement and proof. Such an Introduction, both in its character and its scale of execution, may be compared to the geographical sketch of a country, with which the historian of its fortunes often begins his narration.   So much of Metaphysics is as necessary to us as such a portion of Geography is to the Historian of an Empire; and what has hitherto been said, is intended as a slight outline of the Geography of that Intellectual World, of which we have here to study the History.

To that History we now proceed.

NOTES TO THE INTRODUCTION.

A HISTORY OF THE INDUCTIVE SCIENCES.——This title has the fault of seeming to exclude from the rank of Inductive Sciences those which are not included in the History; as Ethnology and Glossology, Political Economy, Psychology. This exclusion I by no means wish to imply; but I could find no other way of compendiously describing my subject, which was intended to comprehend those Sciences in which, by the observation of facts and the use of reason, systems of doctrine have been established which are universally received as truths among thoughtful men; and which may therefore be studied as examples of the manner in which truth is to be discovered. Perhaps a more exact description of the work would have been, *A History of the principal Sciences hitherto established by Induction.* I may add that I do not include in the phrase " Inductive Sciences," the branches of Pure Mathematics, (Geometry, Arithmetic, Algebra, and the like,) because, as I have elsewhere stated (*Phil. Ind. Sc.*, B. II. c. 1), these are not *Inductive* but *Deductive* Sciences: they do not infer true theories from observed facts, and more general from more limited laws: but they trace the conditions of all theory, the properties of space and number; and deduce results from ideas without the aid of experience. The History of these Sciences is briefly given in Chapter 13 of the Book just referred to.

(A.) p. 7. The points belonging to the *Philosophy of the Sciences*, which are briefly noticed in this Introduction, are considered more fully in my work on that subject. The Antithesis of *Facts and Ideas* is treated of in Book I., chapter 2, 3, 4 of that work : *Successive Generalizations* in chap. 7 : *Technical Terms* in chap. 8 : *Inductive Charts*, such as are here referred to in p. 13, are given with reference to the History of Astronomy and of Optics, in Book XI., chap. 6, of the *Philosophy*.   *Scientific Ideas*, such as are here spoken of in p. 16, are discussed in the *Philosophy*, from Book II. to Book X. ; and the principal controversies are there noticed by which this discussion has been historically carried on.

BOOK I.

HISTORY

OF THE

GREEK SCHOOL PHILOSOPHY,

WITH REFERENCE TO

PHYSICAL SCIENCE.

Τίς γὰρ ἀρχὰ δέξατο ναυτιλίας;
Τίς δὲ κίνδυνος κρατεροῖς ἀδάμαν-
   τος δῆσεν ἅλοις;
  . . . . . Ἐπεὶ δ᾽ ἐμβόλου
Κρεμασαν ἀγκύρας ὕπερθεν
Χρυσέαν χείρεσσι λαβὼν φιάλαν
Ἀρχος εν πρυμνᾳ πατέρ Οὐρανιδᾶν
Ἐγχεικέραυνον Ζῆνα, καὶ ὠκυπόρους
Κυμάτων ῥίπας, ἀνεμων τ᾽ ἐκάλει,
Νύκτας τε, καὶ πόντου κελεύθους,
Ἄματά τ᾽ εὔφρονα, καὶ
Φιλίαν νόστοιο μοῖραν.

PINDAR. Pyth. iv. 124, 349.

Whence came their voyage? them what peril held
With adamantine rivets firmly bound?
    .   .   .   .   .   .
  But soon as on the vessel's bow
    The anchor was hung up,
  Then took the Leader on the prow
    In hands a golden cup,
  And on great Father Jove did call,
  And on the Winds and Waters all,
    Swept by the hurrying blast;
  And on the Nights, and Ocean Ways,
  And on the fair auspicious Days,
    And loved return at last.

BOOK I.

CHAPTER I.

PRELUDE TO THE GREEK SCHOOL PHILOSOPHY.

Sect. 1.—*First Attempts of the Speculative Faculty in Physical Inquiries.*

AT an early period of history there appeared in men a propensity to pursue speculative inquiries concerning the various parts and properties of the material world. What they saw excited them to meditate, to conjecture, and to reason : they endeavoured to account for natural events, to trace their causes, to reduce them to their principles. This habit of mind, or, at least that modification of it which we have here to consider, seems to have been first unfolded among the Greeks. And during that obscure introductory interval which elapsed while the speculative tendencies of men were as yet hardly disentangled from the practical, those who were most eminent in such inquiries were distinguished by the same term of praise which is applied to sagacity in matters of action, and were called *wise* men—σοφοὶ. But when it came to be clearly felt by such persons that their endeavours were suggested by the love of knowledge, a motive different from those which lead to the wisdom of active life, a name was adopted of a more appropriate, as well as of a more modest signification, and they were termed *philosophers*, or lovers of wisdom.   This appellation is said[1] to have been first assumed by Pythagoras.   Yet he, in Herodotus, instead of having this title, is called a powerful *sophist*—Ἑλλήνων οὐ τῷ ἀσθενεστάτῳ σο-φιστῇ Πυθαγόρῃ[2]; the historian using this word, as it would seem, without intending to imply that misuse of reason which the term afterwards came to denote.   The historians of literature place Pytha-goras at the origin of the Italic School, one of the two main lines of succession of the early Greek philosophers: but the other, the Ionic School, which more peculiarly demands our attention, in conse-quence of its character and subsequent progress, is deduced from Thales, who preceded the age of *Phi-losophy*, and was one of the *sophi*, or "wise men of Greece."

The Ionic School was succeeded in Greece by several others; and the subjects which occupied the attention of these schools became very extensive. In fact, the first attempts were, to form systems which should explain the laws and causes of the material universe; and to these were soon added all the great questions which our moral condition and

---

[1] Cic. Tusc. v. 3.   [2] Herod. iv. 95.

faculties suggest. The physical philosophy of these schools is especially deserving of our study, as exhibiting the character and fortunes of the most memorable attempt at universal knowledge which has ever been made. It is highly instructive to trace the principles of this undertaking; for the course pursued was certainly one of the most natural and tempting which can be imagined; the essay was made by a nation unequalled in fine mental endowments, at the period of its greatest activity and vigour; and yet it must be allowed, (for, at least so far as physical science is concerned, none will contest this,) to have been entirely unsuccessful. We cannot consider otherwise than as an utter failure, an endeavour to discover the causes of things, of which the most complete results are the Aristotelian physical treatises; and which, after reaching the point which these treatises mark, left the human mind to remain stationary, at any rate on all such subjects, for nearly two thousand years.

The early philosophers of Greece entered upon the work of physical speculation in a manner which showed the vigour and confidence of the questioning spirit, as yet untamed by labours and reverses. It was for later ages to learn that man must acquire, slowly and patiently, letter by letter, the alphabet in which nature writes her answers to such inquiries: the first students wished to divine, at a single glance, the whole import of her book. They endeavoured to discover the origin and principle of the universe; according to Thales, *water* was the origin of all things, according to Anaximenes, *air*; and Heraclitus considered *fire* as the essential principle of the universe. It has been conjectured, with great plausibility, that this tendency to give to their philosophy the form of a cosmogony, was owing to the influence of the poetical cosmogonies and theogonies which had been produced, and admired at a still earlier age. Indeed, such wide and ambitious doctrines as those which have been mentioned, were better suited to the dim magnificence of poetry, than to the purpose of a philosophy which was to bear the sharp scrutiny of reason. When we speak of the *principles* of things, the term, even now, is very ambiguous and indefinite in its import; but how much more was that the case in the first attempts to use such abstractions! The term which is commonly used in this sense (ἀρχή), signified at first *the beginning*; and in its early philosophical applications implied some obscure mixed reference to the mechanical, chemical, organic, and historical causes of the visible state of things, besides the theological views which at this period were only just beginning to be separated from the physical. Hence we are not to be surprised if the sources from which the opinions of this period appear to be derived are rather vague suggestions and casual analogies, than any reasons which will bear examination. Aristotle conjectures, with considerable probability, that the doctrine of Thales, according to which water was the universal element, resulted from the manifest importance of moisture in the support of animal and vegetable life[3]. But such precarious analyses of these obscure and loose dogmas of early antiquity are of small consequence to our object.

In more limited and more definite examples of inquiry concerning the causes of natural appearances, and in the attempts made to satisfy men's curiosity in such cases, we appear to discern a more genuine prelude to the true spirit of physical inquiry. One of the most remarkable instances of this kind is to be found in the speculations which Herodotus records, relative to the cause of the floods of the Nile. "Concerning the nature of this river," says the father of history[4], "I was not able to learn anything, either from the priests or from any one besides, though I questioned them very pressingly. For the Nile is flooded for a hundred days, beginning with the summer solstice; and after this time it diminishes, and is, during the whole winter, very small. And on this head I was not able to obtain anything satisfactory from any one of the Egyptians, when I asked what is the power by which the Nile is in its nature the reverse of other rivers."

We may see, I think, in the historian's account, that the Grecian mind felt a craving to discover the reasons of things which other nations did not feel. The Egyptians, it appears, had no theory, and felt

[3] Metaph. i. 3.   [4] Herod. ii. 19.

no want of a theory. Not so the Greeks; they had their reasons to render, though they were not such as satisfied Herodotus. "Some of the Greeks," he says, "who wish to be considered great philosophers, (Ἑλλήνων τινὲς ἐπισήμοι βουλόμενοι γενέσθαι σοφίην) have propounded three ways of accounting for these floods. Two of them," he adds, "I do not think worthy of record, except just so far as to mention them." But as these are some of the earliest Greek essays in physical philosophy, it will be worth while, even at this day, to preserve the brief notice he has given of them, and his own reasonings upon the same subject.

"One of these opinions holds that the Etesian winds [which blew from the north] are the cause of these floods, by preventing the Nile from flowing into the sea." Against this the historian reasons very simply and sensibly. "Very often when the Etesian winds do not blow, the Nile is flooded nevertheless. And moreover, if the Etesian winds were the cause, all other rivers, which have their course opposite to these winds, ought to undergo the same changes as the Nile; which the rivers of Syria and Libya so circumstanced do not."

"The next opinion is still more unscientific, (ἀνεπιστημονεστέρη) and is, in truth, marvellous for its folly. This holds that the ocean flows all round the earth, and that the Nile comes out of the ocean, and by that means produces its effects." "Now," says the historian, "the man who talks about this

'ocean-river, goes into the region of fable, where it
is not easy to demonstrate that he is wrong. I
know of no such river. But I suppose that Homer
or some of the earlier poets invented this fiction
and introduced it into their poetry."

. He then proceeds to a third account, which to a
modern reasoner would appear not at all unphilosophical in itself, but which he, nevertheless, rejects
in a manner no less decided than the others. "The
third opinion, though much the most plausible, is
still more wrong than the others; for it asserts an
impossibility, namely, that the Nile proceeds from
the melting of the snow. Now the Nile flows out
of Libya, and through Ethiopia, which are very hot
countries, and thus comes into Egypt, which is a
colder region. How then can it proceed from
snow?" He then offers several other reasons "to
show," as he says, "to any one capable of reasoning
on such subjects" (ἀνδρί γε λογίζεσθαι τοιούτων πέρι
οἵῳ τε ἐόντι), that the assertion cannot be true. The
winds which blow from the southern regions are
hot; the inhabitants are black; the swallows and
kites (ἰκτῖνοι) stay in the country the whole year;
the cranes fly the colds of Scythia, and seek their
warm winter-quarters there; which would not be
if it snowed ever so little." He adds another reason,
founded apparently upon some limited empirical
maxim of weather-wisdom taken from the climate
of Greece. "Libya," he says, "has neither rain nor
ice, and therefore no snow; *for*, in five days after a

fall of snow there must be a fall of rain; so that if it snowed in those regions it must rain too." I need not observe that Herodotus was not aware of the difference between the climate of high mountains and plains in a torrid region; but it is impossible not to be struck both with the activity and the coherency of thought displayed by the Greek mind in this primitive physical inquiry.

But I must not omit the hypothesis which Herodotus himself proposes, after rejecting those which have been already given. It does not appear to me easy to catch his exact meaning, but the statement will still be curious. "If," he says, "one who has condemned opinions previously promulgated may put forwards his own opinion concerning so obscure a matter, I will state why it seems to me that the Nile is flooded in summer." This opinion he propounds at first with an oracular brevity, which it is difficult to suppose that he did not intend to be impressive. "In winter the sun is carried by the seasons away from his former course, and goes to the upper parts of Libya. And *there, in short, is the whole account;* for that region to which this divinity (the sun) is nearest, must naturally be most scant of water, and the river-sources of that country must be dried up."

But the lively and garrulous Ionian immediately relaxes from this apparent reserve. "To explain the matter more at length," he proceeds, "it is thus. The sun, when he traverses the upper parts of Libya, does what he commonly does in summer;—he *draws* the water to him (ἕλκει ἐπ᾽ ἑωῦτὸν τὸ ὕδωρ), and having thus drawn it, he pushes it to the upper regions (of the air probably,) and then the winds take it and disperse it till they dissolve in moisture. And thus the winds which blow from those countries, Libs and Notus, are the most moist of all winds. Now when the winter relaxes and the sun returns to the north, he still draws water from all the rivers, but they are increased by showers and rain-torrents, so that they are in flood till the summer comes; and then, the rain failing and the sun still drawing them, they become small. But the Nile, not being fed by rains, yet being drawn by the sun, is, alone of all rivers, much more scanty in the winter than in the summer. For in summer it is drawn like all other rivers, but in winter it alone has its supplies shut up. And in this way, I have been led to think the sun is the cause of the occurrence in question." We may remark that the historian here appears to ascribe the inequality of the Nile at different seasons to the influence of the sun upon its springs alone, the other cause of change, the rains, being here excluded : and that, on this supposition, the same relative effects would be produced whether the sun increase the sources in winter by melting the snows, or diminish them in summer by what he calls *drawing* them upwards.

This specimen of the early efforts of the Greeks in physical speculations, appears to me to speak strongly for the opinion that their philosophy on such subjects was the native growth of the Greek mind, and owed nothing to the supposed lore of Egypt and the East; an opinion which has been adopted with regard to the Greek philosophy in general by the most competent judges on a full survey of the evidence[5]. Indeed, we have no evidence whatever that, at any period, the African or Asiatic nations, (with the exception perhaps of the Indians,) ever felt this importunate curiosity with regard to the definite application of the idea of cause and effect to visible phenomena; or drew so strong a line between a fabulous legend and a reason rendered; or attempted to ascend to a natural cause by classing together phenomena of the same kind. We may be well excused, therefore, for believing that they could not impart to the Greeks what they themselves did not possess; and so far as our survey goes, physical philosophy has its origin, apparently spontaneous and independent, in the active and acute intellect of Greece.

Sect. 2.—*Primitive Mistake in Greek Physical Philosophy.*

WE now proceed to examine with what success the Greeks followed the track into which they had thus struck. And here we are obliged to confess that

[5] Thirlwall, *Hist. Gr.*, ii. 130; and, as there quoted, Ritter, *Geschichte der Philosophie*, i. 159—173.

they very soon turned aside from the right road to truth, and deviated into a vast field of error, in which they and their successors have wandered almost to the present time. It is not necessary here to inquire why those faculties which appear to be bestowed upon us for the discovery of truth, were permitted by Providence to fail so signally in answering that purpose; whether, like the powers by which we seek our happiness, they involve a responsibility on our part, and may be defeated by rejecting the guidance of a higher faculty; or whether these endowments, though they did not immediately lead man to profound physical knowledge, answered some nobler and better purpose in his constitution and government. The fact undoubtedly was, that the physical philosophy of the Greeks soon became trifling and worthless; and it is proper to point out, as precisely as we can, in what the fundamental mistake consisted.

To explain this, we may in the first place return for a moment to Herodotus's account of the cause of the floods of the Nile.

The reader will probably have observed a remarkable phrase used by Herodotus, in his own explanation of these inundations. He says that the sun *draws*, or attracts, the water; a metaphorical term, obviously intended to denote some more general and abstract conception than that of the visible operation which the word primarily signifies. This abstract notion of 'drawing' is, in the historian, as

D 2

we see, very vague and loose; it might, with equal propriety, be explained to mean what we now understand by mechanical or by chemical attraction, or pressure, or evaporation.   And in like manner, all the first attempts to comprehend the operations of nature, led to the introduction of abstract conceptions, often vague, indeed, but not, therefore, unmeaning; such as *motion* and *velocity*, *force* and *pressure*, *impetus* and *momentum* (ῥοπή).   And the next step in philosophizing, necessarily was to endeavour to make these vague abstractions more clear and fixed, so that the logical faculty should be able to employ them securely and coherently.   But there were two ways of making this attempt; the one, by examining the words only, and the thoughts which they call up; the other, by attending to the facts and things which bring these abstract terms into use.   The latter, the method of *real* inquiry, was the way to success; but the Greeks followed the former, the *verbal* or *notional* course, and failed.

If Herodotus, when the notion of the sun's attracting the waters of rivers had entered into his mind, had gone on to instruct himself, by attention to facts, in what manner this notion could be made more definite, while it still remained applicable to all the knowledge which could be obtained, he would have made some progress towards a true solution of his problem.   If, for instance, he had tried to ascertain whether this Attraction which the sun exerted upon the waters of rivers, depended on his influence at their fountains only, or was exerted over their whole course, and over waters which were not parts of rivers, he would have been led to reject his hypothesis; for he would have found, by observations sufficiently obvious, that the sun's Attraction, as shown in such cases, is a tendency to lessen all expanded and open collections of moisture, whether flowing from a spring or not; and it would then be seen that this influence, operating on the whole surface of the Nile, must diminish it as well as other rivers, in summer, and therefore could not be the cause of its overflow. He would thus have corrected his first loose conjecture by a real study of nature, and might, in the course of his meditations, have been led to available notions of Evaporation, or other natural actions. And, in like manner, in other cases, the rude attempts at explanation, which the first exercise of the speculative faculty produced, might have been gradually concentrated and refined, so as to fall in, both with the requisitions of reason and the testimony of sense.

But this was not the direction which the Greek speculators took. On the contrary; as soon as they had introduced into their philosophy any abstract and general conceptions, they proceeded to scrutinize these by the internal light of the mind alone, without any longer looking abroad into the world of sense. They took for granted that philosophy must result from the relations of those notions which are involved in the common use of language, and they proceeded to seek their philosophical doctrines by studying such notions. They ought to have reformed and fixed their usual conceptions by Observation; they only analyzed and expanded them by Reflection: they ought to have sought by trial, among the Notions which passed through their minds, some one which admitted of exact application to Facts; they selected arbitrarily, and, consequently, erroneously, the Notions according to which Facts should be assembled and arranged: they ought to have collected clear Fundamental Ideas from the world of things by *inductive* acts of thought; they only derived results by *Deduction* from one or other of their familiar Conceptions (B).

When this false direction had been extensively adopted by the Greek philosophers, we may treat of it as the method of their *Schools*. Under that title we must give a further account of it.

CHAPTER II.

THE GREEK SCHOOL PHILOSOPHY.

Sect. 1.—The general Foundation of the Greek School Philosophy.

THE physical philosophy of the Greek Schools was formed by looking at the material world through the medium of that common language which men employ to answer the common occasions of life; and by adopting, arbitrarily, as the grounds of comparison of facts, and of inference from them, notions more abstract and large than those with which men are practically familiar, but not less vague and obscure. Such a philosophy, however much it might be systematized, by classifying and analyzing the conceptions which it involves, could not overcome the vices of its fundamental principle. But before speaking of these defects, we must give some indications of its character.

The propensity to seek for principles in the common usages of language may be discerned at a very early period. Thus we have an example of it in a saying which is reported of Thales, the founder of Greek philosophy[1]. When he was asked " What is the *greatest* thing?" he replied, " *Place;* for all other

---

[1] Plut. *Conv. Sept. Sap.* Diog. Laert. i. 35.

things are *in* the world, but the world is *in* it." In Aristotle we have the consummation of this mode of speculation. The usual point from which he starts in his inquiries is, that *we say* thus or thus in common language. Thus, when he has to discuss the question, whether there be, in any part of the universe, a Void, or space in which there is nothing, he inquires first in how many senses we say that one thing is *in* another. He enumerates many of these[2]; we say the part is in the whole, as the finger is *in* the hand; again we say, the species is in the genus, as man is included *in* animal; again, the government of Greece is *in* the king; and various other senses are described or exemplified, but of all these *the most proper* is when we say a thing is *in* a vessel, and generally, *in place*. He next examines what *place* is, and comes to this conclusion, that "if about a body there be another body including it, it is in place, and if not, not." A body *moves* when it changes its place; but he adds, that if water be in a vessel, the vessel being at rest, the parts of the water may still move, for they are included by each other; so that while the whole does not change its place, the parts may change their places in a circular order. Proceeding then to the question of a *void*, he, as usual, examines the different senses in which the term is used, and adopts, as the most proper, *place without matter*; with no useful result, as we shall soon see.

[2] Physic. Ausc. iv. 3.

Again[3], in a question concerning mechanical action, he says, " When a man moves a stone by pushing it with a stick, *we say* both that the man moves the stone, and that the stick moves the stone, but the latter *more properly*."

Again, we find the Greek philosophers applying themselves to extract their dogmas from the most general and abstract notions which they could detect; for example,—from the conception of the Universe as One or as Many things. They tried to determine how far we may, or must, combine with these conceptions that of a whole, of parts, of number, of limits, of place, of beginning or end, of full or void, of rest or motion, of cause and effect, and the like. The analysis of such conceptions with such a view, occupies, for instance, almost the whole of Aristotle's *Treatise on the Heavens.*

The Dialogue of Plato, which is entitled *Parmenides*, appears at first as if its object were to show the futility of this method of philosophizing; for the philosopher whose name it bears, is represented as arguing with an Athenian named Aristotle, (c) and, by a process of metaphysical analysis, reducing him at least to this conclusion, " that whether *One* exist, or do not exist, it follows that both it and other things, with reference to themselves and to each other, all and in all respects, both are and are not, both appear and appear not." Yet the method of Plato, so far as concerns truth of that

[3] Physic. Ausc. viii. 5.

kind with which we are here concerned, was little more efficacious than that of his rival. It consists mainly, as may be seen in several of the dialogues, and especially in the *Timæus*, in the application of notions as loose as those of the Peripatetics; for example, the conceptions of the Good, the Beautiful, the Perfect; and these are rendered still more arbitrary, by assuming an acquaintance with the views of the Creator of the universe. The philosopher is thus led to maxims which agree with those of the Aristotelians, that there can be no void, that things seek their own place, and the like[4].

Another mode of reasoning, very widely applied in these attempts, was the doctrine of contrarieties, in which it was assumed, that adjectives or substantives which are in common language, or in some abstract mode of conception, opposed to each other, must point at some fundamental antithesis in nature, which it is important to study. Thus Aristotle[5] says, that the Pythagoreans, from the contrasts which number suggests, collected ten principles,— Limited and Unlimited, Odd and Even, One and Many, Right and Left, Male and Female, Rest and Motion, Straight and Curved, Light and Darkness, Good and Evil, Square and Oblong. We shall see hereafter, that Aristotle himself deduced the doctrine of Four Elements, and other dogmas, by oppositions of the same kind.

[4] Timæus, p. 80.   [5] Metaph. 1. 5.

The physical speculator of the present day will learn without surprise, that such a mode of discussion as this, led to no truths of real or permanent value. The whole mass of the Greek philosophy, therefore, shrinks into an almost imperceptible compass, when viewed with reference to the progress of physical knowledge. Still the general character of this system, and its fortunes from the time of its founders to the overthrow of their authority, are not without their instruction, and, it may be hoped, not without their interest. I proceed, therefore, to give some account of these doctrines in their most fully developed and permanently received form, that in which they were presented by Aristotle.

Sect. 2.—The Aristotelian Physical Philosophy.

THE principal physical treatises of Aristotle are, the eight Books of "Physical Lectures," the four Books "Of the Heavens," the two Books "Of Production and Destruction:" for the Book "Of the World" is now universally acknowledged to be spurious ;. and the "Meteorologics," though full of physical explanations of natural phenomena, does not exhibit the doctrines and reasonings of the school in so general a form; the same may be said of the "Mechanical Problems." The treatises on the various subjects of Natural History, "On Animals," "On the Parts of Animals," "On Plants," "On Physiognomonics," "On Colours," "On Sound," contain an extraordinary accumulation of facts, and manifest a wonderful power of systematizing; but are not works which expound principles, and therefore do not require to be here considered.

The Physical Lectures are possibly the work concerning which a well-known anecdote is related by Simplicius, a Greek commentator of the sixth century, as well as by Plutarch. It is said, that Alexander the Great wrote to his former tutor to this effect; " You have not done well in publishing these lectures; for how shall we, your pupils, excel other men, if you make that public to all, which we learnt from you." To this Aristotle is said to have replied; " My Lectures are published and not published; they will be intelligible to those who heard them, and to none beside." This may very easily be a story invented and circulated among those who found the work beyond their comprehension; and it cannot be denied, that to make out the meaning and reasoning of every part, would be a task very laborious and difficult, if not impossible. But we may follow the import of a large portion of the Physical Lectures with sufficient clearness to apprehend the character and principles of the reasoning; and this is what I shall endeavour to do.

The author's introductory statement of his view of the nature of philosophy falls in very closely with what has been said, that he takes his facts and generalizations as they are implied in the structure of language. " We must in all cases proceed," he

says, "from what is known to what is unknown."
This will not be denied; but we can hardly follow
him in his inference. He adds, "we must proceed,
therefore, from universal to particular. And something of this," he pursues, "may be seen in language; for names signify things in a general and
indefinite manner, as *circle*, and by defining we unfold them into particulars." He illustrates this by
saying, "thus children at first call all men *father*,
and all women *mother*, but afterwards distinguish."

In accordance with this view, he endeavours to
settle several of the great questions concerning the
universe, which had been started among subtle and
speculative men, by unfolding the meaning of the
words and phrases which are applied to the most
general notions of things and relations. We have
already noticed this method. A few examples will
illustrate it further:—Whether there was or was
not a *void*, or place without matter, had already been
debated among rival sects of philosophers. The antagonist arguments were briefly these:—There must
be a void, because a body cannot move into a space
except it is empty, and therefore without a void
there could be no motion:—and, on the other hand,
there is no void, for the intervals between bodies
are filled with air, and air is something. These
opinions had even been supported by reference to
experiment. On the one hand, Anaxagoras and
his school had shown, that air when confined, re-
sisted compression, by squeezing a blown bladder,

and pressing down an inverted vessel in the water; on the other hand, it was alleged that a vessel full of fine ashes held as much water as if the ashes were not there, which could only be explained by supposing void spaces among the ashes. Aristotle decides that there is no void, on such arguments as this[6]:—In a void there could be no difference of up and down; for as in nothing there are no differences, so there are none in a privation or negation; but a void is merely a privation or negation of matter; therefore, in a void, bodies could not move up and down, which it is in their nature to do. It is easily seen that such a mode of reasoning elevates the familiar forms of language and the intellectual connexions of terms, to a supremacy over facts; making truth depend upon whether terms are or are not privative, and whether we say that bodies fall *naturally*. In such a philosophy every new result of observation would be compelled to conform to the usual combinations of phrases, as these had become associated by the modes of apprehension previously familiar.

It is not intended here to intimate that the common modes of apprehension, which are the basis of common language, are limited and casual. They imply, on the contrary, universal and necessary conditions of our perceptions and conceptions: thus all things are necessarily apprehended as existing in Time and Space, and as connected by relations of

[6] Physic. Ausc. iv. 7. p. 215.

Cause and Effect; and so far as the Aristotelian philosophy reasons from these assumptions, it has a
real foundation, though even in this case the conclusions are often insecure. We have an example
of this reasoning in the eighth Book[7], where he
proves that there never was a time in which change
and motion did not exist; "For if all things were
at rest, the first motion must have been produced
by some change in some of these things; that is,
there must have been a change before the first
change;" and again, "How can *before* and *after*
apply when time is not? or how can time be when
motion is not? If," he adds, "time is a numeration
of motion, and if time be eternal, motion must be
eternal." But he sometimes introduces principles of
a more arbitrary character; and besides the general
relations of thought, takes for granted the inventions of previous speculators; such, for instance, as
the then commonly received opinions concerning
the frame of the world. From the assertion that
motion is eternal, proved in the manner just stated,
Aristotle proceeds by a curious train of reasoning,
to identify this eternal motion with the diurnal
motion of the heavens. "There must," he says, "be
something which is the First Mover[8]:" this follows
from the relation of causes and effects. Again,
"motion must go on constantly, and, therefore,
must be either continuous or successive. Now what

---

[7] Physic. Ausc. viii. 1. p. 251.
[8] Physic. Ausc. viii. 6. p. 258.

is continuous is more properly said to take place *constantly*, than what is successive. Also the continuous is better ; but we always suppose that which is better to take place in nature, if it be possible. The motion of the First Mover will, therefore, be continuous, if such an eternal motion be possible." We here see the vague judgment of *better* and *worse* introduced, as that of *natural* and *unnatural* was before, into physical reasonings.

I proceed with Aristotle's argument[9]. "We have now, therefore, to show that there may be an infinite, single, continuous motion, and that this is circular." This is, in fact, proved, as may readily be conceived, from the consideration that a body may go on perpetually revolving uniformly in a circle. And thus we have a demonstration, on the principles of this philosophy, that there is and must be a First Mover, revolving eternally with a uniform circular motion.

Though this kind of philosophy may appear too trifling to deserve being dwelt upon, it is important for our purpose so far as to exemplify it, that we may afterwards advance, confident that we have done it no injustice.

I will now pass from the doctrines relating to the motions of the heavens, to those which concern the material elements of the universe. And here it may be remarked that the tendency (of which we are here tracing the developement) to extract specu-

[9] viii. 8.

lative opinions from the relations of words, must be very natural to man; for the very widely accepted doctrine of the Four Elements which appears to be founded on the opposition of the adjectives *hot* and *cold, wet* and *dry*, is much older than Aristotle, and was probably one of the earliest of philosophical dogmas. The great master of this philosophy, however, puts the opinion in a more systematic manner than his predecessors.

"We seek," he says[10], "the principles of sensible things, that is, of tangible bodies. We must take, therefore, not all the contrarieties of quality, but those only which have reference to the touch. Thus black and white, sweet and bitter, do not differ as tangible qualities, and therefore must be rejected from our consideration.

"Now the contrarieties of quality which refer to the touch are these: hot, cold; dry, wet; heavy, light; hard, soft; unctuous, meagre; rough, smooth; dense, rare." He then proceeds to reject all but the four first of these, for various reasons; heavy and light, because they are not active and passive qualities; the others, because they are combinations of the four first, which therefore he infers to be the four elementary qualities.

"[11]Now in four things there are six combinations of two; but the combinations of two opposites, as hot and cold, must be rejected; we have, therefore, four elementary combinations, which agree

[10] De Gen. et Corrupt ii. 2.   [11] iii. 3.

with the four apparently elementary bodies.   Fire
is hot and dry; air is hot and wet (for steam is air);
water is cold and wet, earth is cold and dry."

It may be remarked that this disposition to assume that some common elementary quality must
exist in the cases in which we habitually apply a
common adjective, as it began before the reign of
the Aristotelian philosophy, so also survived its
influence.   Not to mention other cases, it would be
difficult to free Bacon's *Inquisitio in naturam
calidi*, "Examination of the nature of heat," from
the charge of confounding together very different
classes of phenomena under the cover of the word
hot.

The correction of these opinions concerning the
elementary composition of bodies belongs to an advanced period in the history of physical knowledge,
even after the revival of its progress.   But there
are some of the Aristotelian doctrines which particularly deserve our attention, from the prominent
share they had in the very first beginnings of that
revival, I mean the doctrines concerning motion.

These are still founded upon the same mode of
reasoning from adjectives; but in this case, the result follows, not only from the opposition of the
words, but also from the distinction of their being
absolutely or *relatively* true.   "Former writers,"
says Aristotle, "have considered heavy and light
relatively only, taking cases, where both things have
weight, but one is lighter than the other; and they

imagined that, in this way, they defined what was *absolutely* (ἁπλῶς) heavy and light." We now know that things which rise by their lightness do so only because they are pressed upwards by heavier surrounding bodies; and this assumption of absolute levity, which is evidently gratuitous, or rather merely nominal, entirely vitiated the whole of the succeeding reasoning. The inference was, that fire must be absolutely light, since it tends to take its place above the other three elements; earth absolutely heavy, since it tends to take its place below fire, air, and water. The philosopher argued also, with great acuteness, that air, which tends to take its place below fire and above water, must do so *by its nature*, and not in virtue of any combination of heavy and light elements. "For if air were composed of the parts which give fire its levity, joined with other parts which produce gravity, we might assume a quantity of air so large, that it should be lighter than a small quantity of fire, having more of the light parts." It thus follows that each of the four elements tends to its own place, fire being the highest, air the next, water the next, and earth the lowest.

The whole of this train of errors arises from fallacies which have a verbal origin;—from considering light as opposite to heavy; and from considering levity as a quality of a body, instead of regarding it as the effect of surrounding bodies.

It is worth while to notice that a difficulty which

often embarrasses persons on their entrance upon physical speculations,—the difficulty of conceiving that up and down are different directions in different places,—had been completely got over by Aristotle and the Greek philosophers. They were steadily convinced of the roundness of the earth, and saw that this truth led to the conclusion that all heavy bodies tend in converging directions to the centre. And, they added, as the heavy tends to the centre, the light tends to the exterior, "for Exterior is opposite to Centre as heavy is to light[12]."

The tendencies of bodies downwards and upwards, their weight, their fall, their floating or sinking, were thus accounted for in a manner which, however unsound, satisfied the greater part of the speculative world till the time of Galileo and Stevinus, though Archimedes in the mean time published the true theory of floating bodies, which is very different from that above stated. Other parts of the doctrines of motion were delivered by the Stagirite in the same spirit and with the same success. The motion of a body which is thrown along the ground diminishes and finally ceases; the motion of a body which falls from a height goes on becoming quicker and quicker; this was accounted for on the usual principle of opposition, by saying that the former is a *violent*, the latter a *natural* motion. And the later writers of this school expressed the

[12] De Cœlo, iv..4.

characters of such motions in verse. The rule of natural motion was[13]

> Principium tepeat, medium cum fine calebit.
> Cool at the first, it warm and warmer glows.

And of violent motion, the law was—

> Principium fervet, medium calet, ultima friget.
> Hot at the first, then barely warm, then cold.

It appears to have been considered by Aristotle a difficult problem to explain why a stone thrown from the hand continues to move for some time, and then stops. If the hand was the cause of the motion, how could the stone move at all when left to itself? if not, why does it ever stop? And he answers this difficulty by saying[14], "that there is a motion communicated to the air, the successive parts of which urge the stone onwards; and that each part of this medium continues to act for some while after it has been acted on, and the motion ceases when it comes to a particle which cannot act after it has ceased to be acted on." It will be readily seen that the whole of this difficulty, concerning a body which moves forwards and is retarded till it stops, arises from ascribing the retardation, not to the real cause, the surrounding resistances, but to the body itself.

One of the doctrines which was the subject of the warmest discussion between the defenders and opposers of Aristotle, at the revival of physical

---

[13] Alsted. Encyc. tom i. p. 687.   [14] Phys. Ausc. viii. 10.

knowledge, was that in which he asserts[15] "That body is heavier than another which in an equal bulk moves downward quicker." The opinion maintained by the Aristotelians at the time of Galileo was, that bodies fall quicker exactly in proportion to their weight. The master himself asserts this in express terms, and reasons upon it[16]. Yet in another passage he appears to distinguish between weight and actual motion downwards[17]. "In physics, we call bodies heavy and light from their *power* of motion; but these names are not applied to their actual operations (ἐνέργειαις) except any one thinks *momentum* (ῥοπή) to be a word of both applications. But heavy and light are, as it were, the *embers* or *sparks* of motion, and therefore proper to be treated of here."

The distinction just alluded to between Power or Faculty of Action, and actual Operation or Energy, is one very frequently referred to by Aristotle; and though not by any means useless, may easily be so used as to lead to mere verbal refinements instead of substantial knowledge.

The Aristotelian distinction of Causes has not any very immediate bearing upon the parts of physics of which we have here mainly spoken; but it was so extensively accepted, and so long retained, that it may be proper to notice it[18]. "One kind of

[15] De Cœlo, iv. 1, p. 308.   [16] De Cœlo, iii. 2.
[17] De Cœlo, iv. 1, p. 307.   [18] Phys. ii. 3.

Cause is the matter of which any thing is made, as bronze of a statue, and silver of a phial ; another is the form and pattern, as the Cause of an octave is the ratio of two to one ; again, there is the Cause which is the origin of the production, as the father of the child ; and again, there is the End, or that for the sake of which anything is done, as health is the cause of walking." These four kinds of Cause, the *material*, the *formal*, the *efficient*, and the *final*, were long leading points in all speculative inquiries; and our familiar forms of speech still retain traces of the influence of this division.

It is my object here to present to the reader in an intelligible shape, the principles and mode of reasoning of the Aristotelian philosophy, not its results. If this were not the case, it would be easy to excite a smile by insulating some of the passages which are most remote from modern notions. I will only mention, as specimens, two such passages, both very remarkable.

In the beginning of the book " On the Heavens," he proves[19] the world to be *perfect*, by reasoning of the following kind : " The bodies of which the world is composed are solids, and therefore have three dimensions; now three is the most perfect number ; it is the first of numbers, for of *one* we do not speak as a number ; of *two* we say *both* ; but *three* is the first number of which we say *all* ; moreover, it has a beginning, a middle, and an end."

[19] De Cœlo, i. 1.

The reader will still perceive the verbal foundations of opinions thus supported.

" The simple elements must have simple motions, and thus fire and air have their natural motions upwards, and water and earth have their natural motions downdards; but besides these motions, there is motion in a circle, which is unnatural to these elements, but which is a more perfect motion than the other, because a circle is a perfect line, and a straight line is not; and there must be something to which this motion is natural. From this it is evident," he adds, with obvious animation, "that there is some essence of body different from those of the four elements, more divine than those, and superior to them. If things which move in a circle move contrary to nature, it is marvellous, or rather absurd, that this, the unnatural motion, should alone be continuous and eternal; for unnatural motions decay speedily. And so, from all this, we must collect, that besides the four elements which we have here and about us, there is another removed far off, and the more excellent in proportion as it is more distant from us." This fifth element was the " *quinta essentia* " of after writers, of which we have a trace in our modern literature, in the word *quintessence*.

Sect. 3.—Technical Forms of the Greek Schools.

WE have hitherto considered only the principle of the Greek Physics; which was, as we have seen, to deduce its doctrines by an analysis of the notions which common language involves. But though the Grecian philosopher began by studying words in their common meanings, he soon found himself led to fix upon some special shades or applications of these meanings as the permanent and standard notion, which they were to express; that is, he made his language *technical*. The invention and establishment of technical terms is an important step in any philosophy, true or false; we must, therefore, say a few words on this process, as exemplified in the ancient systems.

1. *Technical Forms of the Aristotelian Philosophy.*—We have already had occasion to cite some of the distinctions introduced by Aristotle, which may be considered as technical; for instance, the classification of Causes as *material, formal, efficient, and final;* and the opposition of Qualities as *absolute* and *relative*. A few more of the most important examples may suffice. An analysis of objects into *Matter* and *Form*, when metaphorically extended from visible objects to things conceived in the most general manner, became an habitual hypothesis of the Aristotelian school. Indeed this metaphor is even yet one of the most significant of those which we can employ, to suggest one of the most compre-

hensive and fundamental antitheses with which philosophy has to do ;—the opposition of sense and
reason, of impressions and laws. In this application,
the German philosophers have, up to the present
time, rested upon this distinction a great part of the
weight of their systems ; as when Kant says, that
Space and Time are the *Forms of Sensation*. Even
in our own language, we retain a trace of the influence of this Aristotelian notion, in the word
Information, when used for that knowledge, which
may be conceived as moulding the mind into a
definite shape, instead of leaving it a mere mass of
unimpressed susceptibility.

Another favourite Aristotelian antithesis is that
of *Power* and *Act* (δύναμις, ἐνέργεια). This distinction is made the basis of most of the physical philosophy of the school ; being, however, generally
introduced with a peculiar limitation. Thus, Light
is defined to be "the Act of what is lucid, as being
lucid. And if," it is added, "the lucid be so in
power but not in act, we have darkness." The
reason of the limitation, "as being lucid," is, that a
lucid body may act in other ways ; thus a torch may
move as well as shine, but its moving is not its act
as being a lucid body.

Aristotle appears to be well satisfied with this
explanation, for he goes on to say, "Thus Light is
not Fire, nor any body whatever, or the emanation
of any body, (for that would be a kind of body,) but
it is the presence of something like Fire in the

body; it is, however, impossible that two bodies should exist in the same place, so that it is not a body;" and this reasoning appears to leave him more satisfied with his doctrine, that Light is an *Energy* or *Act*.

But we have a more distinctly technical form given to this notion. Aristotle introduced a word formed by himself, to express the act which is thus opposed to inactive power: this is the celebrated word ἐντελέχεια. Thus the noted definition of Motion in the third book of the Physics[20], is that it is "the *Entelechy*, or Act, of a moveable body in respect of being moveable;" and the definition of the Soul is[21] that it is "the *Entelechy* of a natural body which has life by reason of its power." This word has been variously translated by the followers of Aristotle, and some of them have declared it untranslateable. *Act* and *Action* are held to be inadequate substitutes; the *very act, ipse cursus actionis* is employed by some; *primus actus* is employed by many, but another school use *primus actus* of a non-operating form. Budæus uses *efficacia*. Cicero[22] translates it "quasi quandam continuatam motionem, et perennem;" but this paraphrase, though it may fall in with the description of the soul, which is the subject with which Cicero is concerned, does not appear to agree with the general applications of the term. Hermolaus Barbarus is said to have been so much oppressed with

[20] Phys. iii. 1.   [21] De Animâ. ii. 1.   [22] Tusc. i. 10.

this difficulty of translation, that he consulted the evil spirit by night, entreating to be supplied with a more common and familiar substitute for this word: the mocking fiend, however, suggested only a word equally obscure, and the translator, discontented with this, invented for himself the word *perfectihabia*.

We need not here notice the endless apparatus of technicalities which was, in later days, introduced into the Aristotelian philosophy; but we may remark, that their long continuance and extensive use show us how powerful technial phraseology is, for the perpetuation either of truth or error. The Aristotelian terms, and the metaphysical views which they tend to preserve, are not yet extinct among us. In a very recent age of our literature it was thought a worthy employment by some of the greatest writers of the day, to attempt to expel this system of technicalities by ridicule.

"Crambe regretted extremely that *substantial forms*, a race of harmless beings, which had lasted for many years, and afforded a comfortable subsistence to many poor philosophers, should now be hunted down like so many wolves, without a possibility of retreat. He considered that it had gone much harder with them than with *essences*, which had retired from the schools into the apothecaries' shops, where some of them had been advanced to the degree of *quintessences*[23].

[23] Martinus Scriblerus, cap. vii.

ˋ We must now say a few words on the technical terms which others of the Greek philosophical sects introduced.

2. *Technical Forms of the Platonists.*—The other sects of the Greek philosophy, as well as the Aristotelians, invented and adopted technical terms, and thus gave fixity to their tenets and consistency to their traditionary systems; of these I will mention a few.

A technical expression of a contemporary school has acquired perhaps greater celebrity than any of the terms of Aristotle. I mean the *Ideas* of Plato. The account which Aristotle gives of the origin of these will serve to explain their nature[24]. "Plato," says he, "who, in his youth, was in habits of communication first with Cratylus and the Heraclitean opinions, which represent all the objects of sense as being in a perpetual flux, so that concerning these no science nor certain knowledge can exist, entertained the same opinions at a later period also. When, afterwards, Socrates treated of moral subjects, and gave no attention to physics, but in the subjects which he did discuss, arrived at universal truths, and before any other man, turned his thoughts to definitions, Plato adopted similar doctrines on this subject also; and construed them in this way, that these truths and definitions must be applicable to something else, and not to sensible

[24] Arist. Metaph. i. 6. The same account is repeated, and the subject discussed, Metaph. xii. 4.

things: for it was impossible, he conceived, that there should be a general common definition of any sensible object, since such were always in a state of change. The things, then, which were the subjects of universal truths he called *Ideas;* and held that objects of sense had their names according to Ideas and after them; so that things participated in that Idea which had the same name as was applied to them."

In agreement with this, we find the opinions suggested in the *Parmenides* of Plato, the dialogue which is considered by many to contain the most decided exposition of the doctrine of Ideas. In this dialogue, Parmenides is made to say to Socrates, then a young man[25], "O Socrates, philosophy has not yet claimed you for her own, as, in my judgment, she will claim you, and you will not dishonour her. As yet, like a young man as you are, you look to the opinions of men. But tell me this: it appears to you, as you say, that there are certain *Kinds* or *Ideas* (εἴδη) of which things partake and receive applications according to that of which they partake: thus those things which partake of *Likeness* are called *like;* those things which partake of *Greatness* are called *great;* those things which partake of *Beauty* and *Justice* are called *beautiful* and *just.*" To this Socrates assents. And in another part of the dialogue he shows that these Ideas are not included in our common knowledge, from whence

[25] Parmenid. p. 131.

he infers that they are objects of the Divine mind.

. In the Phædo the same opinion is maintained, and is summed up in this way, by a reporter of the last conversation of Socrates[26] εἶναι τι ἕκαστον τῶν εἰδῶν, καὶ τούτων τ'ἄλλα μεταλαμβάνοντα αὐτῶν τούτων τὴν ἐπωνυμίαν ἴσχειν; "that each *Kind* has an existence, and that other things partake of these Kinds, and are called according to the Kind of which they partake."

. The inference drawn from this view was, that in order to obtain true and certain knowledge, men must elevate themselves, as much as possible, to these Ideas of the qualities which they have to consider: and as things were thus called after the Ideas, the Ideas had a priority and pre-eminence assigned them. The *Idea* of Good, Beautiful, and Wise, was the "First Good," the "First Beautiful," the "First Wise." This dignity and distinction were ultimately carried to a large extent. Those Ideas were described as eternal and self-subsisting, forming an "Intelligible World," full of the models or archetypes of created things. But it is not to our purpose here to consider the Platonic Ideas in their theological bearings. In physics they were applied in the same form as in morals. The *primum calidum, primum frigidum*, were those Ideas or fundamental Principles by participation of which, all things were hot or cold.

[26] Phædo, p. 102.

This school did not much employ itself in the developement of its principles as applied to physical inquiries: but we are not without examples of such speculations. Plutarch's Treatise Περι τοῦ Πρώτου Ψυχροῦ, "On the First Cold," may be cited as one. It is in reality a discussion of a question which has been agitated in modern times also;—whether cold be a positive quality or a mere privation. " Is there, O Favorinus," he begins, " a First Power and Essence of the Cold, as Fire is of the Hot; by a certain presence and participation of which all other things are cold: or is rather coldness a privation of heat, as darkness is of light, and rest of motion?"

3. *Technical Forms of the Pythagoreans.*—The *Numbers* of the Pythagoreans, when propounded as the explanation of physical phenomena, as they were, are still more obscure than the ideas of the Platonists. There were, indeed, considerable resemblances in the way in which these two kinds of notions were spoken of. Plato called his Ideas *unities, monads ;* and as, according to him, Ideas, so, according to the Pythagoreans, Numbers, were the causes of things being what they are[27]. But there was this difference, that things shared the nature of the Platonic Ideas " by participation," while they shared the nature of Pythagorean Numbers " by imitation." Moreover, the Pythagoreans followed their notion out into much greater developement than any other school, investing particular numbers

[27]. Arist. Metaph. i. 6.

with extraordinary attributes, and applying them by very strange and forced analogies. Thus the number Four, to which they gave the name of *Tetractys*, was held to be the most perfect number, and was conceived to correspond to the human soul, in some way which appears to be very imperfectly understood by the commentators of this philosophy.

It has been observed by a distinguished modern scholar[28], that the place which Pythagoras ascribed to his numbers is intelligible only by supposing that he confounded, first a numerical unit with a geometrical point, and then this with a material atom. But this criticism appears to place systems of physical philosophy under requisitions too severe. If all the essential properties and attributes of things were fully represented by the relations of number, the philosophy which supplied such an explanation of the universe, might well be excused from explaining also that existence of objects which is distinct from the existence of all their qualities and properties. The Pythagorean love of numerical speculations might have been combined with the doctrine of atoms, and the combination might have led to results well worth notice. But so far as we are aware, no such combination was attempted in the ancient schools of philosophy; and perhaps we of the present day are only just beginning to perceive, through the disclosures of chemistry and

[28] Thirlwall's *Hist. Gr.* ii. 142.

crystallography, the importance of such a line of inquiry.

4. *Technical Forms of the Atomists and Others.* —The atomic doctrine, of which we have just spoken, was one of the most definite of the physical doctrines of the ancients, and was applied with most perseverance and knowledge to the explanation of phenomena. Though, therefore, it led to no success of any consequence in ancient times, it served to transmit, through a long series of ages, a habit of really physical inquiry; and on this account, has been thought worthy of an historical disquisition by Bacon[29].

The technical term, *Atom*, marks sufficiently the nature of the opinion. According to this theory, the world consists of a collection of simple particles, of one kind of matter, and of indivisible smallness, (as the name indicates,) and by the various configurations and motions of these particles, all kinds of matter and all material phenomena are produced.

To this, the Atomic Doctrine of Leucippus and Democritus, was opposed the *Homoiomeria* of Anaxagoras; that is, the opinion that material things consist of particles which are homogeneous in each kind of body, but various in different kinds: thus for example, since by food the flesh and blood and bones of man increase, the author of this doctrine held that there are in food particles of flesh,

---

[29] Parmenidis et Telesii et præcipue Democriti Philosophia, &c., Works, vol. ix. 317.

and blood, and bone. As the former tenet points to the corpuscular theories of modern times, so the latter may be considered as a dim glimpse of the idea of chemical analysis. The Stoics also, who were, especially at a later period, inclined to materialist views, had their technical modes of speaking on such subjects. They asserted that matter contained in itself tendencies or dispositions to certain forms, which dispositions they called λόγοι σπερματικοὶ, *seminal proportions*, or *seminal reasons*.

·Whatever of sound view, or right direction, there might be in the notions which suggested these and other technical expressions, was, in all the schools of philosophy (so far as physics was concerned), quenched and overlaid by the predominance of trifling and barren speculations; and by the love of subtilizing and commenting upon the works of earlier writers, instead of attempting to interpret the book of nature. Hence these technical terms served to give fixity and permanence to the traditional dogmas of the sect, but led to no progress of knowledge.

. The advances which were made in physical science proceeded, not from these schools of philosophy, (if we except, perhaps, the obligations of the science of Harmonics to the Pythagoreans,) but from reasoners who followed an independent path. The sequel of the ambitious hopes, the vast schemes, the confident undertakings of the philosophers of

ancient Greece, was an entire failure in the physical knowledge of which it is our business to trace
the history.   Yet we are not, on that account, to
think slightingly of these early speculators.   They
were men of extraordinary acuteness, invention, and
range of thought; and above all, they had the
merit of first completely unfolding the speculative
faculty;—of starting in that keen and vigorous
chase of knowledge, out of which all the subsequent
culture and improvement of man's intellectual stores
have arisen.   The sages of early Greece form the
heroic age of science.   Like the first navigators in
their own mythology, they boldly ventured their
untried bark in a distant and arduous voyage, urged
on by the hopes of a supernatural success; and
though they missed the imaginary golden prize
which they sought, they unlocked the gates of distant regions, and opened the seas to the keels of
the thousands of adventurers, who, in succeeding
times, sailed to and fro, to the indefinite increase of
the mental treasures of mankind.

But inasmuch as their attempts, in one sense,
and at first, failed, we must proceed to offer some
account of this failure, and of its nature and causes.

CHAPTER III.

FAILURE OF THE PHYSICAL PHILOSOPHY OF THE GREEK SCHOOLS.

Sect. 1.—Result of the Greek School Philosophy.

THE methods and forms of philosophizing which we have described as employed by the Greek Schools, failed altogether in their application to physics. No discovery of general laws, no explanation of special phenomena, rewarded the acuteness and boldness of these early students of nature. Astronomy, which made considerable progress during the existence of the sects of Greek philosophers, gained perhaps something by the authority with which Plato taught the supremacy and universality of mathematical rule and order; and the truths of Harmonics, which had probably given rise to the Pythagorean passion for numbers, were cultivated with much care by that school. But after these first impulses, the sciences owed nothing to the philosophical sects; and the vast and complex accumulations and apparatus of the Stagirite do not appear to have led to any theoretical physical truths.

This assertion hardly requires proof, since in the existing body of science there are no doctrines for which we are indebted to the Aristotelian School. Real truths, when once established, remain to the end of time a part of the mental treasure of man, and may be discerned through all the additions of later days. But we can point out no physical doctrine now received, of which we trace the anticipation in Aristotle, in the way in which we see the Copernican system anticipated by Aristarchus, the resolution of the heavenly appearances into circular motions suggested by Plato, and the numerical relations of musical intervals ascribed to Pythagoras. But it may be worth while to look at this matter more closely.

Among the works of Aristotle, are thirty-eight chapters of "Problems," which may serve to exemplify the progress he had really made in the reduction of phenomena to laws and causes. Of these Problems, a large proportion are physiological, and these I here pass by, as not illustrative of the state of physical knowledge. But those which are properly physical are, for the most part, questions concerning such facts and difficulties as it is the peculiar business of theory to explain. Now it may be truly said, that in scarcely any one instance are the answers, which Aristotle gives to his questions, of any value. For the most part, indeed, he propounds his answer with a degree of hesitation or vacillation, which of itself shows the absence of all scientific distinctness of thought; and the opinions so offered never appear to involve any settled or general principle.

We may take, as examples of this, the problems of the simplest kind, where the principles lay nearest at hand,—the mechanical ones. " Why," he asks[1], " do small forces move great weights by means of a lever, when they have thus to move the lever added to the weight? Is it," he suggests, "because a greater radius moves faster?" " Why does a small wedge split great weights[2]? Is it because the wedge is composed of two opposite levers?" " Why[3], when a man rises from a chair, does he bend his leg and his body to acute angles with his thigh? Is it because a right angle is connected with equality and rest?" " Why[4] can a man throw a stone further with a sling than with his hand? Is it that when he throws with his hand he moves the stone from rest, but when he uses the sling he throws it already in motion?" " Why[5], if a circle be thrown on the ground, does it first describe a straight line and then a spiral, as it falls? Is it that the air first presses equally on the two sides and supports it, and afterwards presses on one side more?" " Why[6] is it difficult to distinguish a musical note from the octave above? Is it that proportion stands in the place of equality?" It must be allowed that these are very vague and worthless surmises; for even if we were, as some commentators have done, to interpret some of them so as to agree with sound philosophy, we should still be unable to point out, in this author's

[1] Mech. Prob. 4.   [2] Ib. 18.   [3] Ib. 31.   [4] Ib. 13.
[5] Περι 'Αψυχα. 11.   [6] Περι 'Αρμον. 14.

works, any clear or permanent apprehension of the general principles which such an interpretation implies.

Thus the Aristotelian physics cannot be considered as otherwise than a complete failure. It collected no general laws from facts; and consequently, when it tried to explain facts, it had no principles which were of any avail.

The same may be said of the physical speculations of the other schools of philosophy. They arrived at no doctrines from which they could deduce, by sound reasoning, such facts as they saw; though they often venture so far to trust their principles as to infer from them propositions beyond the domain of sense. Thus, the principle that each element seeks *its own place,* led to the doctrine, that, the place of fire being the highest, there is, above the air, a Sphere of Fire; of which doctrine the word *Empyrean,* used by our poets, still conveys a reminiscence. The Pythagorean tenet that ten is a perfect number[7], led some persons to assume that the heavenly bodies are in number ten; and as nine only were known to them, they asserted that there was an *antichthon,* or *counter-earth,* on the other side of the sun, invisible to us. Their opinions respecting numerical ratios, led to various other speculations concerning the distances and positions of the heavenly bodies: and as they had, in other cases, found a connexion between propor-

[7] Arist. Metaph. i. 5.

tions of distance and musical notes, they assumed, on this suggestion, *the music of the spheres.*

Although we shall look in vain in the physical philosophy of the Greek Schools, for any results more valuable than those just mentioned, we shall not be surprised to find, recollecting how much an admiration for classical antiquity has possessed the minds of men, that some writers estimate their claims much more highly than they are stated here. Among such writers we may notice Dutens, who, in 1766, published his "Origin of the Discoveries attributed to the Moderns; in which it is shown that our most celebrated Philosophers have received the greatest part of their knowledge from the Works of the Ancients." The thesis of this work is attempted to be proved, as we might expect, by very large interpretations of the general phrases used by the ancients. Thus, when Timæus, in Plato's dialogue, says of the Creator of the world[8], "that he infused into it two powers, the origins of motions, both of that of the same thing, and of that of different things;" Dutens[9] finds in this a clear indication of the projectile and attractive forces of modern science. And in some of the common declamation of the Pythagoreans and Platonists, concerning the general prevalence of numerical relations in the universe, he discovers their acquaintance with the law of the inverse square of the distance by which gravitation is regulated, though he allows[10] that it

[8] Tim. 96. [9] 3d ed. p. 83. [10] Ib. p. 88.

required all the penetration of Newton and his followers to detect this law in the scanty fragments
by which it is transmitted.

Argument of this kind is palpably insufficient to
cover the failure of the Greek attempts at a general
physical philosophy; or rather we may say, that
such arguments, since they are as good as can be
brought in favour of such an opinion, show more
clearly how entire the failure was. I proceed now
to endeavour to point out its causes.

Sect. 2.—Cause of the Failure of the Greek Phy-sical Philosophy.

THE cause of the failure of so many of the attempts of the Greeks to construct physical science
is so important, that we must endeavour to bring it
into view here; though the full developement of
such subjects belongs rather to the philosophy of induction. The subject must, at present, be treated
very briefly.

I will first notice some errors which may naturally occur to the reader's mind, as possible causes
of failure, but which, we shall be able to show,
were not the real reasons in this case.

The cause of failure was *not the neglect of facts.*
It is often said that the Greeks disregarded experience, and spun their philosophy out of their own
thoughts alone; and this is supposed by many to be
their essential error. It is, no doubt, true, that the
disregard of experience is a phrase which may be

so interpreted as to express almost any defect of philosophical method; since coincidence with experience is requisite to the truth of all theory. But if we fix a more precise sense on our terms, I conceive it may be shown that the Greek philosophy did, in its opinions, recognize the necessity and paramount value of observations; did, in its origin, proceed upon observed facts; and did employ itself to no small extent in classifying and arranging phenomena. We must endeavour to illustrate these assertions, because it is important to show that these steps alone do not necessarily lead to science.

1. The acknowledgment of experience as the main ground of physical knowledge is so generally understood to be a distinguishing feature of later times, that it may excite surprise to find that Aristotle, and other ancient philosophers, not only asserted in the most pointed manner that all our knowledge must begin from experience, but also stated in language much resembling the habitual phraseology of the most modern schools of philosophising, that particular facts must be *collected*; that from these, general principles must be obtained by *induction*; and that these principles, when of the most general kind, are *axioms*. A few passages will show this.

"The way[11] must be the same," says Aristotle, in speaking of the rules of reasoning, "with respect to philosophy, as it is with respect to any art or

[11] Anal. Prior. i. 30.

science whatever; we must collect the facts, and the things to which the facts happen, in each subject, and provide as large a supply of these as possible." He then proceeds to say that "we are not to look at once at all this collected mass, but to consider small and definite portions"..."And thus it is the office of observation to supply principles in each subject; for instance, astronomical observation supplies the principles of astronomical science. For the phenomena being properly assumed, the astronomical demonstrations were from these discovered. And the same applies to every art and science. So that if we take the facts (τὰ ὑπάρχοντα) belonging to each subject, it is *our* task to mark out clearly the course of the demonstrations. For if *in our natural history* (κατὰ τὴν ἱστορίαν) we have omitted nothing of the facts and properties which belong to the subject, we shall learn what we can demonstrate and what we cannot."

These facts, τὰ ὑπάρχοντα, he, at other times, includes in the term *sensation*. Thus he says[12], "It is obvious that if any sensation is wanting, there must be also some knowledge wanting which we are thus prevented from having, since we arrive at knowledge either by induction or by demonstration. Demonstration proceeds from universal propositions, induction from particulars. But we cannot have universal theoretical propositions except from induction; and we cannot make inductions without

[12] Anal. Post. i. 18.

having sensation ; for sensation has to do with particulars."

In another place[13], after stating that principles must be prior to, and better known than conclusions, he distinguishes such principles into absolutely prior, and prior relative to us; " The prior principles, relative to us, are those which are nearer to the sensation; but the principles absolutely prior are those which are more remote from the sensation. The most general principles are the more remote, the more particular are nearer. The general principles which are necessary to knowledge are *axioms*."

We may add to these passages, that in which he gives an account of the way in which Leucippus was led to the doctrine of atoms. After describing the opinions of some earlier philosophers, he says[14], " Thus, proceeding in violation of sensation, and disregarding it, because, as they held, they must follow reason, some came to the conclusion that the universe was one, and infinite, and at rest. As it appeared, however, that though this ought to be by reasoning, it would go near to madness to hold such opinions in practice, (for no one was ever so mad as to think fire and ice to be one,) Leucippus, therefore, pursued a line of reasoning which was in accordance with sensation, and which was not irreconcileable with the production and decay, the motion and multitude of things." It is obvious that the school to

[13] Anal. Post. i. 2.   [14] De Gen. et Cor. i. 8.

which Leucippus belonged (the Eclectic) must have
been, at least in its origin, strongly impressed with
the necessity of bringing its theories into harmony
with the observed course of nature.

2.   Nor was this recognition of the fundamental
value of experience a mere profession.   The Greek
philosophy did, in its beginning, proceed upon observation.   Indeed it is obvious that the principles
which it adopted were, in the first place, assumed in
order to account for some classes of facts, however
imperfectly they might answer their purpose.   The
principle of things seeking their own places, was invented in order to account for the falling and floating of bodies.   Again, Aristotle says, that heat is
that which brings together things of the same kind,
cold is that which brings together things whether of
the same or of different kinds: it is plain that in
this instance he intended by his principle to explain
some obvious facts, as the freezing of moist substances, and the separation of heterogeneous things
by fusion; for, as he adds, if fire brings together
things which are akin, it will separate those which
are not akin.   It would be easy to illustrate the
remark further, but its truth is evident from the nature of the case; for no principles could be accepted
for a moment, which were the result of an arbitrary caprice of the mind, and which were not in
some measure plausible, and apparently confirmed
by facts.

But the works of Aristotle show, in another way,

how unjust it would be to accuse him of disregarding facts. Many large treatises of his consist almost entirely of collections of facts, as for instance, those "On Colours," "On Sounds," and the collection of Problems to which we have already referred; to say nothing of the numerous collection of facts bearing on natural history and physiology, which form a great portion of his works, and are even now treasuries of information. A moment's reflection will convince us that the physical sciences of our own times, for example, mechanics and hydrostatics, are founded almost entirely upon facts with which the ancients were as familiar as we are. The defect of their philosophy, therefore, wherever it may lie, exists neither in the speculative depreciation of the value of facts, nor in the practical neglect of their use.

3. Nor again, should we hit upon the truth, if we were to say that Aristotle and other ancient philosophers, did indeed collect facts; but that they took no steps in classifying and comparing them; and that thus they failed to obtain from them any general knowledge. For, in reality, the treatises of Aristotle which we have mentioned, are as remarkable for the power of classifying and systematizing which they exhibit, as for the industry shown in the accumulation. But it is not classification of facts merely which can lead us to knowledge, except we adopt that special arrangement, which, in each case, brings into view the principles of the subject. We may easily show how unprofitable an arbitrary or

random classification is, however orderly and systematic it may be.

For instance, for a long period all unusual fiery appearances in the sky were classed together as *meteors*. Comets, shooting-stars, and globes of fire, and the aurora borealis in all its forms, were thus grouped together, and classifications of considerable extent and minuteness were proposed with reference to these objects. But this classification was of a mixed and arbitrary kind. Figure, colour, motion, duration, were all combined as characters, and the imagination lent its aid, transforming these striking appearances into fiery swords and spears, bears and dragons, armies and chariots. The facts so classified were, notwithstanding, worthless; and would not have been one jot the less so, had they and their classes been ten times as numerous as they were. No rule or law that would stand the test of observation was or could be thus discovered. Such classifications have, therefore, long been neglected and forgotten. Even the ancient descriptions of these objects of curiosity are unintelligible, or unworthy of trust, because the spectators had no steady conception of the usual order of such phenomena. For, however much we may fear to be misled by preconceived opinions, the caprices of imagination distort our impressions far more than the anticipations of reason. In this case men had, indeed we may say with regard to many of these meteors, they still have, no science : not for want of facts, nor even for want of classification of facts; but because the clas-sification was one in which no real principle was contained.

4. Since, as we have said before, two things are requisite to science,—Facts and Ideas; and since, as we have seen, Facts were not wanting in the physical speculations of the ancients, we are naturally led to ask, Were they then deficient in Ideas? Was there a want among them of mental activity, and logical connexion of thought? But it is so obvious that the answer to this inquiry must be in the negative, that we need not dwell upon it. No one who knows anything of the history of the ancient Greek mind, can question, that in acuteness, in ingenuity, in the power of close and distinct reasoning, they have never been surpassed. The common opinion, which considers the defect of their philosophical character to reside rather in the exclusive activity of such qualities, than in the absence of them, is at least so far just.

5. We come back again, therefore, to the question, What was the radical and fatal defect in the physical speculations of the Greek philosophical schools?

To this I answer: The defect was, that though they had in their possession Facts and Ideas, *the Ideas were not distinct and appropriate to the Facts* (D).

The peculiar characteristics of scientific ideas, which I have endeavoured to express by speaking of them as *distinct* and *appropriate to the facts*, must be more fully and formally set forth, when we come to the philosophy of the subject.   In the mean time, the reader will probably have no difficulty in conceiving that, for each class of Facts, there is some special set of Ideas, by means of which the facts can be included in general scientific truths; and that these Ideas, which may thus be termed *appropriate*, must be possessed with entire distinctness and clearness, in order that they may be successfully applied. It was the want of Ideas having this reference to material phenomena, which rendered the ancient philosophers, with very few exceptions, helpless and unsuccessful speculators on physical subjects.

This must be illustrated by one or two examples. One of the facts which Aristotle endeavours to explain is this ; that when the sun's light passes through a hole, whatever be the form of the hole, the bright image, if formed at any considerable distance from the hole, is round, instead of imitating the figure of the hole, as shadows resemble their objects in form. We shall easily perceive this appearance to be a necessary consequence of the circular figure of the sun, if we conceive light to be diffused from the luminary by means of straight *rays* proceeding from every point of the sun's disk and passing through every point within the boundary of the hole.   By attending to the consequences of this mode of conception, it will be seen that each point of the hole will be the vertex of a double cone of rays which has the sun's disk for its base on one side and an image of the sun on the other; and the figure of the image of the hole will be determined by supposing a series of equal bright circles, images of the sun, to be placed along the boundary of an image equal to the hole itself. The figure of the image thus determined will partake of the form of the hole, and of the circular form of the sun's image: let these circular images become larger and larger as they are farther from the hole, while the central image of the hole remains always of the original size; and thus at a considerable distance from the hole, the trace of the hole's form is nearly obliterated, and the image is nearly a perfect circle. Instead of this distinct conception of a cone of rays which has the sun's disk for its basis, Aristotle has the following loose conjecture[15]. " Is it because light is emitted in a conical form; and of a cone, the base is a circle; so that on whatever the rays of the sun fall, they appear more circular?" And thus though he applies the notion of rays to this problem, he possesses this notion so *indistinctly* that his explanation is of no value. He does not introduce into his explanation the consideration of the sun's circular figure, and is thus prevented from giving a true account of this very simple optical phenomenon.

Again, to pass to a more extensive failure: why was it that Aristotle, knowing the property of the

[15] Problem. 15. ὅσα μαθηματίκης, &c.

lever, and many other mechanical truths, was unable to form them into a science of mechanics, as Archimedes afterwards did ?

The reason was, that, instead of considering rest and motion directly, and distinctly, with reference to the Idea of Cause, that is Force, he wandered in search of reasons among other ideas and notions, which could not be brought into steady connexion with the facts;—the ideas of properties of circles, of proportions of velocities,—the notions of "strange" and "common," of "natural" and "unnatural." Thus, in the Proem to his Mechanical Problems, after stating some of the difficulties which he has to attack, he says, "Of all such cases, the circle contains the principle of the cause. And this is what might be looked for; for it is nothing absurd, if something *wonderful* is derived from something more wonderful still. Now the most wonderful thing is, that opposites should be combined; and the circle is constituted of such combinations of opposites. For it is constructed by a stationary point and a moving line, which are contrary to each other in nature; and hence we may the less be surprised at the resulting contrarieties. And in the first place, the circumference of the circle, though a line without breadth, has opposite qualities; for it is both *convex* and *concave*. In the next place, it has, at the same time, opposite motions, for it moves forward and backward at the same time. For the circumference, setting out from any point, comes to the same point again, so that by a continuous progression, the last point becomes the first. So that, as was before stated, it is not surprising that the circle should be the principle of all wonderful properties."

Aristotle afterwards proceeds to explain more specially how he applies the properties of the circle in this case. "The reason," he says, in his fourth Problem, "why a force, acting at a greater distance from the fulcrum, moves a weight more easily, is, that it describes a greater circle." He had already asserted that when a body at the end of a lever is put in motion, it may be considered as having two motions; one in the direction of the tangent, and one in the direction of the radius; the former motion is, he says, *according to nature*, the latter, *contrary to nature*. Now in the smaller circle, the motion, contrary to nature, is more considerable than it is in the larger circle. "Therefore," he adds, "the mover or weight at the larger arm will be transferred further by the same force than the weight moved, which is at the extremity of the shorter arm."

These loose and inappropriate notions of "natural" and "unnatural" motions, were unfit to lead to any scientific truths; and, with the habits of thought which dictated these speculations, a perception of the true grounds of mechanical properties was impossible.

Thus, in this instance, the error of Aristotle was the neglect of the Idea *appropriate* to the facts,

namely, the Idea of Mechanical Cause, which is
Force; and the substitution of vague or inappli-
cable notions involving only relations of space, or
emotions of wonder. The errors of those who failed
similarly in other instances, were of the same kind.
To detail or classify these would lead us too far into
the philosophy of science; since we should have to
enumerate the Ideas which are appropriate, and the
various class of Facts on which the different sciences
are founded,—a task not to be now lightly under-
taken. But it will be perceived, without further
explanation, that it is necessary, in order to obtain
from facts any general truth, that we should apply
to them that appropriate Idea, by which permanent
and definite relations are established among them.

In such ideas the ancients were very poor, and
the stunted and deformed growth of their physical
science was the result of this penury. The Ideas of
Space and Time, Number and Motion, they did indeed possess distinctly; and so far as these went,
their science was tolerably healthy. They also
caught a glimpse of the Idea of a Medium by which
the qualities of bodies, as colours and sounds, are
perceived. But the idea of Substance remained
barren in their hands; in speculating about elements
and qualities, they went the wrong way, assuming
that the properties of the Compounds must *resemble*
those of the Elements which determine them; and
their loose notions of Contrariety never approached
the form of those ideas of Polarity, which, in mo-

dern times, regulate many parts of physics and chemistry.

If this statement should seem to any one to be technical or arbitrary, we must refer, for the justification of it, to the Philosophy of Science, of which we hope hereafter to treat. But it will appear, even from what has been here said, that there are certain Ideas or Forms of mental apprehension, which may be applied to Facts in such a manner as to bring into view fundamental principles of science ; while the same Facts, however arrayed or reasoned about, so long as these appropriate Ideas are not employed, cannot give rise to any exact or substantial knowledge.

We shall, in the next Book, see the influence of the appropriate general Ideas, in the formation of various sciences. It need only be observed, before we proceed, that, in order to do full justice to the physical knowledge of the Greek Schools of philosophy, it is not necessary to study their course after the time of their founders. Their fortunes, in respect of such acquisitions as we are now considering, were not progressive. The later chiefs of the Schools followed the earlier masters; and though they varied much, they added little. The Romans adopted the philosophy of their Greek subjects; but they were always, and, indeed, acknowledged themselves to be, inferior to their teachers. They were as arbitrary and loose in their ideas as the Greeks, without possessing their invention, acuteness, and spirit of system.

In addition to the vagueness which was combined with the more elevated trains of philosophical speculation among the Greeks, the Romans, introduced into their treatises a kind of declamatory rhetoric, which arose probably from their forensic and political habits, and which still further obscured the waning gleams of truth. Yet we may also trace, in the Roman philosophers to whom this charge mostly applies (Lucretius, Pliny, Seneca), the national vigour and ambition. There is something Roman in the public spirit and anticipation of universal empire which they display, as citizens of the intellectual republic. Though they speak sadly or slightingly of the achievements of their own generation, they betray a more abiding and vivid belief in the dignity and destined advance of human knowledge as a whole, than is obvious among the Greeks.

We must, however, turn back, in order to describe steps of more definite value to the progress of science than those which we have hitherto noticed.

NOTES TO BOOK I.

(B.) p. 38. THE course by which the Sciences were formed, and which is here referred to as that which the Greeks did *not* follow, is described in detail in the *Philosophy*, Book xi., *Of the Construction of Science.*

(c.) p. 41. This Aristotle is not the Stagirite, who was forty-five years younger than Plato, but one of the "thirty tyrants," as they were called.

(D.) p. 81. This account of the cause of failure in the physical speculations of the ancient Greek philosophers has been objected to as unsatisfactory. I will offer a few words in explanation of it.

The mode of accounting for the failure of the Greeks in physics is, in substance ;—that the Greeks in their physical speculations fixed their attention upon the wrong aspects and relations of the phenomena ; and that the aspects and relations in which phenomena are to be viewed in order to arrive at scientific truths may be arranged under certain heads, which I have termed *Ideas ;* such as Space, Time, Number, Cause, Likeness. In every case, there is an Idea to which the phenomena may be referred so as to bring into view the Laws by which they are governed ; this Idea I term the *appropriate* Idea in such case ; and in order that the reference of the phenomena to the Law may be clearly seen, the Idea must be *distinctly* possessed.

Thus the reason of Aristotle's failure in his attempts at Mechanical Science is, that he did not refer the facts to the appropriate Idea, namely Force, the Cause of Motion, but to relations of Space and the like; that is, he introduces *Geometrical* instead of *Mechanical* Ideas. It may be said that we learn little by being told that Aristotle's failure in this and the like cases arose from his referring to the wrong class of Ideas; or, as I have otherwise expressed it, fixing his attention upon the wrong aspects and relations of the facts; since, it may be said, this is only to state in other words that he *did* fail. . But this criticism is, I think, ill-founded, The account which I have given is not only a statement that Aristotle, and others who took a like course, did fail; but also, that they failed in one certain point out of several which are enumerated. They did not fail because they neglected to observe facts; they did not fail because they omitted to class facts; they did not fail because they had not ideas to reason from; but they failed because they did not take the right ideas in each case. And so long as they were in the wrong in this point, no industry in collecting facts, or ingenuity in classing them and reasoning about them, could lead them to solid truth. Nor is this account of the nature of their mistake without its instruction for us; although we are not to expect to derive from the study of their failure any technical rule which shall necessarily guide us to scientific discovery. For their failure teaches us that, in the formation of science, an Errour in the Ideas is as fatal to the discovery of Truth as an Errour in the Facts; and may as completely impede the progress of knowledge. I have in Books II. to x. of the *Philosophy*, shown historically how large a portion of the progress of Science consists in the establishment of Appropriate Ideas as the basis of each science.

Of the two main processes by which science is constructed, as stated in Book xi. of that work, namely the *Explication of Conceptions* and the *Colligation of Facts*, the former must precede the latter. In Book xii. chap. 5, of the *Philosophy*, I have stated the maxim concerning appropriate Ideas in this form, that *the Idea and the Facts must be homogeneous.*

When I say that the failure of the Greeks in physical science arose from their not employing *appropriate* Ideas to connect the facts, I do not use the term "appropriate" in a loose popular sense; but I employ it as a somewhat technical term, to denote *the* appropriate Idea, out of that series of Ideas which have been made (as I have shown in the *Philosophy*) the foundation of sciences; namely Space, Time, Number, Cause, Likeness, Substance, and the rest. It appears to me just to say that Aristotle's failure in his attempts to deal with problems of equilibrium, arose from his referring to circles, velocities, notions of natural and unnatural, and the like,—conceptions depending upon Ideas of Space, of Nature, &c.—which are not appropriate to these problems, and from his missing the Idea of Mechanical Force or Pressure, which is the appropriate Idea.

I give this, not as an account of *all* failures in attempts at science, but only as the account of such radical and fundamental failures as this of Aristotle; who, with a knowledge of the facts, failed to connect them into a really scientific view. If I had to compare rival theories of a more complex kind, I should not necessarily say that one involved an appropriate Idea and the other did not, though I might judge one to be true and the other to be false. For instance, in comparing the emissive and the undulatory theory of light, we see that both involve the same Idea ;—the Idea of a Medium acting by certain mechanical properties. The question there is, what is the true view of the mechanism of the Medium?

The other example of Aristotle's failure in physics, given in p. 82, namely, his attempted explanation of the round image of a square hole, is a specimen rather of indistinct than of inappropriate ideas. In the first edition I had not accurately represented Aristotle's statement.

The geometrical explanation of this phenomena, which I have inserted in the text, was given by Maurolycus, and before him, by Leonardo da Vinci.

BOOK II.

HISTORY

OF THE

PHYSICAL SCIENCES

IN

ANCIENT GREECE.

Ναρθηκοπλήρωτον δὲ θηρῶμαι πυρὸς
Πηγὴν κλοπαίαν, ἣ διδάσκαλος τέχνης
Πάσης βροτοῖς πεφῆνε καὶ μέγας πόρος.

Prom. Vinct. 109.

I brought to earth the spark of heavenly fire,
Concealed at first, and small, but spreading soon
Among the sons of men, and burning on,
Teacher of art and use, and fount of power.

BOOK II.

INTRODUCTION.

IN order to the acquisition of any such exact and real knowledge of nature as that which we properly call Physical Science, it is requisite, as has already been said, that men should possess Ideas both distinct and appropriate, and should apply them to ascertained Facts. They are thus led to propositions of a general character, which are obtained by Induction, as will elsewhere be more fully explained. We proceed now to trace the formation of Sciences among the Greeks by such processes. The provinces of knowledge which thus demand our attention are, Astronomy, Mechanics and Hydrostatics, Optics and Harmonics; of which I must relate, first, the earliest stages, and next, the subsequent progress.

Of these portions of human knowledge, Astronomy is, beyond doubt or comparison, much the most ancient and the most remarkable; and probably existed, in somewhat of a scientific form, in Chaldea and Egypt, and other countries, before the period of the intellectual activity of the Greeks. But I will give a brief account of some of the other Sciences before I proceed to Astronomy, for two reasons; first, because the origin of Astronomy is lost in the obscurity of a remote antiquity; and therefore we cannot exemplify the conditions of the first rise of science so well in that subject as we can in others which assumed their scientific form at known periods; and next, in order that I may not have to interrupt, after I have once begun it, the history of the only progressive Science which the ancient world produced (E).

CHAPTER I.

EARLIEST STAGES OF MECHANICS AND HYDRO-STATICS.

Sect. 1.—Mechanics.

ASTRONOMY is a science so ancient that we can hardly ascend to a period when it did not exist; Mechanics, on the other hand, is a science which did not begin to be till after the time of Aristotle; for Archimedes must be looked upon as the author of the first sound knowledge on this subject. What is still more curious, and shows remarkably how little the continued progress of science follows inevitably from the nature of man, this department of knowledge, after the right road had been fairly entered upon, remained absolutely stationary for nearly two thousand years; no single step was made, in addition to the propositions established by Archimedes, till the time of Galileo and Stevinus. This extraordinary halt will be a subject of attention hereafter; at present we must consider the original advance.

The great step made by Archimedes in Mechanics was the establishing, upon true grounds, the general proposition concerning a straight lever, loaded with two heavy bodies, and resting upon a

H

fulcrum. The proposition is, that two bodies so circumstanced will balance each other, when the distance of the smaller body from the fulcrum is greater than the distance of the other, in exactly the same proportion in which the weight of the body is less.

This proposition is proved by Archimedes in a work which is still extant; and the proof holds its place in our treatises to this day, as the simplest which can be given. The demonstration is made to rest on assumptions which amount in effect to such Definitions and Axioms as these:—That those bodies are of equal weight which balance each other at equal arms of a straight lever; and that in every heavy body there is a definite point called a *Centre of Gravity*, in which point we may suppose the weight of the body collected.

The principle, which is really the foundation of the validity of the demonstration thus given, and which is the condition of all experimental knowledge on the subject, is this;—that when two equal weights are supported on a lever, they act on the fulcrum of the lever with the same effect as if they were both together supported immediately at that point. Or more generally, we may state the principle to be this;—that the pressure by which a heavy body is supported continues the same, however we alter the form or position of the body, so long as the magnitude and material continue the same.

The experimental truth of this principle is a matter of obvious and universal experience. The weight of a basket of stones is not altered by shaking the stones into new positions. We cannot make the direct burden of a stone less by altering its position in our hands; and if we try the effect on a balance or a machine of any kind, we shall see still more clearly and exactly that the altered position of one weight, or the altered arrangement of several, produces no change in their effect, so long as their point of support remains unchanged.

This general fact is obvious, when we possess in our minds the ideas which are requisite to apprehend it clearly. But when we are so prepared, the truth appears to be manifest, even independent of experience, and is seen to be a rule to which experience must conform. What then is the leading Idea which thus enables us to reason effectively upon mechanical subjects? By attention to the course of such reasonings, we perceive that it is the Idea of *Pressure;* Pressure being conceived as a measurable effect of heavy bodies at rest, distinguishable from all other effects, such as motion, change of figure, and the like. It is not here necessary to attempt to trace the history of this Idea in our minds; but it is certain that such an Idea may be distinctly formed, and that upon it the whole science of statics may be built. *Pressure, load, weight,* are names by which this Idea is denoted when the effect tends directly downwards; but we

H 2

may have pressure without motion, or *dead pull*, in other cases, as at the critical instant when two nicely-matched wrestlers are balanced by the exertion of the utmost strength of each.

Pressure in any direction may thus exist without any motion whatever. But the causes which produce such pressure are capable of producing motion, and are generally seen producing motion, as in the above instance of the wrestlers, or in a pair of scales employed in weighing; and thus men come to consider pressure as the exception, and motion as the rule; or perhaps they image to themselves the motion which *might* or *would* take place; for instance, the motion which the arms of a lever *would* have if they *did* move. They turn away from the case really before them, which is that of bodies at rest, and balancing each other, and pass to another case, which is arbitrarily assumed to represent the first. Now this arbitrary and capricious evasion of the question we consider as opposed to the introduction of the distinct and proper Idea of Pressure, by means of which the true principles of this subject can be apprehended.

We have already seen that Aristotle was in the number of those who thus evaded the difficulties of the problem of the lever, and consequently lost the reward of success. He failed, as has before been stated, in consequence of his seeking his principles in notions, either vague and loose, as the distinction of natural and unnatural motions, or else inappropriate, as the circle which the weight *would* describe, the velocity which it *would* have if it moved; circumstances which are not part of the fact under consideration. The influence of such modes of speculation was the main hinderance to the prosecution of the true Archimedean form of the science of Mechanics.

. The mechanical doctrine of Equilibrium, is *Statics.* It is to be distinguished from the mechanical doctrine of Motion which is termed *Dynamics,* and which was not successfully treated till the time of Galileo.

Sect. 2.—*Hydrostatics.*

ARCHIMEDES not only laid the foundations of the Statics of solid bodies, but also solved the principal problem of *Hydrostatics,* or the Statics of Fluids; namely, the conditions of the floating of bodies. This is the more remarkable, since not only did the principles which Archimedes established on this subject remain unpursued till the revival of science in modern times, but, when they were again put forward, the main proposition was so far from obvious that it was termed, and is to this day called, the *hydrostatic paradox.* The true doctrine of Hydrostatics, however, assuming the Idea of Pressure, which it involves, in common with the Mechanics of solid bodies, requires also a distinct Idea of a Fluid, as a body of which the parts are perfectly moveable among each other by the slightest partial pressure, and in which all pressure exerted on one part is transferred to all other parts. From this idea of Fluidity, necessarily follows that multiplication of pressure which constitutes the hydrostatic paradox; and the notion being seen to be verified in nature, the consequences were also realized as facts. This notion of Fluidity is expressed in the postulate which stands at the head of Archimedes's " Treatise on Floating Bodies." And from this principle are deduced the solutions, not only of the simple problems of the science, but of some problems of considerable complexity.

The difficulty of holding fast this Idea of Fluidity so as to trace its consequences with infallible strictness of demonstration, may be judged of from the circumstance that, even at the present day, men of great talents, not unfamiliar with the subject, sometimes admit into their reasonings an oversight or fallacy with regard to this very point. The importance of the Idea when clearly apprehended and securely held, may be judged of from this, that the whole science of Hydrostatics in its most modern form is only the developement of the Idea. And what kind of attempts at science would be made by persons destitute of this Idea, we may see in the speculations of Aristotle concerning light and heavy bodies, which we have already quoted;

where, by considering light and heavy as opposite qualities, residing in things themselves, and by an inability to apprehend the effect of surrounding fluids in supporting bodies, the subject was made a mass of false or frivolous assertions, which the utmost ingenuity could not reconcile with facts, and could still less deduce from the asserted doctrines any new practical truths.

In the case of Statics and Hydrostatics, the most important condition of their advance was undoubtedly the distinct apprehension of these two *appropriate Ideas, Statical Pressure*, and *Hydrostatical Pressure* as included in the idea of Fluidity. For the Ideas being once clearly possessed, the experimental laws which they served to express (that the whole pressure of a body downwards was always the same ; and that water, and the like, were fluids according to the above idea of fluidity) were so obvious, that there was no doubt nor difficulty about them. These two ideas lie at the root of all mechanical science ; and the firm possession of them is, to this day, the first requisite for a student of the subject. After being clearly awakened in the mind of Archimedes, these ideas slept for many centuries, till they were again called up in Galileo, and more remarkably in Stevinus. This time, they were not destined again to slumber ; and the results of their activity have been the formation of two Sciences, which are as certain and severe in their demonstrations as geometry itself, and as copious and interesting in their conclusions; but which, besides this recommendation, possess one of a different order;—that they exhibit the exact impress of the laws of the physical world; and unfold a portion of the rules according to which the phenomena of nature take place, and must take place, till nature herself shall alter.

CHAPTER II.

Earliest Stages of Optics.

THE progress made by the ancients in Optics was nearly proportional to that which they made in Statics. As they discovered the true grounds of the doctrine of Equilibrium, without obtaining any sound principles concerning Motion, so they discovered the law of the Reflection of light, but had none but the most indistinct notions concerning Refraction.

The extent of the principles which they really possessed is easily stated. They knew that vision is performed by *rays* which proceed in straight lines, and that these rays are *reflected* by certain surfaces (mirrors) in such manner that the angles which they make with the surface on each side are equal. They drew various conclusions from these premises by the aid of geometry; as, for instance, the convergence of rays which fall on a concave speculum.

It may be observed that the *Idea* which is here introduced, is that of visual *rays*, or lines along which vision is produced and light carried. This idea once clearly apprehended, it was not difficult to show that these lines are straight lines, both in the case of light and of sight. In the beginning of Euclid's "Treatise on Optics," some of the arguments are mentioned by which this was established. We are told in the Proem, "In explaining what concerns the sight, he adduced certain arguments from which he inferred that all light is carried in straight lines. The greatest proof of this is shadows, and the bright spots which are produced by light coming through windows and cracks, and which could not be, except the rays of the sun were carried in straight lines. So in fires, the shadows are greater than the bodies if the fire be small, but less than the bodies if the fire be greater." A clear comprehension of the principle would lead to the perception of innumerable proofs of its truth on every side.

The Law of Equality of Angles of Incidence and Reflection was not quite so easy to verify; but the exact resemblance of the object and its image in a plane mirror, (as the surface of still water, for instance,) which is a consequence of this law, would afford convincing evidence of its truth in that case, and would be confirmed by the examination of other cases.

With these true principles was mixed much error and indistinctness, even in the best writers. Euclid, and the Platonists, maintained that vision is exercised by rays proceeding *from* the eye, not *to* it; so that when we see objects, we learn their form as a blind man would do, by feeling it out with his staff. This mistake, however, though Mon-

tucla speaks severely of it, was neither very dis-
creditable nor very injurious; for the mathematical
conclusions on each supposition are necessarily the
same. Another curious, and false assumption is,
that these visual rays are not close together, but
separated by intervals, like the fingers when the
hand is spread. The motive for this invention was
the wish to account for the fact, that in looking
for a small object, as a needle, we often cannot
see it when it is under our nose; which it was
conceived would be impossible if the visual rays
reached to all points of the surface before us.

These errours would not have prevented the progress of the science. But the Aristotelian physics,
as usual, contained speculations more essentially
faulty. Aristotle's views led him to try to describe the kind of causation by which vision is produced, instead of the laws by which it is exercised;
and the attempt consisted, as in other subjects, of
indistinct principles, and ill-combined facts. According to him, vision must be produced by a
Medium,—by something *between* the object and the
eye,—for if we press the object on the eye, we
do not see it; this Medium is Light, or " the transparent in action;" darkness occurs when the transparency is potential not actual; colour is not the
"absolute visible," but something which is *on* the
absolute visible; colour has the power of setting
the transparent in action; it is not, however, all
colours that are seen by means of light, but only

the proper colour of each object; for some things, as the heads, and scales, and eyes of fish, are seen in the dark; but then they are not seen with their proper colour[1].

In all this there is no steady adherence either to one notion, or to one class of facts. The distinction of Power and Act is introduced to modify the Idea of Transparency, according to the formula of the school; then Colour is made to be something unknown in addition to Visibility; and the distinction of "proper" and "improper" colours is assumed, as sufficient to account for a phenomenon. Such classifications have in them nothing of which the mind can take steady hold; nor is it difficult to see that they do not come under those conditions of successful physical speculation, which we have laid down (F).

[1] De Anim. ii. 6.

CHAPTER III.

EARLIEST STAGES OF HARMONICS.

AMONG the ancients, the science of Music was an application of Arithmetic, as Optics and Mechanics were of Geometry. The story which is told concerning the origin of their arithmetical music, is the following, as it stands in the Arithmetical Treatise of Nicomachus.

Pythagoras, walking one day, meditating on the means of measuring musical notes, happened to pass near a blacksmith's shop, and had his attention arrested by hearing the hammers, as they struck the anvil, produce sounds which had a musical relation to each other. On listening further, he found that the intervals were a Fourth, a Fifth, and an Octave; and on weighing the hammers, it appeared that the one which gave the Octave was *one-half* the heaviest, the one which gave the Fifth was *two-thirds*, and the one which gave the Fourth was *three-quarters*. He returned home, reflected upon this phenomenon, made trials, and finally discovered, that if he stretched musical strings of equal length, by weights which have the proportion of one-half, two-thirds, and three-fourths, they produced intervals which were an Octave, a Fifth, and a Fourth. This observation gave an arithmetical measure of the principal musical intervals, and made Music an arithmetical subject of speculation.

This story, if not entirely a philosophical fable, is undoubtedly inaccurate; for the musical intervals thus spoken of, would not be produced by striking with hammers of the weights there stated. But it is true that the notes of strings have a definite relation to the forces which stretch them; and this truth is still the groundwork of the theory of musical concords and discords (G).

It may at first appear that the truth, or even the possibility of this history, by referring the discovery to accident, disproves our doctrine, that this, like all other fundamental discoveries, required a distinct and well-pondered Idea as its condition. In this, however, as in all cases of supposed accidental discoveries in science, it will be found, that it was exactly the possession of such an Idea which made the accident possible.

Pythagoras, assuming the truth of the tradition, must have had an exact and ready apprehension of those relations of musical sounds, which are called respectively an Octave, a Fifth, and a Fourth. If he had not been able to conceive distinctly this relation, the sounds of the anvil would have struck his ears to no more purpose than they did those of the smiths themselves. He must have had, too, a ready familiarity with numerical ratios; and, moreover, (that in which, probably, his superiority most consisted,) a disposition to connect one notion with the other—the musical relation with the arithmetical, if it were found possible. When the connexion was once suggested, it was easy to devise experiments by which it might be confirmed.

"The philosophers of the Pythagorean School[1], and in particular, Lasus of Hermione, and Hippasus of Metapontum, made many such experiments upon strings; varying both their lengths and the weights which stretched them; and also upon vessels filled with water, in a greater or less degree." And thus was established that connexion of the Idea with the Fact, which this science, like all others, requires.

———

I shall quit the Physical Sciences of Ancient Greece, with the above brief statement of the discovery of the fundamental principles which they involved; not only because such initial steps must always be the most important in the progress of science, but because, in reality, the Greeks made no advances beyond these. There took place among them no additional inductive processes, by which new facts were brought under the dominion of principles, or by which principles were presented in a more comprehensive shape than before. Their

[1] Montucla, iii. 10.

advance terminated in a single stride. Archimedes had stirred the intellectual world, but had not put it in progressive motion: the science of mechanics stopped where he left it. And though, in some subjects, as in Harmonics, much was written, the works thus produced consisted of deductions from the fundamental principles, by means of arithmetical calculations; occasionally modified, indeed, by reference to the pleasures which music, as an art, affords, but not enriched by any new scientific truths.

NOTES TO BOOK II.

(E.) p. 96.   IT has been objected to the arrangement
here employed that it is not symmetrical; and that
Astronomy, as being one of the Physical Sciences, ought
to have occupied a chapter in this Second Book, instead
of having a whole Book to itself (BOOK III).   I do not
pretend that the arrangement is symmetrical, and have
employed it only on the ground of convenience.   The
importance and extent of the history of Astronomy are
such that this science could not, with a view to our
purposes, be made co-ordinate with Mechanics or Optics.

(F.) p. 108.   It is proper to notice more distinctly
the nature of the Geometrical Propositions contained in
Euclid's work.   The *Optica* contains Propositions concerning Vision and Shadows, derived from the principle
that the rays of light are rectilinear: as, that the shadow
is greater than the object if the illuminating body be less,
and *vice versa*.   The *Catoptrica* contains Propositions concerning the effects of Reflection, derived from the principle that the Angles of Incidence and Reflection are
equal: as, that in a convex mirror the object appears convex, and smaller than the object.   We see here an example of the promptitude of the Greeks in deduction.   When
they had once obtained a knowledge of a principle, they
followed it to its mathematical consequences with great
acuteness.   The subject of concave mirrors is pursued
further in Ptolemy's *Optics*.

The Greek writers also cultivated the subject of *Perspective* speculatively, in mathematical treatises, as well as practically, in pictures. The whole of this theory is a consequence of the principle that vision takes place in straight lines drawn from the object to the eye.

The ancients were in some measure acquainted with the Refraction as well as the Reflection of Light, as I have noticed in Book ix. Chap. 2. The current knowledge on this subject must have been very slight and confused; for it does not appear to have enabled them to account for one of the simplest results of Refraction, the magnifying effect of convex transparent bodies. I have noticed in the passage just referred to, Seneca's crude notions on this subject; and in like manner Ptolemy in his *Optics* asserts that an object placed in water must always appear larger than when taken out. Aristotle uses the term ἀνάκλασις, (*Meteorol.* iii. 2), but apparently in a very vague manner. It is not evident that he distinguished Refraction from Reflection. His Commentators however do distinguish these as διάκλασις and ἀνάκλασις. See Olympiodorus in Schneider's *Eclogæ Physicæ*, vol. i. p. 397. And Refraction had been the subject of special attention among the Greek Mathematicians. Archimedes had noticed (as we learn from the same writer) that in certain cases, a ring which cannot be seen over the edge of the empty vessel in which it is placed, becomes visible when the vessel is filled with water. The same fact is stated in the *Optics* of Euclid. We do not find this fact explained in that work as we now have it: but in Ptolemy's *Optics* the fact is explained by a flexure of the visual ray: it is noticed that this flexure is different at different angles from the perpendicular, and there is an elaborate collection of measures of the flexure at different angles, made by means of an instrument devised for the purpose. There is also a collection of similar measures of the refraction when the ray passes from air to glass, and when it passes from glass to water. This part of Ptolemy's work is, I think, the 6ldest extant example of a collection of experimental measures, in any other subject than astronomy; and in astronomy, our measures are the result of *observation*, rather than of *experiment*. As Delambre says (*Astron. Anc.* vol. ii. p. 427.) "On y voit des expériences de physique bien faites, ce qui est sans example chez les anciens."

Ptolemy's Optical work was known only by Roger Bacon's references to it (*Opus Majus*, p. 286, &c.) till 1816 : but copies of Latin translations of it were known to exist in the Royal Library at Paris, and in the Bodleian at Oxford. Delambre has given an account of the contents of the Paris copy in his *Astron. Anc.* ii. 414. and in the *Connoissance des Temps* for 1816; and Prof. Rigaud's account of the Oxford copy is given in the article *Optics*, in the *Encyclopædia Britannica*. Ptolemy shews great sagacity in applying the notion of Refraction to the explanation of the displacement of astronomical objects which is produced by the atmosphere,—*Astronomical Refraction*, as it is commonly called. He represents the visual ray as refracted in passing from the *ether*, which is above the air, into the air; the air being bounded by a spherical surface which has for its center "the center of all the elements, the center of the earth;" and the refraction being a flexure towards the line drawn perpendicular to this surface. He thus constructs, says Delambre, the same figure on which Cassini afterwards founded the whole of his theory; and gives a theory more complete than that of any astronomer previous to him. Tycho for instance believed that astronomical refraction was caused only by the *vapours* of the atmosphere, and did not exist above the altitude of 45°.

Cleomedes, about the time of Augustus, had guessed at Refraction as an explanation of an eclipse in which the sun and moon are both seen at the same time. " Is it not possible," he says, " that the ray which proceeds from the eye and traverses moist and cloudy air may bend downwards to the sun, even when he is below the horizon?" And Sextus Empiricus, a century later, says, " The air being dense, by the refraction of the visual ray, a constellation may be seen above the horizon when it is yet below the horizon." But from what follows, it appears doubtful whether he clearly distinguished Refraction and Reflection.

In order that we may not attach too much value to the vague expressions of Cleomedes and Sextus Empiricus, we may remark that Cleomedes conceives such an eclipse as he describes not to be possible, though he offers an explanation of it if it be : (the fact must occur whenever the moon is seen in the horizon in the middle of an eclipse) : and that Sextus Empiricus gives his suggestion of the effect of refraction as an argument why the Chaldean astrology cannot be true, since the constellation which appears to be rising at the moment of a birth is not the one which is truly rising. The Chaldeans might have answered, says Delambre, that the star begins to shed its influence, not when it is really in the horizon, but when its light is seen. (*Ast. Anc.* vol. i. p. 231, and vol. ii. p. 548.)

It has been said that Vitellio, or Vitello, whom we shall have hereafter have to speak of in the history of Optics, took his Tables of Refractions from Ptolemy. This is contrary to what Delambre states. He says that Vitello may be accused of plagiarism from Alhazen, and that Alhazen did not borrow his Tables from Ptolemy. Roger Bacon had said (*Opus Majus*, p. 288), " Ptolemeus in libro de Opticis, id est, de Aspectibus, seu in Perspectivâ sua, qui prius quam Alhazen dedit hanc sententiam, quam a Ptolemæo acceptam Alhazen exposuit." This refers only to the opinion that visual rays proceed from the eye. But this also is erroneous; for Alhazen maintains the contrary: " Visio fit radiis a visibili extrinsecus ad visum manantibus." (*Opt.* Lib. i. cap. 5.) Vitello says of his Table of Refractions, " acceptis instrumentaliter, prout potuimus propinquius, angulis omnium refractionum... invenimus quod semper iidem sunt anguli refractionum: ...secundum hoc fecimus has tabulas."

(G.) p. 110. Nicomachus says that Pythagoras found the weights to be, as I have mentioned, in the proportion of 12, 6, 8, 9; and the intervals, an Octave, corresponding to the proportion 12 to 6, or 2 to 1; a Fifth, corresponding to the proportion 12 to 8, or 3 to 2; and a Fourth, corresponding to the proportion 12 to 9, or 4 to 3. There is no doubt that this statement of the ancient writer is inexact as to the physical fact, for the rate of vibration of a string, on which its note depends, is, other things being equal, not as the weight, but as the square root of the weight. But he is right as to the essential point, that those ratios of 2 to 1, 3 to 2, and 4 to 3, are the characteristic ratios of the Octave, Fifth and Fourth. In order to produce these intervals, the appended weights must be, not as 12, 9, 8, and 6, but as 12, $6\frac{3}{4}$, $5\frac{1}{3}$, and 3.

The numerical relations of the other intervals of the musical scale, as well as of the Octave, Fifth and Fourth, were discovered by the Greeks. Thus they found that the proportion in a Major Third was 5 to 4 ; in a Minor Third 6 to 5; in a Major Tone 9 to 8 ; in a Semitone or *Diesis* 16 to 15. They even went so far as to determine the *Comma*, in which the interval of two notes is so small that they are in the proportion of 81 to 80. This is the interval between two notes each of which may be called the Seventeenth above the key-note;—the one note being obtained by ascending a Fifth four times over ; the other being obtained by ascending through two Octaves and a Major Third. The want of coincidence between these two notes is an inherent arithmetical imperfection in the musical scale, of which the consequences are very extensive.

The numerical properties of the musical scale were worked out to a very great extent by the Greeks; and many of their Treatises on this subject remain to us. The principal ones are the seven authors published by Meibomius*. These arithmetical elements of Music are to the present day important and fundamental portions of the Science of Harmonics.

* *Antiquæ Musicæ Scriptores septem*, 1652.

BOOK III.

HISTORY

OF

GREEK ASTRONOMY.

Τόδε δὲ μηδέις ποτε φοβηθῇ τῶν Ἑλλήνων, ὡς οὐ χρη περι τὰ θεῖα ποτὲ πραγματεύεσθαι θνητοὺς ὄντας· πᾶν δε τούτου διανοηθῆναι τοὐναντίον, ὡς οὔτε ἄφρον εστι ποτὲ το θεῖον, οὔτε ἀγνοεῖ που τὴν ἀνθρωπίνην φυσιν· ἀλλ᾽ οἶδεν ὅτι, διδάσκοντος αυτοῦ, ξυνακαλουθήσει καὶ μαθήσεται τα διδάσκομενα.

PLATO, *Epinomis*, p. 988.

Nor should any Greek have any misgiving of this kind; that it is not fitting for us to inquire narrowly into the operations of superior Powers, such as those by which the motions of the heavenly bodies are produced: but, on the contrary, men should consider that the Divine Powers never act without purpose, and that they know the nature of man: they know that by their guidance and aid, man may follow and comprehend the lessons which are vouchsafed him on such subjects.

INTRODUCTION.

THE earliest and fundamental conceptions of men respecting the objects with which Astronomy is concerned, are formed by familiar processes of thought, without appearing to have in them anything technical or scientific. Days, Years, Months, the Sky, the Constellations, are notions which the most uncultured and incurious minds possess. Yet these are elements of the Science of Astronomy. The reasons why, in this case alone, of all the provinces of human knowledge, men were able, at an early and unenlightened period, to construct a science out of the obvious facts of observation, with the help of the common furniture of their minds, will be more apparent in the course of the philosophy of science; but I may here barely mention two of these reasons. They are, first, that the familiar act of thought, exercised for the common purposes of life, by which we give to an assemblage of our impressions such a unity as is implied in the above notions and terms, a Month, a Year, the Sky, and the like, is, in reality, an *inductive act,* and shares the nature of the processes by which all sciences are formed; and, in the next place, that the ideas appropriate to the induction in this case, are those which, even in the least cultivated minds, are very clear and definite; namely, the ideas of Space and Figure, Time and Number, Motion and Recurrence. Hence, from their first origin, the modifications of those ideas assume a scientific form.

We must now trace in detail the peculiar course which, in consequence of these causes, the knowledge of man respecting the heavenly bodies took, from the earliest period of his history.

CHAPTER I.

EARLIEST STAGES OF ASTRONOMY.

Sect. 1.—*Formation of the Notion of a Year.*

THE notion of a *Day* is early and obviously impressed upon man in almost any condition in which we can imagine him. The recurrence of light and darkness, of comparative warmth and cold, of noise and silence, of the activity and repose of animals;—the rising, mounting, descending, and setting of the sun;—the varying colours of the clouds, generally, notwithstanding their variety, marked by a daily progression of appearances;—the calls of the desire of food and of sleep in man himself, either exactly adjusted to the period of this change, or at least readily capable of being accom+modated to it;—the recurrence of these circumstances at intervals, equal, so far as our obvious judgment of the passage of time can decide; and these intervals so short that the repetition is noticed with no effort of attention or memory;—this as+semblage of suggestions makes the notion of a day necessarily occur to man, if we suppose him to have the conception of Time, and of Recurrence. He naturally marks by a term such a portion of time, and such a cycle of recurrence; he calls each portion of time, in which this series of appearances and occurrences come round, *a Day :* and such a group of particulars are considered as appearing or happening *in* the same day.

A Year is a notion formed in the same manner; implying in the same way the notion of recurring facts; and also the faculty of arranging facts in time, and of appreciating their recurrence. But the notion of a Year, though undoubtedly very obvious, is, on many accounts, less so than that of a Day. The repetition of similar circumstances, at equal intervals, is less manifest in this case, and the intervals being much longer, some exertion of memory becomes requisite in order that the recurrence may be perceived. A child might easily be persuaded that successive years were of unequal length; or, if the summer were cold, and the spring and autumn warm, might be made to believe, if all who spoke in its hearing agreed to support the delusion, that one year was two. It would be impossible to practise such a deception with regard to the day, without the use of some artifice beyond mere words.

Still, the recurrence of the appearances which suggest the notion of a Year is so obvious, that we can hardly conceive man without it. But though, in all climes and times, there would be a recurrence, and at the same interval in all, the recurring appearances would be extremely different in different countries; and the contrasts and resemblances of the seasons would be widely varied. In some places the winter utterly alters the face of the country, converting grassy hills, deep leafy woods of various hues of green, and running waters, into snowy and icy wastes, and bare snow-laden branches; while in others, the field retains its herbage, and the tree its leaves, all the year; and the rains and the sunshine alone, or various agricultural employments quite different from ours, mark the passing seasons. Yet in all parts of the world the yearly cycle of changes has been singled out from all others, and designated by a peculiar name. The inhabitant of the equatorial regions has the sun vertically over him at the end of every period of six months, and similar trains of celestial phenomena fill up each of these intervals, yet we do not find years of six months among such nations. The Arabs alone[1], who practise neither agriculture nor navigation, have a year depending upon the moon only; and borrow the word from other languages, when they speak of the solar year.

In general nations have marked this portion of time by some word which has a reference to the returning circle of seasons and employments. Thus the Latin *annus* signified a ring, as we see in the derivative *annulus:* the Greek term ἐνιαυτός implies

[1] Ideler, *Berl. Trans.* 1813. p. 51.

something which *returns into itself:* and the word as it exists in Teutonic languages, of which our word *year* is an example, is said to have its origin in the word *yra,* which means a ring in Swedish, and is perhaps connected with the Latin *gyrus.*

Sect. 2.—*Fixation of the Civil Year..*

THE year, considered as a recurring cycle of seasons and of general appearances, must attract the notice of man as soon as his attention and memory suffice to bind together the parts of a succession of the length of several years. But to make the same term imply a certain fixed number of days, we must know how many days the cycle of the seasons occupies; a knowledge which requires faculties and artifices beyond what we have already mentioned. For instance, men cannot reckon as far as any number at all approaching the number of days in the year, without possessing a system of numeral terms, and methods of practical numeration on which such a system of terms is always founded[2]. The South American Indians, the Koussa Caffres and Hottentots, and the natives of New Holland, all of whom are said to be unable to reckon further than the fingers of their hands and feet[3], cannot as we do, include, in their notion of a year, the fact of its consisting of 365 days. This fact is not

[2] Arithm. in *Encyc. Metrop.* (by Dr. Peacock,) Art. 8.
[3] Ibid. Art. 32.

likely to be known to any nation except those which have advanced far beyond that which may be considered as the earliest scientific process which we can trace in the history of the human race, the formation of a method of designating the successive numbers to an indefinite extent, by means of names, framed according to the decimal, quinary, or vigenary scale.

But even if we suppose men to have the habit of recording the passage of each day, and of counting the score thus recorded, it would be by no means easy for them to determine the exact number of days in which the cycle of the seasons recurs; for the indefiniteness of the appearances which mark the same season of the year, and the changes to which they are subject as the seasons are early or late, would leave much uncertainty respecting the duration of the year. They would not obtain any accuracy on this head, till they had attended for a considerable time to the motions and places of the sun; circumstances which require more precision of notice than the general facts of the degrees of heat and light. The motions of the sun, the succession of the places of his rising and setting at different times of the year, the greatest heights which he reaches, the proportion of the length of day and night, would all exhibit several cycles. The turning back of the sun, when he had reached his greatest distance to the south or to the north, as shown either by his rising or by his

height at noon, would perhaps be the most observable of such circumstances. Accordingly the τροπαὶ
ἠελίοιο, the turnings of the sun, are used repeatedly
by Hesiod as a mark from which he reckons the
seasons of various employments. "Fifty days," he
says, "after the turning of the sun, is a seasonable
time for beginning a voyage⁴."

The phenomena would be different in different
climates, but the recurrence would be common to
all.   Any one of these kinds of phenomena, noted
with moderate care for a year, would show what
was the number of days of which a year consisted;
and if several years were included in the interval
through which the scrutiny extended, the knowledge of the length of the year so acquired would
be proportionally more exact.

Besides those notices of the sun, which offered
exact indications of the seasons, other more indefinite natural occurrences were used; as the arrival
of the swallow (χελιδών) and the kite (ἰκτίν).   The
birds, in Aristophanes's play of that name, mention
it, as one of their offices, to mark the seasons;
Hesiod similarly notices the cry of the crane as an
indication of the departure of winter⁵.

Among the Greeks the seasons were at first
only summer and winter (θέρος and χειμών), the

---

⁴ Ἤματα πεντήκοντα μετα τροπὰς ἠελίοιο
   Ες τέλος ἐλθόντος θέρεος.

                                    Op. et Dies, 661.

⁵ Ideler, i. 240.

latter including all the rainy and cold portion of the year. The winter was then subdivided into the χειμών and ἔαρ, and the summer, less definitely, into θέρος and ὀπώρα. Tacitus says that the Germans knew neither the blessings nor the name of autumn, "Autumni perinde nomen ac bona ignorantur." Yet *harvest, herbst,* is certainly an old German word[6].

In the same period in which the sun goes through his cycle of positions, the stars also go through a cycle of appearances belonging to them; and these appearances were perhaps employed at as early a period as those of the sun in determining the exact length of the year. Many of the groups of fixed stars are readily recognized, as exhibiting always the same configuration; and particular bright stars are singled out as objects of attention. These are observed, at particular seasons, to appear in the west after sunset; but it is noted that when they do this, they are found nearer and nearer to the sun every successive evening, and at last disappear in his light. It is observed also, that at a certain interval after this, they rise visibly before the dawn of day renders the stars invisible; and after they are seen to do this, they rise every day at a longer interval before the sun. The risings and settings of the stars under these circumstances, or under others which are easily recognized, were, in countries where the sky is usually clear, employed at an early period, to mark the

[6] Ideler, i. 243.

seasons of the year.   Eschylus[7] makes Prometheus
mention this among the benefits of which he, the
teacher of arts to the earliest race of men, was the
communicator.

Thus, for instance, the rising[8] of the Pleiades in
the evening was a mark of the approach of winter.
The rising of the waters of the Nile in Egypt coin-
cided with the heliacal rising of Sirius, which star
the Egyptians called Sothis.   Even without any
artificial measure of time or position, it was not
difficult to carry observations of this kind to such
a degree of accuracy as to learn from them the
number of days which compose the year; and to
fix the precise season from the appearance of the
stars.

[7] Οὐκ ἦν γαρ αυτοῖς οὔτε χείματος τέκμαρ,
"Ουτ' ἀνθεμώδους ἦρος, οὐδε καρπίμου
Θέρους βέβαιον· ἀλλ' ἄτερ γνώμης τὸ πᾶν
"Επρασσον, ἔστε δή σφιν ἀνατολὰς ἐγὼ
"Αστρων ἔδειξα, τάς τε δυσκρίτους δύσεις.
Prom. V. 454.

[8] Ideler (Chronol. i. 242) says that *this* rising of the Pleiades
took place at a time of the year which corresponds to our 11th
May, and the setting to the 20th October; but this does not
agree with the forty days of their being "concealed," which,
from the context, must mean, I conceive, the interval between
their setting and rising.   Pliny, however, says, "Vergiliarum
exortu æstas incipit, occasu hiems; *semestri* spatio intra se
messes vindemiasque et omnium maturitatem complexæ. (H. N.
xviii. 69.)

The autumn of the Greeks, ὀπώρα, was earlier than our
autumn, for Homer calls Sirius ἀστὴρ ὀπωρινός, which rose at
the end of July.

A knowledge concerning the stars appears to have been first cultivated with the last-mentioned view, and makes its first appearance in literature with this for its object. Thus Hesiod directs the husbandman when to reap by the rising, and when to plough by the setting of the Pleiades[9]. In like manner Sirius[10], Arcturus[11], the Hyades and Orion[12], are noticed.

By such means it was determined that the year consisted, at least, nearly, of 365 days. The Egyptians, as we learn from Herodotus[13], claimed the

[9] Πληίαδων 'Ατλαγενέων ἐπιτελλομενάων.
"Αρχεσθ' ἀμητοῦ· ἀρότοιο δὲ, δυσομενάων.
"Αι δή τοι νύκτας τε καὶ ἤματα τεσσεράκοντα
Κεκρύφαται, αὖτις δὲ περιπλομένου ἐνιαυτοῦ
Φαίνονται.
Op. et Dies, l. 381.

[10] l. 413.

[11] Εὔτ' ἂν δ' ἑξήκοντα μετὰ τροπὰς ἡελίοιο
Χειμέρι', ἐκτελέσῃ Ζεὺς ἤματα, δή ρα τότ' ἀστὴρ
'Αρκτοῦρος, προλιπὼν ἱερὸν ῥόον' 'Ωκεανοῖο
Πρῶτον παμφαίνων ἐπιτέλλεται ἀκροκνέφαιος.
Ib. 562.
'Εὔτ' ἂν δ' Ωρίων και Σείριος ἐς μέσον ἔλθῃ
'Ουρανὸν, Αρκτοῦρον δ' ἐσίδῃ ῥοδοδάκτυλος ἠώς.
Ib. 607.

[12] . . . . αὐτὰρ ἐπὴν δὴ
Πληϊάδες Ύάδες τε τό τε σθένος 'Ωρίωνος
Δύνωσιν.
Ib. 612.

These methods were employed to a late period, because the Greek months, being lunar, did not correspond to the seasons. Tables of such motions were called παραπήγματα.—Ideler, Hist. Untersuchungen, p. 209.

[13] ii. 4.

K 2

honour of this discovery. The priests informed him, he says, "that the Egyptians were the first men who discovered the year, dividing it into twelve equal parts; and this they asserted that they discovered from the stars." Each of these parts or months consisted of 30 days, and they added 5 days more at the end of the year, "and thus the circle of the seasons comes round." It seems, also, that the Jews, at an early period, had a similar reckoning of time, for the Deluge which continued 150 days (Gen. vii. 24,) is stated to have lasted from the 17th day of the second month (Gen. vii. 11) to the 17th day of the seventh month (Gen. viii. 4,) that is, 5 months of 30 days.

A year thus settled as a period of a certain number of days is called a *Civil Year*. It is one of the earliest discoverable institutions of states possessing any germ of civilization; and one of the earliest portions of human systematic knowledge is the discovery of the length of the civil year, so that it should agree with the natural year, or year of the seasons.

Sect. 3.—Correction of the Civil Year. (Julian Calendar.)

IN reality, by such a mode of reckoning as we have described, the circle of the seasons would not come round exactly. The real length of the year is very nearly 365 days and a quarter. If a year of 365 days were used, in four years the year would begin a day too soon, when considered with reference to the sun and stars; and in 60 years it would begin 15 days too soon, a quantity perceptible to the loosest degree of attention. The civil year would be found not to coincide with the year of the seasons; the beginning of the former would take place at different periods of the latter; it would *wander* into various seasons, instead of remaining fixed to the same season; the term year, and any number of years, would become ambiguous; some correction, at least some comparison, would be requisite.

We do not know by whom the insufficiency of the year of 365 days was first discovered[14]; we find this knowledge diffused among all civilized nations, and various artifices used in making the correction. The method which we employ, and which consists in reckoning an additional day at the end of February every fourth or *leap* year, is an example of the principle of *intercalation*, by which the correction was most commonly made. Methods of intercalation for the same purpose were found to exist in the new world. The Mexicans added 13 days at the end of every 52 years. The method of the Greeks was more complex; (by means of the *octaëteris* or cycle of 8 years;) but it had the additional object of accommodating itself

---

[14] Syncellus (*Chronographia*, p. 123), says, that according to the legend, it was King Aseth who first added the 5 additional days to 360, for the year, in the eighteenth century B. C.

to the motions of the moon, and therefore must be treated of hereafter. The Egyptians, on the other hand, knowingly permitted their civil year to wander, at least so far as their religious observances were concerned. "They do not wish," says Geminus[15], "the same sacrifices of the gods to be made perpetually at the same time of the year, but that they should go through all the seasons, so that the same feast may happen in summer and winter, in spring and autumn." The period in which any festival would thus pass through all the seasons of the year is 1461 years; for 1460 years of $365\frac{1}{4}$ days are equal to 1461 years of 365 days. This period of 1461 years is called the *Sothic* period, from Sothis, the name of the dog-star, by which their *fixed* year was determined; and for the same reason it is called the *canicular* period[16].

Other nations did not regulate their civil year by intercalation at short intervals, but rectified it by a *reform* when this became necessary. The Persians are said to have added a month of 30 days every 120 years. The Roman calendar, at first very rude in its structure, was reformed by Numa, and was directed to be kept in order by the perpetual interposition of the augurs. This, however, was, from various causes, not properly done; and the consequence was, that the reckoning fell into utter disorder, in which state it was found by

[15] Uranol. p. 33.
[16] Censorinus de Die Natali, c. 18.

Julius Cæsar, when he became dictator. By the advice of Sosigenes, he adopted the mode of inter-calation of one day in 4 years, which we still retain; and in order to correct the derangement which had already been produced, he added 90 days to a year of the usual length, which thus became what was called *the year of confusion*. The *Julian Calen-dar*, thus reformed, came into use, January 1, B. C. 45.

Sect. 4.—Attempts at the Fixation of the Month.

THE circle of changes through which the moon passes in about thirty days, is marked, in the earliest stages of language, by a word which implies the space of time which one such circle occupies; just as the circle of changes of the seasons is desig-nated by the word *year*. The lunar changes are, indeed, more obvious to the sense, and strike a more careless person, than the annual; the moon, when the sun is absent, is almost the sole natural object which attracts our notice; and we look at her with a far more tranquil and agreeable atten-tion than we bestow on any other celestial object. Her changes of form and place are definite and striking to all eyes; they are uninterrupted, and the duration of their cycle is so short as to require no effort of memory to embrace it. Hence it ap-pears to be more easy, and in earlier stages of civilization more common, to count time by *moons* than by years.

The words by which this period of time is designated in various languages, seem to refer us to the early history of language. Our word *month* is connected with the word *moon*, and a similar connexion is noticeable in the other branches of the Teutonic. The Greek word μὴν in like manner is related to μήνη, which, though not the common word for the moon, is found in Homer with that signification. The Latin word *mensis* is probably connected with the same group[17].

The month is not any exact number of days, being more than 29 and less than 30. The latter number was first tried, for men more readily select numbers possessing some distinction of regularity. It existed for a long period in many countries. A very few months of 30 days, however, would suffice to derange the agreement between the days of the months and the moon's appearance. A little further trial would show that months of 29 and 30 days alternately, would preserve, for a considerable period, this agreement.

[17] Cicero derives this word from the verb *to measure;* "quia *mensa* spatia conficiunt *menses* nominantur:" and other etymologists, with similar views, connect the above-mentioned words with the Hebrew *manah*, to measure, (with which the Arabic work *almanach* is connected.) Such a derivation would have some analogy with that of *annus*, &c., noticed above: but if we are to attempt to ascend to the earliest condition of language, we must conceive it probable that men would have a name for a most conspicuous visible object, *the moon*, before they would have a verb denoting the very abstract and general notion, *to measure*.

The Greeks adopted this calendar, and, in consequence, considered the days of their month as representing the changes of the moon : the last day of the month was called ἔνη καὶ νέα, " the old and new," as belonging to both the waning and the reappearing moon[18] : and their festivals and sacrifices, as determined by the calendar, were conceived to be necessarily connected with the same periods of the cycles of the sun and moon. " The laws and the oracles," says Geminus, " which directed that they should in sacrifices observe three things, months, days, years, were so understood." With this persuasion, a correct system of intercalation became a religious duty.

The above rule of alternate months of 29 and 30 days, supposes the length of the months 29 days and a half, which is not exactly the length of a lunar month. Accordingly the Months and the Moon were soon at variance. Aristophanes, in " The Clouds," makes the Moon complain of the disorder when the calendar was deranged.

Οὐκ ἄγειν τὰς ἡμέρας
Οὐδὲν ὀρθῶς, ἀλλ' ἄνω τε καὶ κάτω κυδοιδοπᾶν
῞Ωστ' ἀπειλεῖν φησὶν αὐτῇ τοὺς θεοὺς ἑκάστοτε

[18] Aratus says of the moon, in a passage quoted by Geminus, p. 33 :

῎Αιει δ' ἄλλοθεν ἄλλα παρακλίνουσα μετωπὰ
῎Ειρῃ, ὁποστάιη μῆνος περιτέλλεται ἠώς.

As still her shifting visage changing turns
By her we count the monthly round of morns.

'Ηνίκ' ἄν ψευσθῶσι δείπνου κἀπίωσιν οἴκαδε
Τῆς ἑορτῆς μὴ τυχόντες κατὰ λόγον τῶν ἡμερῶν.
Nubes, 615—19.

CHORUS OF CLOUDS.

The Moon by us to you her greeting sends,
But bids us say that she's an ill-used moon,
And takes it much amiss that you should still
Shuffle her days, and turn them topsy-turvy;
And that the gods (who know their feast-days well,)
By your false count are sent home supperless,
And scold and storm at her for your neglect[19].

The correction of this inaccuracy, however, was not pursued separately, but was combined with another object, the securing a correspondence between the lunar and solar years, the main purpose of all early cycles.

Sect. 5.—Invention of Lunisolar Years.

THERE are 12 complete lunations in a year; which according to the above rule, would make 354 days, leaving $12\frac{1}{4}$ days of difference between such a lunar year and a solar year. It is said, that at an early period, this was attempted to be corrected by interpolating a month of 30 days every alternate year; and Herodotus[20] relates a conversation of Solon, implying a still ruder mode of intercalation. This

[19] This passage is supposed by the commentators to be intended as a satire upon those who had introduced the cycle of Meton (spoken of in Sect. 5), which had been done at Athens a few years before "The Clouds" was acted.

[20] B. i. c. 15.

can hardly be considered as an improvement in the Greek calendar already described.

The first cycle which produced any near correspondence of the reckoning of the moon and the sun, was the *Octaëteris*, or period of 8 years: 8 years of 354 days, together with 3 months of 30 days each, making up (in 99 lunations,) 2922 days; which is exactly the amount of 8 years of $365\frac{1}{4}$ days each. Hence this period would answer its purpose so far as the above lengths of the lunar and solar cycles are exact; and it might assume various forms, according to the manner in which the three intercalary months were distributed. The customary method was to add a thirteenth month at the end of the third, fifth, and eighth year of the cycle. This period is ascribed to various persons and times; probably different persons proposed different forms of it. Dodwell places its introduction in the 59th Olympiad, or in the 6th century, B. C.: but Ideler thinks the astronomical knowledge of the Greeks of that age was too limited to allow of such a discovery.

This cycle, however, was imperfect. The duration of 99 lunations is something more than 2922 days; it is more nearly $2923\frac{1}{2}$; hence in 16 years there was a deficiency of 3 days, with regard to the motions of the moon. This cycle of 16 years (*Heccædecaëteris*), with 3 interpolated days at the end, was used, it is said, to bring the calculation right with regard to the moon; but in this way

the origin of the year was displaced with regard to
the sun.   After 10 revolutions of this cycle, or
160 years, the interpolated days would amount to
30, and hence the end of the lunar year would be
a month in advance of the end of the solar.   By
terminating the lunar year at the end of the preceding month, the two years would again be
brought into agreement : and we have thus a cycle
of 160 years[21].

This cycle of 160 years, however, was calculated from the cyle of 16 years; and was probably
never used in civil reckoning; which the others, or
at least that of 8 years, appear to have been.

The cycles of 16 and 160 years, were corrections of the cycle of 8 years; and were readily
suggested, when the length of the solar and lunar
periods became known with accuracy.   But a much
more exact cycle, independent of these, was discovered and introduced by Meton[22], 432 years B. C.
This cycle consisted of 19 years, and is so correct
and convenient, that it is in use among ourselves
to this day.   The time occupied by 19 years, and
by 235 lunations, is very nearly the same; (the
former time is less than 6940 days by $9\frac{1}{2}$ hours,
the latter, by $7\frac{1}{2}$ hours.)   Hence, if the 19 years
be divided into 235 months, so as to agree with the
changes of the moon, at the end of that period
the same succession may begin again with great
exactness.

[21] Geminus. Ideler.   [22] Ideler, Hist. Unters. p. 208.

· In order that 235 months, of 30 and 29 days, may make up 6940 days, we must have 125 of the former, which were called *full* months, and 110 of the latter, which were termed *hollow.* An artifice was used in order to distribute 110 hollow months among 6940 days. It will be found that there is a hollow month for each 63 days nearly. Hence if we reckon 30 days to every month, but at every 63d day leap over a day in the reckoning, we shall, in the 19 years, omit 110 days; and this accordingly was done. Thus the 3d day of the 3d month, the 6th day of the 5th month, the 9th day of the 7th, must be omitted, so as to make these months 'hollow.' Of the 19 years, seven must consist of 13 months; and it does not appear to be known according to what order these seven years were selected. Some say they were the 3d, 6th, 8th, 11th, 14th, 17th, and 19th; others, the 3d, 5th, 8th, 11th, 13th, 16th, and 19th.

The near coincidence of the solar and lunar periods in this cycle of 19 years, was undoubtedly a considerable discovery at the time when it was first accomplished. It is not easy to trace the way in which such a discovery was made at that time; for we do not even know the manner in which men then recorded the agreement or difference between the calendar day and the celestial pheno-menon which ought to correspond to it. It is most probable, that the length of the month was obtained with some exactness, by the observation of eclipses, at considerable intervals of time from each other; for eclipses are very noticeable phe-nomena, and must have been very soon observed to occur only at new and full moon[23].

The exact length of a certain number of months being thus known, the discovery of a cycle which should regulate the calendar with sufficient accu-racy, would be a business of arithmetical skill, and would depend, in part, on the existing knowledge of arithmetical methods; but in making the dis-covery, a natural arithmetical sagacity was pro-bably more efficacious than method. It is very possible that the *Cycle of Meton* is correct more nearly than its author was aware, and more nearly than he could ascertain from any evidence and calculation known to him. It is so exact that it is still used in calculating the new moon for the time of Easter; and the *Golden Number*, which is spoken of in stating such rules, is the number of this Cycle corresponding to the current year[24].

Meton's Cycle was corrected a hundred years later (330 B. C.), by Calippus, who discovered the

---

[23] Thucyd. vii. 50. Ἡ σελήνη ἐκλείπει· ἐτύγχανε γὰρ πανσέ-ληνος οὖσα. iv. 52. Τοῦ ἡλίου ἐκλιπές τι ἐγένετο περὶ νου-μηνίαν. ii. 28. Νουμηνίᾳ κατὰ σελήνην (ὥσπερ καὶ μόνον δοκεῖ εἶναι γίγνεσθαι δυνατὸν) ὁ ἥλιος ἐξέλιπε μετὰ μεσημβρίαν καὶ πάλιν ἂν επληρώθη, γενόμενος μηνοειδὴς καὶ ἀστέρων τινῶν ἐκφανέντων.

[24] The same cycle of 19 years has been used by the Chinese for a very great length of time; their civil year consisting, like that of the Greeks, of months of 29 and 30 days.

The Siamese also have this period. (*Astron.* Lib. U. K.)

error of it by observing an eclipse of the moon six years before the death of Alexander[25]. In this corrected period, four cycles of 19 years were taken, and a day left out at the end of the 76 years, in order to make allowance for the hours by which, as already observed, 6940 days are greater than 19 years, and than 235 lunations: and this *Calippic period* is used in Ptolemy's Almagest, in stating observations of eclipses.

The Metonic and Calippic periods undoubtedly imply a very considerable degree of accuracy in the knowledge which the astronomers, to whom they are due, had of the length of the month; and the first is a very happy invention for bringing the solar and lunar calendars into agreement.

The Roman Calendar, from which our own is derived, appears to have been a much less skilful contrivance than the Greek; though scholars are not agreed on the subject of its construction, we can hardly doubt that months, in this as in other cases, were intended originally to have a reference to the moon. In whatever manner the solar and lunar motions were intended to be reconciled, the attempt seems altogether to have failed, and to have been soon abandoned. The Roman months, both before and after the Julian correction, were portions of the year, having no reference to full and new moons; and we, having adopted this division of the year, have thus, in our common calen-

[25] Delamb. A. A. p. 17.

dar, the traces of one of the early attempts of mankind to seize the law of the succession of celestial phenomena, in a case where the attempt was a complete failure.

Considered as a part of the progress of our astronomical knowledge, improvements in the calendar do not offer many points to our observation, but they exhibit a few very important steps. Calendars which, belonging apparently to unscientific ages and nations, possess a great degree of accordance with the true motions of the sun and moon, like the solar calendar of the Mexicans, and the lunar calendar of the Greeks, contain the only record now extant of discoveries which must have required a great deal of observation, of thought, and probably of time. The later improvements in calendars, which take place when astronomical observation has been attentively pursued, are of little consequence to the history of science; for they are generally founded on astronomical determinations, and are posterior in time, and inferior in accuracy, to the knowledge on which they depend. But cycles of correction, which are both short and close to exactness, like that of Meton, may perhaps be the original form of the knowledge which they imply; and certainly require both accurate facts and sagacious arithmetical reasonings. The discovery of such a cycle must always have the appearance of a happy guess, like other discoveries of laws of nature. Beyond this point, the interest of the study of calendars, as bearing on our subject, ceases: they may be considered as belonging rather to art than to science; rather as an application of a part of our knowledge to the uses of life, than a means or an evidence of its extension.

Sect. 6.—The Constellations.

SOME tendency to consider the stars as formed into groups, is inevitable when men begin to attend to them; but how men were led to the fanciful system of names of Stars and of Constellations, which we find to have prevailed in early times, it is very difficult to determine. Single stars, and very close groups, as the Pleiades, were named in the time of Homer and Hesiod, and at a still earlier period, as we find in the book of Job[26].

Two remarkable circumstances with respect to the Constellations are, first, that they appear in most cases to-be arbitrary combinations; the artificial figures which are made to include the stars, not having any resemblance to their obvious configurations; and, second, that these figures, in different

---

[26] Job xxxviii. 31. " Canst thou bind the sweet influences of Chima (the Pleiades), or loose the bands of Kesil (Orion)? Canst thou bring forth Mazzaroth (Sirius) in his season? or canst thou guide Ash (or Aisch) (Arcturus) with his sons?"

And ix. 9. "Which maketh Arcturus, Orion, and Pleiades, and the chambers of the south."

Dupuis, vi. 545, thinks that Aisch was αἴξ, the goat and kids. See Hyde, Ulughbeigh.

countries, are so far similar, as to imply some communication. The arbitrary nature of these figures shows that they were rather the work of the imaginative and mythological tendencies of man, than of mere convenience and love of arrangement. " The constellations," says an astronomer of our own time[27], " seem to have been almost purposely named and delineated to cause as much confusion and inconvenience as possible. Innumerable snakes twine through long and contorted areas of the heavens, where no memory can follow them : bears, lions, and fishes, large and small, northern and southern, confuse all nomenclature. A better system of constellations might have been a material help as an artificial memory." , When men indicate the stars by figures, borrowed from obvious resemblances, they are led to combinations quite different from the received constellations. Thus the common people in our own country find a wain or waggon, or a plough, in a portion of the great bear[28].

. The similarity of the constellations recognized in different countries is very remarkable. The Chaldean, the Egyptian, and the Grecian skies have a resemblance which cannot be overlooked. Some

---

[27] Sir J. Herschel.
[28] So also the Greeks, Homer. *Il.* xviii. 487.

$$\text{"}A\rho\kappa\tau o\nu \ \mathring{\eta}\nu \ \kappa\alpha\grave{\iota} \ \mathring{\alpha}\mu\alpha\xi\alpha\nu \ \mathring{\epsilon}\pi\iota\kappa\lambda\eta\sigma\iota\nu \ \kappa\alpha\lambda\acute{\epsilon}o\nu\sigma\iota\nu.$$

The northern bear which oft the wain they call.

"$A\rho\kappa\tau o\varsigma$ was the traditional name, $\mathring{\alpha}\mu\alpha\xi\alpha$, that suggested by the form.

have conceived that this resemblance may be traced also in the Indian and Arabic constellations, at least in those of the zodiac[29]. But while the figures are the same, the names and traditions connected with them are different, according to the histories and localities of each country[30]; the river among the stars which the Greeks called the Eridanus, the Egyptians asserted to be the Nile. Some conceive that the signs of the zodiac, or path along which the sun and moon pass, had its divisions marked by signs which had a reference to the course of the seasons, to the motion of the sun, or the employments of the husbandman. If we take the position of the heavens, which, from the knowledge we now possess, we are sure they must have had 15000 years ago, the significance of the signs of the zodiac, in which the sun was, as referred to the Egyptian year, becomes very marked[31], and has led some to suppose that the zodiac was invented at such a period. Others have rejected this as an improbably great antiquity, and have thought it more likely that the constellation assigned to each season was that which at that season rose at the beginning of the night: thus the balance (which is conceived to designate the equality of days and nights) was placed among the stars which

---

. [29] Dupuis, vi. 548. The Indian zodiac contains, in the place of our Capricorn, a ram *and* a fish, which proves the resemblance without chance of mistake. Bailly, i. p. 157.

[30] Dupuis, vi. 549.   [31] Laplace, *Hist. Astron.* p. 8.

rose in the evening when the spring began: this would fix the origin of these signs 2500 years before our era.

It is clear, as has already been said, that fancy, and probably superstition, had a share in forming the collection of constellations. It is certain that, at an early period, superstitious notions were associated with the stars[32]. Astrology is of very high antiquity in the East. The stars were supposed to influence the character and destiny of man, and to be in some way connected with superior natures and powers.

We may, I conceive, look upon the formation of the constellations, and the notions thus connected with them, as a very early attempt to find a meaning in the relations of the stars; and as an utter failure. The first effort to associate the appearances and motions of the skies by conceptions implying unity and connexion, was made in a wrong direction, as may very easily be supposed. Instead of considering the appearances only with reference to space, time, number, in a manner purely rational, a number of other elements, imagination, tradition, hope, fear, awe of the supernatural, belief in destiny, were called into action. Man, still young, as a philosopher at least, had yet to learn what notions his successful guesses on these subjects must involve, and what they must exclude. At that period, nothing could be more natural or

[32] Dupuis, vi. 546.

excusable than this ignorance ; but it is curious to see how long obstinately the belief lingered (if indeed it be yet extinct) that the motions of the stars, and the dispositions and fortunes of men, may come under some common conceptions and laws, by which a connexion between the one and the other may be established.

We cannot, therefore, agree with those who consider astrology in the early ages as "only a degraded astronomy, the abuse of a more ancient science[32]." It was the first step to astronomy, by leading to habits and means of grouping phenomena ; and, after a while, by showing that pictorial and mythological relations among the stars had no value, or at least no very obvious value. From that time, the inductive process went on steadily in the true road, under the guidance of ideas of space, time, and number.

Sect. 7.—The Planets.

WHILE men were becoming familiar with the fixed stars, the planets must have attracted their notice. Venus, from her brightness, and from her accompanying the sun at no great distance, and thus appearing as the morning and evening star, was very conspicuous. Pythagoras is said to have maintained that the evening and morning star are the same body; which certainly must have been one

[33.] Dupuis, vi. 546.

of the earliest discoveries on this subject; and
indeed, we can hardly conceive men noticing the
stars for a year or two without coming to this
conclusion.

Jupiter and Mars, sometimes still brighter than
Venus, were also very noticeable.   Saturn and Mercury were less so, but in fine climates they and
their motion would soon be detected by persons
observant of the heavens.   To reduce to any rule
the movements of these luminaries must have taken
time and thought; probably before this was done,
certainly very early, these heavenly bodies were
brought more peculiarly under those views which
we have noticed as leading to astrology.

At a time beyond the reach of certain history,
the planets, along with the sun and moon, had
been arranged in a certain recognized order by the
Egyptians or some other ancient nation.   Probably
this arrangement had been made according to the
slowness of their motions among the stars; for
though the motion of each is very variable, the
gradation of their velocities is, on the whole, very
manifest; and the different rate of travelling of
the different planets, and probably other circumstances of difference, led, in the ready fancy of early
times, to the attribution of a peculiar character to
each luminary.   Thus Saturn was held to be of
a cold and gelid nature; Jupiter, who, from his
more rapid motion, was supposed to be lower in

place, was temperate ; Mars, fiery, and the like[34].

It is not necessary to dwell on the details of these speculations, but we may notice a very remarkable evidence of their antiquity and generality in the structure of one of the most familiar of our measures of time, the *Week*. This distribution of time according to periods of seven days, comes down to us, as we learn from the Jewish scriptures, from the beginning of man's existence on the earth. The same usage is found over all the East; it existed among the Arabians, Assyrians, Egyptians[35]. The same week is found in India among the Bramins; it has, there also, its days marked by those of the heavenly bodies; and it has been ascertained that the same day has, in that country, the name corresponding with its designation in other nations.

The notion which led to the usual designations of the days of the week is not easily unravelled. The days each correspond to one of the heavenly bodies, which were, in the earliest systems of the world, conceived to be the following, enumerating

---

[34] Achilles Tatius (*Uranol.* pp. 135, 136,) gives the Grecian and Egyptian names of the planets.

	Egyptian.	Greek.	
Saturn . .	Νεμεσέως	Κρόνου ἀστὴρ	φαίνων
Jupiter . .	Ὀσίριδος	Δῖος	φαέθων
Mars . .	Ἡρακλεοῦς		πυρόεις
Venus . .		Ἀφροδίτης	ἐώσφορος
Mercury .	Ἀπόλλωνος	Ἑρμοῦ	στίλβων

[35] Laplace, *Hist. Astron.* p. 16.

them in the order of their remoteness from the earth[36]; Saturn, Jupiter, Mars, the Sun, Venus, Mercury, the Moon. At a later period, the received systems placed the seven luminaries in *the seven spheres.* The knowledge which was implied in this view, and the time when it was obtained, we must consider hereafter. · The order in which the names are assigned to the days of the week (beginning with Saturday,) is, Saturn, the Sun, the Moon, Mars, Mercury, Jupiter, Venus; and various accounts are given of the manner in which one of these orders is obtained from the other; all the methods proceeding upon certain arbitrary arithmetical processes, connected in some way with astrological views. It is perhaps not worth our while here to examine further the steps of this process; it would be difficult to determine with certainty why the former order of the planets was adopted, and how and why the latter was deduced from it. But there is something very remarkable in the universality of the notions, apparently so fantastic, which have produced this result; and we may probably consider the Week, with Laplace[37], as "the most ancient monument of astronomical knowledge." This period has gone on without interruption or irregularity from the earliest recorded times to our own days, traversing the extent of ages and the revolutions of empires; the names of the ancient deities which were associated with the

[36] *Philol. Mus.* No. 1.   [37] *Hist. Ast.* p. 17.

stars have been replaced by those of the objects of the worship of our Teutonic ancestors, according to their views of the correspondence of the two mythologies; and the Quakers, in rejecting these names of days, have cast aside the most ancient existing relic of astrological as well as idolatrous superstition.

Sect. 8.—*The Circles of the Sphere.*

THE inventions hitherto noticed, though undoubtedly they were steps in astronomical knowledge, can hardly be considered as purely abstract and scientific speculations; for the exact reckoning of time is one of the wants, even of the least civilized nations. But the distribution of the places and motions of the heavenly bodies by means of a celestial sphere with imaginary lines drawn upon it, is a step in *speculative* astronomy, and was occasioned and rendered important by the scientific propensities of man.

It is not easy to say with whom this notion originated. Some parts of it are obvious. The appearance of the sky naturally suggests the idea of a concave Sphere, with the stars fixed on its surface. Their motions during any one night, it would be readily seen, might be represented by supposing this Sphere to turn round a Pole or Axis; for there is a conspicuous star in the heavens which apparently stands still (the Pole-star); all the others travel round this in circles, and keep the

same positions with respect to each other. This
stationary star is every night the same, and in the
same place; the other stars also have the same
relative position; but their general position at the
same time of night varies gradually from night to
night, so as to go through its cycle of appearances
once a year. All this would obviously agree with
the supposition that the sky is a concave sphere
or dome, that the stars have fixed places on this
sphere, and that it revolves perpetually and uniformly about the Pole or fixed point.

But this supposition does not at all explain the
way in which the appearances of different nights
succeed each other. This, however, may be explained, it appears, by supposing the *sun* also *to
move among the stars* on the surface of the concave sphere. The sun by his brightness makes the
stars invisible which are on his side of the heavens;
this we can easily believe; for the moon, when
bright, also puts out all but the largest stars; and
we see the stars appearing in the evening, each
in its place, according to their degree of splendour,
as fast as the declining light of day allows them
to become visible. And as the sun brings day, and
his absence night, if he move through the circuit
of the stars in a year, we shall have, in the course
of that time, every part of the starry sphere in
succession presented to us as our nocturnal sky.

This notion, that *the sun moves round among
the stars in a year*, is the basis of astronomy,

and a considerable part of the science is only the developement and particularization of this general conception. It is not easy to ascertain either the exact method by which the path of the sun among the stars was determined, or the author and date of the discovery. That there is some difficulty in tracing the course of the sun among the stars will be clearly seen, when it is considered that no star can ever be seen at the same time with the sun. If the whole circuit of the sky be divided into twelve parts or *signs*, it is estimated by Autolycus, the oldest writer on these subjects whose works remain to us[38], that the stars which occupy one of these parts are obsorbed by the solar rays, so that they cannot be seen. Hence the stars which are seen nearest to the place of the setting and the rising sun in the evening and in the morning, are distant from him by the half of a sign; the evening stars being to the west, and the morning stars to the east of him. If the observer had previously obtained a knowledge of the places of all the principal stars, he might in this way determine the position of the sun each night, and thus trace his path in a year.

In this, or some such way, the sun's path was determined by the early astronomers of Egypt. Thales, who is mentioned as the father of Greek astronomy, probably learnt among the Egyptians the results of such speculations, and introduced

[38] Delamb. A. A. p. xiii.

them into his own country. His knowledge, indeed, must have been a great deal more advanced than that which we are now describing, if it be true, as is asserted, that he predicted an eclipse. But his having done so is not very consistent with what we are told of the steps which his successors had still to make.

The Circle of the Signs, in which the sun moves among the stars, is obliquely situated with regard to the circles in which the stars move about the poles. Pliny[39] states that Anaximander[40], a scholar of Thales, was the first person who pointed out this obliquity, and thus, as he says, "opened the gate of nature." Certainly the person who first had a clear view of the nature of the sun's path in the celestial sphere, made that step which led to all the rest; but it is difficult to conceive that the Egyptians and Chaldeans had not already advanced so far.

The diurnal motion of the celestial sphere, and the motion of the moon in the circle of the signs, gave rise to a mathematical science, *the Doctrine of the Sphere*, which was one of the earliest branches of applied mathematics. A number of technical conceptions and terms were soon introduced. The *Sphere* of the heavens was conceived to be complete, though we see but a part of it; it

[39] Lib. ii. c. (viii.)

[40] Plutarch, De Plac. Phil. lib. ii. cap. xii. says Pythagoras was the author of this discovery.

was supposed to turn about the visible *pole* and another pole opposite to this, and these poles were connected by an imaginary *Axis*. The circle which divided the sphere. exactly midway between these poles was called the *Equator* (ἰσημέρινος). The two circles parallel to this which bounded the sun's path among the stars were called *Tropics* (τροπικαί), because the sun turns back again towards the equator when he reaches them. The stars which never set are bounded by a circle called the *Arctic Circle* (ἄρκτικος, and ἄρκτος, the Bear, the constellation to which some of the principal stars. within that circle belong). A circle about the opposite pole is called *Antarctic*, and the stars which are within it can never rise to us[41]. The sun's path or circle of the signs is called the *Zodiac*, or circle of animals ; the points where this circle meets the equator are the *Equinoctial Points*, the days and nights being equal when the sun is in them ; the *Solstitial Points* are those where the sun's. path touches the tropics ; his motion to the south or to. the north ceases when he is there, and he appears in that respect to stand still. The *Colures* (κόλουροι, *mutilated*) are circles which pass through the poles and through the equinoctial and solstitial points ; they have their name because they are only visible in part, a portion of them being below the horizon.

.⁴¹. The Arctic and Antarctic Circles of modern astronomers are different from these.

The *Horizon* (ὁρίζων) is commonly understood as the boundary of the visible earth and heaven. In the doctrine of the sphere, this boundary is *a great circle*, that is, a circle of which the plane passes through the centre of the sphere; and, therefore, an entire hemisphere is always above the horizon. The term occurs for the first time in the work of Euclid, called *Phœnomena* (Φαινόμενα). We possess two treatises written by Autolycus[42] (who lived about 300 B. C.) which trace *deductively* the results of the doctrine of the sphere. Supposing its diurnal motion to be uniform, in a work entitled Περὶ Κινουμένης Σφαίρας, "On the Moving Sphere," he demonstrates various properties of the diurnal risings, settings, and motions of the stars. In another work, Περὶ Ἐπιτολῶν καὶ Δύσεων, "On Risings and Settings[43]," *tacitly* assuming the sun's motion in his circle to be uniform, he proves certain propositions, with regard to the risings and settings of the stars, at the same time when the sun rises and sets[44], or *vice versâ*[45]; and also their *apparent* risings and settings when they cease to be visible after sun-set, or begin to be visible after sun-rise[46]. Several of the propositions contained in the former of these treatises are still necessary to be understood, as fundamental parts of astronomy.

The work of Euclid, just mentioned, is of the

---

[42] Delambre, *Astron. Ancienne*, p. 19. [43] Ib. p. 25.
[44] *Cosmical* setting and rising. [45] *Acronical.*
[46] *Heliacal.*

same kind. Delambre[47] finds in it evidence that Euclid was merely a book-astronomer, who had never observed the heavens.

We may here remark the first instance of that which we shall find abundantly illustrated in every part of the history of science; that man is *prone* to become a deductive reasoner;—that as soon as he obtains principles which can be traced to details by logical consequence, he sets about forming a body of science, by making a system of such reasonings. Geometry has always been a favourite mode of exercising this propensity: and that science, along with Trigonometry, Plane and Spherical, to which the early problems of astronomy gave rise, have, up to the present day, been a constant field for the exercise of mathematical ingenuity; a few simple astronomical truths being assumed as the basis of the reasoning.

Sect. 9.—*The Globular Form of the Earth.*

THE establishment of the globular form of the earth is an important step in astronomy, for it is the first of those convictions, directly opposed to the apparent evidence of the senses, which astronomy irresistibly proves. To make men believe that *up* and *down* are different directions in different places; that the sea, which seems so level, is, in fact, convex; that the earth, which appears to rest on a solid foundation, is, in·fact, not sup-

[47] A. A. p. 53.

ported at all ; are great triumphs both of the power of discovering and the power of convincing. We may readily allow this, when we recollect how recently the doctrine of the *antipodes*, or the existence of inhabitants of the earth, who stand on the opposite side of it, with their feet turned towards ours, was considered both monstrous and heretical.

Yet the different positions of the horizon at different places, necessarily led the student of spherical astronomy toward this notion of the earth as a round body. Anaximander[48] is said by some to have held the earth to be globular, and to be detached or suspended ; he is also stated to have constructed a sphere, on which were shown the extent of land and water. As, however, we do not know the arguments upon which he maintained the earth's globular form, we cannot judge of the value of his opinion ; it may have been no better founded than a different opinion ascribed to him by Laertius, that the earth had the shape of a pillar. Probably, the authors of the doctrine of the globular form of the earth were led to it, as we have said, by observing the different height of the pole at different places. They would find that the space which they passed over from north to south on the earth, was proportional to the change of place of the horizon in the celestial sphere ; and as the horizon is, at every place, in the direction.

[48] See Brucker, *Hist. Phil.* vol. i. p. 486.

of the earth's apparently level surface, this observation would naturally suggest to them the opinion that the earth is placed within the celestial sphere, as a small globe in the middle of a much larger one.

We find this doctrine so distinctly insisted on by Aristotle, that we may almost look on him as the establisher of it[49]. "As to the figure of the earth, it must necessarily be spherical." This he proves, first by the tendency of things, in all places, downwards. He then adds[50], " And, moreover, from the phenomena according to the sense: for if it were not so, the eclipses of the moon would not have such sections as they have. For in the configurations in the course of a month, the deficient part takes all different shapes; it is straight, and concave, and convex ; but in eclipses it always has the line of division convex; wherefore, since the moon is eclipsed in consequence of the interposition of the earth, the periphery of the earth must be the cause of this by having a spherical form. And again, from the appearances of the stars, it is clear, not only that the earth is round, but that its size is not very large: for when we make a small removal to the south or the north, the circle of the horizon becomes palpably different, so that the stars overhead undergo a great change, and are not the same to those that travel to the north

[49] Arist. de Cœlo. Lib. ii. cap. xiv. ed. Casaub. p. 290.
[50] p. 291 C.

and to the south. For some stars are seen in Egypt or at Cyprus, but are not seen in the countries to the north of these; and the stars that in the north are visible while they make a complete circuit, there undergo a setting. So that from this it is manifest, not only that the form of the earth is round, but also that it is a part of not a very large sphere: for otherwise the difference would not be so obvious to persons making so small a change of place. Wherefore we may judge that those persons *who connect the region in the neighbourhood of the pillars of Hercules with that towards India, and who assert that in this way the sea is* ONE, do not assert things very improbable. They confirm this conjecture moreover by the elephants, which are said to be of the same species (γένος) towards each extreme; as if this circumstance was a consequence of the conjunction of the extremes. The mathematicians, who try to calculate the measure of the circumference, make it amount to 400,000 stadia; whence we collect that the earth is not only spherical, but is not large compared with the magnitude of the other stars."

When this notion was once suggested, it was defended and confirmed by such arguments as we find in later writers: for instance[51], that the tendency of all things was to fall to the place of heavy bodies, and that this place being the center of the

[51] Pliny, *Nat. Hist.* ii. LXV.

earth, the whole earth had no such tendency; that the inequalities on the surface were so small as not materially to affect the shape of so vast a mass; that drops of water naturally form themselves into figures with a convex surface; that the end of the ocean would fall if it were not rounded off; that we see ships, when they go out to sea, disappearing downwards, which shows the surface to be convex. These are the arguments still employed in impressing the doctrines of astronomy upon the student of our own days; and thus we find that, even at the early period of which we are now speaking, truths had begun to accumulate which form a part of our present treasures.

Sect. 10.—*The Phases of the Moon.*

WHEN men had formed a steady notion of the moon as a solid body, revolving about the earth, they had only further to conceive it spherical, and to suppose the sun to be beyond the region of the moon, and they would find that they had obtained an explanation of the varying forms which the bright part of the moon assumes in the course of a month. For the convex side of the crescent-moon, and her full edge when she is gibbous, are always turned towards the sun. And this explanation, once suggested, would be confirmed, the more it was examined. For instance, if there be near us a spherical stone, on which the sun is shining, and if we place ourselves so that this stone and the moon are seen in the same direction, (the moon appearing just over the top of the stone;) we shall find that the visible part of the stone; which is then illuminated by the sun, is exactly similar in form to the moon, at whatever period of her changes she may be. The stone and the moon being in the same position with respect to us, and both being enlightened by the sun, the bright parts are the same in figure; the only difference is, that the dark part of the moon is usually not visible at all.

This doctrine is ascribed to Anaximander. Aristotle was fully aware of it[52]. It could not well escape the Chaldeans and Egyptians, if they speculated at all about the causes of the appearances in the heavens.

Sect. 11.—Eclipses.

ECLIPSES of the sun and moon were from the earliest times regarded with a peculiar interest. The notions of superhuman influences and relations, which, as we have seen, were associated with the luminaries of the sky, made men look with alarm at any sudden and striking change in those objects; and as the constant and steady course of the celestial revolutions was contemplated with a feeling of admiration and awe, any marked interrup-

[52] Probl. Cap. xv. Art. 7.

tion :and deviation in this course, was regarded with surprize and terror. This appears to be the case with all nations at an early stage of their civilization.

This impression would cause Eclipses to be noted and remembered; and accordingly we find that the records of Eclipses are the earliest astronomical information which we possess. When men had discovered some of the laws of succession of other astronomical phenomena, for instance, of the usual appearances of the moon and sun, it might then occur to them that these unusual appearances also might probably be governed by some rule.

· · The search after this rule was successful at an early period. The Chaldeans were able to predict Eclipses of the Moon. This they did, probably, by means of their cycle of 223 months, or about 18 years; for at the end of this time, the eclipses of the moon begin to return, at the same intervals and in the same order as at the beginning[53]. Probably this was the first instance of the prediction of peculiar astronomical phenomena. The Chinese have, indeed, a legend, in which it is related that a solar eclipse happened in the reign of Tchong-kang, above 2000 years before Christ, and that the emperor was so much irritated against two great officers of state, who had neglected to predict this eclipse, that he put them to death. But this can-

[53] The eclipses of the sun are more difficult to calculate; since they depend upon the place of the spectator on the earth.

not be accepted as a real event: for during the next ten centuries, we find no single observation, or fact, connected with astronomy, in the Chinese histories; and their astronomy has never advanced beyond a very rude and imperfect condition.

We can only conjecture the mode in which the Chaldeans discovered their period of 18 years; and we may make very different suppositions with regard to the degree of science by which they were led to it. We may suppose, with Delambre[54], that they carefully recorded ' the eclipses which happened, and then, by the inspection of their registers, discovered that those of the moon recurred after a certain period. Or we may suppose, with other authors, that they sedulously determined the motions of the moon, and having obtained these with considerable accuracy, sought and found a period which should include cycles of these motions. This latter mode of proceeding would imply a considerable degree of knowledge.

It appears probable rather that such a period was discovered by noticing the *recurrence* of eclipses, than by studying the moon's *motions*. After $6585\frac{1}{3}$ days, or 223 lunations, the same eclipses nearly will recur. It is not contested that the Chaldeans were acquainted with this period, which they called *Saros;* or that they calculated eclipses by means of it.

[54] A. A.; p. 212.

Sect. 12.—*Sequel to the Early Stages of Astronomy.*

EVERY stage of science has its train of practical applications and systematic inferences, arising both from the demands of convenience and curiosity, and from the pleasure, which, as we have already said, ingenious and active-minded men feel in exercising the process of deduction. The earliest condition of astronomy in which it can be looked upon as a science, exhibits several examples of such applications and inferences, of which we may mention a few.

Prediction of Eclipses.—The cycles which served to keep in order the calendar of the early nations of antiquity, in some instances enabled them also, as has just been stated, to predict eclipses; and this application of knowledge necessarily excited great notice. Cleomedes, in the time of Augustus, says, "we never see an eclipse happen which has not been. predicted by those who make use of the Tables." (ὑπό τῶν κανονικῶν.)

Terrestrial Zones.—The globular form of the earth being assented to, the doctrine of the sphere was appplied to the earth as well as the heavens; and its surface was divided by various imaginary circles; among the rest, the equator, the tropics, and circles at the same distance from the poles as the tropics are from the equator. One of the curious consequences of this division was the *assumption*, that there must be some marked difference in the stripes or *zones* into which the earth's surface was thus divided. In going to the south, Europeans found countries hotter and hotter, in going to the north, colder and colder; and it was supposed that the space between the tropical circles must be uninhabitable from heat, and that within the polar circles, again, uninhabitable from cold. · This fancy was, as we now know, entirely unfounded. But the principle of the globular form of the earth, when dealt with by means of spherical geometry, led to many true and important propositions concerning the lengths of days and nights at·different places. These propositions still form a part of our Elementary Astronomy.

Gnomonick.——Another important result of the doctrine of the sphere was *Gnomonick* or *Dialling*. Anaximenes is said by Pliny to have first·taught this art in Greece; and both he and Anaximander are reported to have erected the first dial·at Lacedemon. Many of the ancient dials remain to us; some of these are of complex forms, and must have required great ingenuity and considerable geometrical knowledge in their construction. ·

Measure of the Sun's Distance.——The explanation of the phases of the moon led to no result·so remarkable as the attempt of Aristarchus of Samos to obtain from this doctrine a measure of the distance of the sun as compared with that of the moon. If the moon was a perfectly smooth sphere, when she was exactly midway between the·new and full in position (that is a quadrant from the sun) she would be somewhat more than a half moon; and the place when she was *dichotomized*, that is, was an exact semicircle, the bright part being bounded by a straight line, would depend upon the sun's distance from the earth. Aristarchus endeavoured to fix the exact place of this Dichotomy; but the irregularity of the edge which bounds the bright part of the moon, and the difficulty of measuring with accuracy, by means then in use, either the precise time, when the boundary was most nearly a straight line or the exact distance of the moon from the sun at that time, rendered his conclusion false and valueless. He collected that the sun is at 18 times the distance of the moon from us; we now know that he is at 400 times the moon's distance.

It would be easy to dwell longer on subjects of this kind; but we have already perhaps entered too much in detail. We have been tempted to do this by the interest which the mathematical spirit of the Greeks gave to the earliest astronomical discoveries, when these were the subjects of their reasonings: but we must now proceed to contemplate them engaged in a worthier employment, namely, in adding to these discoveries.

CHAPTER II.

PRELUDE TO THE INDUCTIVE EPOCH OF HIPPARCHUS.

WITHOUT pretending that we have exhausted the consequences of the elementary discoveries which we have enumerated, we now proceed to consider the nature and circumstances of the next great discovery which makes an Epoch in the history of astronomy; and this we shall find to be the Theory of Epicycles and Eccentrics. Before, however, we relate the establishment of this theory, we must, according to the general plan we have marked out, notice some of the conjectures and attempts by which it was preceded, and the growing acquaintance with facts, which made the want of such an explanation felt.

In the steps previously made in astronomical knowledge, no ingenuity had been required, to devise the view which was adopted. The motions of the stars and sun were most naturally and almost irresistibly conceived as the results of motion in a revolving sphere; the indications of position which we obtain from different places on the earth's surface, when clearly combined, obviously imply a globular shape. In these cases, the first conjectures, the supposition of the simplest form, of the most uniform motion, required no after-correction. But this manifest simplicity, this easy and obvious explanation, did not apply to the movement of all the heavenly bodies. The planets, the "wandering stars," could not be so easily understood ; the motion of each, as Cicero says, "undergoing very remarkable changes in its course, going before and behind, quicker and slower, appearing in the evening, but gradually lost there, and emerging again in the morning[1]." A continued attention to these stars would, however detect a kind of intricate regularity in their motions, which might naturally be described as "a dance." The Chaldeans are stated by Diodorus[2], to have observed assiduously the risings and settings of the planets, from the top of the temple of Belus. By doing this, they would find the times in which the forwards and backwards movements of Saturn, Jupiter, and Mars recur ; and also the time in which they come round to the same part of the heavens[3]. Venus and Mercury never recede far from the sun, and the intervals which elapse while either of them leaves its greatest distance from

---

[1] Cic. de Nat. D. lib. ii. p. 450. " Ea quæ Saturni stella dicitur, φαίνωνque a Græcis nominatur, quæ a terra abest plurimum, xxx fere annis cursum suum conficit ; in quo cursu multa mirabiliter efficiens, tum antecedendo, tum retardando, tum vespertinis temporibus delitescendo, tum matutinis se rursum aperiendo, nihil immutat sempiternis sæculorum ætatibus, quin eadem iisdem temporibus efficiat." And so of the other planets.

[2] Del. A. A.; i. p. 4.   [3] Plin. H. N. ii. p. 204.

the sun and returns again to the greatest distance on the same side, would easily be observed. .

Probably the manner in which the motions of the planets were originally reduced to rule was something like the following:—In about 30 of our years, Saturn goes 29 times through his *Anomaly*, that is, the succession of varied motions by which he sometimes goes forwards and sometimes backwards among the stars. During this time, he goes once round the heavens, and returns nearly to the same place. This is the cycle of his apparent motions.

Perhaps the eastern nations contented themselves with thus referring these motions to cycles of time, so as to determine their recurrence. Something of this kind was done at an early period, as we have seen.

But the Greeks soon attempted to frame to themselves a sensible image of the mechanism by which these complex motions were produced: nor did they find this difficult. Venus, for instance, who, upon the whole, moves from west to east among the stars, is seen, at certain intervals, to return or move *retrograde* a short way back from east to west, then to become for a short time *stationary*, then to turn again and resume her *direct* motion westward, and so on. Now this can be explained by supposing that she is placed in the rim of a wheel, which is turned edgeways to us, and of which the center turns round in the heavens from west to east, while the wheel, carrying the planet in its motion, moves round its own center. In: this way the motion of the wheel about its center, would, in some situations, counterbalance the general motion of the center, and make the planet retrograde, while, on the whole, the westerly motion would prevail. Just as if we suppose that a person, holding a lamp in his hand in the dark, and at a distance, so that the lamp alone is ·visible, should run on turning himself round; we·should see the light sometimes stationary, sometimes retrograde, but on the whole progressive.

: A mechanism of this kind was imagined for each of the planets, and the wheels of which we have spoken were, in the end, called *Epicycles*.

The application of such mechanism to the planets, appears to have arisen in Greece about the time of Aristotle. In the works of Plato we find a strong taste for this kind of mechanical speculation. In the tenth book of the " Polity," we have the apologue of Alcinus the Pamphylian, who, being supposed to be killed in battle, revived when he was placed on the funeral pyre, and related what he had seen during his trance. Among other revelations, he beheld the machinery by which all the celestial bodies revolve. The axis of these revolutions is the adamantine distaff which Destiny holds between her knees; on this are fixed, by means of different sockets, flat rings, by which the planets are carried. The order and magnitude of these spindles are minutely detailed. Also, in the "Epilogue to the Laws" (Epinomis), he again describes the various movements of the sky, so as to show a distinct acquaintance with the general character of the planetary motions: and, after speaking of the Egyptians and Syrians as the original cultivators of such knowledge, he adds some very remarkable exhortations to his countrymen to prosecute the subject. " Whatever we Greeks," he says, " receive from the barbarians, we improve and perfect; there is good hope and promise, therefore, that Greeks will carry this knowledge far beyond that which was introduced from abroad." To this task, however, he looks with a due appreciation of the qualities and preparation which it requires. " An astronomer must be," he says, " the wisest of men; his mind must be duly disciplined in youth; especially is mathematical study necessary; both an acquaintance with the doctrine of number, and also with that other branch of mathematics, which, closely connected as it is with the science of the *heavens*, we very absurdly call *geometry*, the measurement of the *earth*[4]."

These anticipations were very remarkably verified in the subsequent career of the Greek astronomy.

The theory, once suggested, probably made rapid progress. Simplicius[5] relates, that Eudoxus

[4] *Epinomis*, pp. 988, 990.
[5] Lib. ii. de Cœlo. Bullialdus, p. 18.

us introduced the hypothesis of revolving
_____ or spheres. Calippus of Cyzicus, having
visited Polemarchus, an intimate friend of Eudoxus,
they went together to Athens, and communicated
to Aristotle the invention of Eudoxus, and with his
help improved and corrected it.

Probably at first this hypothesis was applied
only to account for the general phenomena of the
progressions, retrogradations, and stations of the
planet; but it was soon found that the motions of
the sun and moon, and the circular motions of
the planets, which the hypothesis supposed, had
other *anomalies* or irregularities, which made a
further extension of the hypothesis necessary.

The defect of uniformity in these motions of the
sun and moon, though less apparent than in the
planets, is easily detected, as soon as men endeavour to obtain any accuracy in their observations.
We have already stated (Chap. I.) that the Chaldeans were in possession of a period of about 18
years, which they used in the calculation of eclipses,
and which might have been discovered by close
observation of the moon's motions; although it
was probably rather hit upon by noting the recurrence of eclipses. The moon moves in a manner
which is not reducible to regularity without considerable care and time. If we trace her path
among the stars, we find that, like the path of the
sun, it is oblique to the equator, but it does not,
like that of the sun, pass over the same stars in

successive revolutions. Thus its *latitude,* or distance from the equator, has a cycle different from
its revolution among the stars ; and its *Nodes,* or
the points where it cuts the equator, are perpetually changing their position.   In addition to this,
the moon's motion in her own path is not uniform ;
in the course of each lunation, she moves alternately slower and quicker, passing gradually through
the intermediate degrees of velocity ; and goes
through the cycle of these changes in something
less than a month : this is called a revolution of
Anomaly.   When the moon has gone through a
complete number of revolutions of Anomaly, and
has, in the same time, returned to the same position with regard to the Sun, and also with regard
to her Nodes, her motions with respect to the sun
will thenceforth be the same as at the first, and
all the circumstances on which lunar eclipses depend being the same, the eclipses will occur in
the same order.   In 6585⅓ days there are 239
revolutions of anomaly, 241 revolutions with regard
to one of the nodes, and, as we have said, 223
lunations or revolutions with regard to the sun.
Hence this period will bring about a succession of
the same lunar eclipses.

If the Chaldeans observed the moon's motion
among the stars with any considerable accuracy,
so as to detect this period by that means, they
could hardly avoid discovering the anomaly or unequal motion of the moon ; for in every revolution,

her daily progression in the heavens varies from about 22 to 26 times her own diameter.   But there is not, in the existence of this period, any evidence that they had measured the amount of this variation; and Delambre[6] is probably right in attributing all such observations to the Greeks.

The sun's motion would also be seen to be irregular as soon as men had any exact mode of determining the lengths of the four seasons, by means of the passage of the sun through the equinoctial and solstitial points.   For spring, summer, autumn, and winter, which would each consist of an equal number of days if the motions were uniform, are, in fact, found to be unequal in length.

It was not very difficult to see that the mechanism of epicycles might be applied so as to explain irregularities of this kind.   A wheel travelling round the earth, while it revolved upon its center, might produce the effect of making the sun or moon fixed in its rim go sometimes faster and sometimes slower in appearance, just in the same way as the same suppositions would account for a planet going sometimes forwards and sometimes backwards: the epicycles of the sun and moon would, for this purpose, be less than those of the planets.   Accordingly, it is probable that, at the time of Plato and Aristotle, philosophers were already endeavouring to apply the hypothesis to

[6] *Astronomie Ancienne*, i. 212.

these cases, though it does not appear that any one fully succeeded before Hipparchus.

The problem which was thus present to the minds of astronomers, and which Plato is said to have proposed to them in a distinct form, was, " To reconcile the celestial phenomena by the combination of equable circular motions." That the circular motions should likewise be equable, was a condition, which, if it had been merely tried at first, as the most simple and definite conjecture, would have deserved praise. But this condition, which is, in reality, inconsistent with nature, was, in the sequel, adhered to with a pertinacity which introduced endless complexity into the system. The history of this assumption is one of the most marked instances of that love of simplicity and symmetry, which is the source of all general truths, though it so often produces and perpetuates errour. At present we can easily see how fancifully the notion of simplicity and perfection was interpreted, in the arguments by which the opinion was defended, that the real motions of the heavenly bodies must be circular and uniform. The Pythagoreans, as well as the Platonists, maintained this dogma. According to Geminus, "They supposed the motions of the sun, and the moon, and the five planets, to be circular and equable: for they would not allow of such disorder among divine and eternal things, as that they should sometimes move quicker, and sometimes slower, and sometimes stand still; for no one would tolerate such anomaly in the movements, even of a man, who was decent and orderly. The occasions of life, however, are often reasons for men going quicker or slower, but in the incorruptible nature of the stars, it is not possible that any cause can be alleged of quickness and slowness. Whereupon they propounded this question, how the phenomena might be represented by equable and circular motions."

These conjectures and assumptions led naturally to the establishment of the various parts of the Theory of Epicycles. It is probable that this theory was adopted with respect to the planets at or before the time of Plato. And Aristotle gives us an account of the system thus devised[7]. "Eudoxus," he says," "attributed four spheres to each Planet: the first revolved with the fixed stars (and this produced the diurnal motion); the second gave the planet a motion along the ecliptic (the mean motion in longitude); the third had its axis perpendicular[8] to the ecliptic (and this gave the inequality of each planetary motion); the fourth produced the oblique motion transverse to this (the motion in latitude)." He is also said to have attributed a motion in latitude and a correspond-

[7] Metaph. xi. 8.

[8] Aristotle says "has its poles in the ecliptic," but this must be a mistake of his. He professes merely to receive these opinions from the professed astronomers "ἐκ τῆς οἰκειοτάτης φιλυσοφίας τῶν μαθηματικῶν."

ing sphere to the Sun as well as to the Moon, of which it is difficult to understand the meaning, if Aristotle has reported rightly of the theory; for it would be absurd to ascribe to Eudoxus a know-. of the motions by which the sun deviates from the ecliptic. Calippus conceived that two addi-. tional spheres must be given to the sun and to the moon, in order to explain the phenomena: probably he was aware of the inequalities of the. motions of these luminaries. He also proposed an additional sphere for each planet, to account, we: may suppose, for the results of the eccentricity of the orbits.

The hypothesis, in this form, does not appear: to have been reduced to measure, and was, more-over, unnecessarily complex. The resolution of the oblique motion of the moon into two separate mo-. tions, by Eudoxus, was not the simplest way of conceiving it; and Calippus imagined the con-nexion of these spheres in some way which made: it necessary nearly to double their number; in this manner his system had no less than 55 spheres.

Such was the progress which the *Idea* of the hypothesis of epicycles had made in men's minds, previously to the establishment of the theory by. Hipparchus. There had also been a preparation for this step, on the other side, by the collection of *Facts*. We know that observations of the eclipses of the moon were made by the Chaldeans 367 B.C. at Labylon, and were known to the Greeks; for

Hipparchus and Ptolemy founded their theory of the moon on these observations. Perhaps we cannot consider, as equally certain, the story that, at the time of Alexander's conquest, the Chaldeans possessed a series of observations, which went back 1903 years, and which Aristotle caused Callisthenes to bring to him in Greece. All the Greek observations which are of any value, begin with the school of Alexandria. Aristyllus and Timocharis appear, by the citations of Hipparchus, to have observed the places of stars and planets, and the times of the solstices, at various periods from B.C. 295 to B.C. 269. Without their observations, indeed, it would not have been easy for Hipparchus to establish either the theory of the sun or the precession of the equinoxes.

In order that observations at distant intervals may be compared with each other, they must be referred to some common era. The Chaldeans dated by the era of Nabonassar, which commenced 749 B.C. The Greek observations were referred to the Calippic periods of 76 years, of which the first began 331 B.C. These are the dates used by Hipparchus and Ptolemy.

CHAPTER III.

INDUCTIVE EPOCH OF HIPPARCHUS.

Sect. 1.—*Establishment of the Theory of Epicycles and Eccentrics.*

ALTHOUGH, as we have already seen, at the time of Plato, the Idea of Epicycles had been suggested, and the problem of its general application proposed, and solutions of this problem offered by his followers; we still consider Hipparchus as the real discoverer and founder of that theory; inasmuch as he not only guessed that it *might*, but showed that it *must*, account for the phenomena, both as to their nature and as to their quantity. The assertion that "he only discovers who proves," is just; not only because, until a theory is proved to be the true one, it has no pre-eminence over the numerous other guesses among which it circulates, and above which the proof alone elevates it; but also because he who takes hold of the theory so as to apply calculation to it, possesses it with a distinctness of conception which makes it peculiarly his.

In order to establish the Theory of Epicycles, it was necessary to assign the magnitudes, distances, and positions of the circles or spheres in which the heavenly bodies were moved, in such a manner as to account for their apparently irregular motions. We may best understand what was the problem to be solved, by calling to mind what we now know to be the real motions of the heavens. The true motion of the earth round the sun, and therefore the apparent annual motion of the sun, is performed, not in a circle of which the earth is the center, but in an ellipse or oval, the earth being nearer to one end than to the other; and the motion is most rapid when the sun is at the nearer end of this oval. But instead of an oval, we may suppose the sun to move uniformly in a circle, the earth being now, not in the center, but nearer to one side; for on this supposition, the sun will appear to move most quickly when he is nearest to the earth, or in his *Perigee*, as that point is called. Such an orbit is called an *Eccentric*, and the distance of the earth from the center of the circle is called the *Eccentricity*. It may easily be shown by geometrical reasoning, that the inequality of apparent motion so produced, is exactly the same in detail, as the inequality which follows from the hypothesis of a small *Epicycle*, turning uniformly on its axis, and carrying the sun in its circumference, while the center of this epicycle moves uniformly in a circle of which the earth is the center. This identity of the results of the hypothesis of the Eccentric and the Epicycle is proved by Ptolemy in the third book of the "Almagest."

The Sun's Eccentric.—When Hipparchus had clearly conceived these hypotheses, as *possible* ways of accounting for the sun's motion, the task which he had to perform, in order to show that they deserved to be adopted, was to assign a place to the *Perigee,* a magnitude to the *Eccentricity,* and an *Epoch* at which the sun was at the perigee ; and to show that, in this way, he had produced a true representation of the motions of the sun. This, accordingly, he did ; and having thus determined, with considerable exactness, both the law of the solar irregularities, and the numbers on which their amount depends, he was able to assign the motions and places of the sun for any moment of future time with corresponding exactness ; he was able, in short, to construct *Solar Tables,* by means of which the sun's place with respect to the stars could be correctly found at any time. These tables (as they are given by Ptolemy[1],) give the *Anomaly,* or inequality of the sun's motion; and this they exhibit by means of the *Prosthapheresis,* the quantity which, at any distance of the sun from the *Apogee,* it is requisite to add to or subtract from the arc, which he would have described if his motion had been equable.

The reader might perhaps expect that the calculations which thus exhibited the motions of the sun for an indefinite future period must depend upon a considerable number of observations made at all seasons of the year. That, however, was not the

[1] Syntax. 1. iii.

case; and the genius of the discoverer appeared, as such genius usually does appear, in his perceiving how small a number of facts, rightly considered, were sufficient to form a foundation for the theory. The number of days contained in two seasons of the year sufficed for this purpose to Hipparchus. " Having ascertained," says Ptolemy, " that the time from the vernal equinox to the summer tropic is $94\frac{1}{2}$ days, and the time from the summer tropic to the autumnal equinox $92\frac{1}{2}$ days, from these phenomena alone he demonstrates that the straight line joining the centre of the sun's eccentric path with the centre of the zodiac (the spectator's eye) is nearly the 24th part of the radius of the eccentric path; and that its *apogee* precedes the summer solstice by $24\frac{1}{2}$ degrees nearly, the zodiac containing 360."

The exactness of the Solar Tables, or *Canon*, which was founded on these data, was manifested, not only by the coincidence of the sun's calculated place with such observations as the Greek astronomers of this period were able to make, (which were indeed very rude,) but by its enabling them to calculate solar and lunar eclipses; phenomena which are a very precise and severe trial of the accuracy of such tables, inasmuch as a very minute change in the apparent place of the sun or moon would completely alter the obvious features of the eclipse. Though the tables of this period were by no means perfect, they bore with tolerable credit this trying and perpetually recurring test; and thus proved the soundness of the theory on which the tables were calculated.

The Moon's Eccentric.—The moon's motions have many irregularities; but when the hypothesis of an Eccentric or an Epicycle had sufficed in the case of the sun, it was natural to try to explain, in the same way, the motions of the moon; and it was shown by Hipparchus that such hypotheses would account for the more obvious anomalies. It is not very easy to describe the several ways in which these hypotheses were applied, for it is, in truth, very difficult to explain in words even the mere facts of the moon's motion. If she were to leave a visible bright line behind her in the heavens wherever she moved, the path thus exhibited would be of an entremely complex nature; the circle of each revolution slipping away from the preceding, and the traces of successive revolutions forming a sort of band of net-work running round the middle of the sky[2]. In each revolution, the motion in longitude is affected by an anomaly of the same nature as the sun's anomaly already spoken of; but besides this, the path of the moon deviates from the ecliptic to the north and to the south of the ecliptic, and thus she has a motion in latitude. This motion in latitude would be sufficiently known if we knew the

---

[2] The reader will find an attempt to make the nature of this path generally intelligible in the *Companion to the British Almanack* for 1834.

period of its *restoration*, that is, the time which the moon occupies in moving from any latitude till she is restored to the same latitude; as, for instance, from the ecliptic on one side of the heavens to the ecliptic on the same side of the heavens again. But it is found that the period of the restoration of the latitude is not the same as the period of the restoration of the longitude, that is, as the period of the moon's revolution among the stars; and thus the moon describes a different path among the stars in every successive revolution, and her path, as well as her velocity, is constantly variable.

Hipparchus, however, reduced the motions of the moon to rule and to Tables, as he did those of the sun, and in the same manner. He determined, with much greater accuracy than any preceding astronomer, the *mean* or average equable motions of the moon in longitude and in latitude; and he then represented the anomaly of the motion in longitude by means of an eccentric, in the same manner as he had done for the sun.

But here there occurred still an additional change, besides those of which we have spoken. The Apogee of the Sun was always in the same place in the heavens; or at least so nearly so, that Ptolemy could detect no error in the place assigned to it by Hipparchus 250 years before. But the Apogee of the Moon was found to have a motion among the stars. It had been observed before the time of Hipparchus, that in $6585\frac{1}{3}$ days, there are

241 revolutions of the moon with regard to the stars, but only 239 revolutions with regard to the anomaly. This difference could be suitably represented by supposing the eccentric, in which the moon moves, to have itself an angular motion, perpetually carrying its apogee in the same direction in which the moon travels; but this supposition being made, it was necessary to determine, not only the eccentricity of the orbit, and place of the apogee at a certain time, but also the rate of motion of the apogee itself, in order to form tables of the moon.

This task, as we have said, Hipparchus executed; and in this instance, as in the problem of the reduction of the sun's motion to tables, the data which he found it necessary to employ were very few. He deduced all his conclusions from six eclipses of the moon[3]. Three of these, the records of which were brought from Babylon, where a register of such occurrences was kept, happened in the 366th and 367th years from the era of Nabonassar, and enabled Hipparchus to determine the eccentricity and apogee of the moon's orbit at that time. The three others were observed at Alexandria, in the 547th year of Nabonassar, which gave him another position of the orbit at an interval of 180 years; and he thus became acquainted with the motion of the orbit itself, as well as its form[4].

[3] Ptol. Syn. iv. 10.

[4] Ptolemy uses the hypothesis of an epicycle for the moon's first inequality: but Hipparchus employs an eccentric.

The moon's motions are really affected by several other inequalities, of very considerable amount, besides those which were thus considered by Hipparchus; but the lunar paths, constructed on the above data, possessed a considerable degree of correctness, and especially when applied, as they were principally, to the calculation of eclipses; for the greatest of the additional irregularities which we have mentioned disappear at new and full moon, which are the only times when eclipses take place.

The numerical explanation of the motions of the sun and moon, by means of the hypothesis of eccentrics, and the consequent construction of Tables, was one of the great achievements of Hipparchus. The general explanation of the motions of the planets, by means of the hypothesis of epicycles, was in circulation previously, as we have seen. But the special motions of the planets, in their epicycles, are, in reality, affected by anomalies of the same kind as those which render it necessary to introduce eccentrics in the cases of the sun and moon.

Hipparchus determined, with great exactness, the *mean motions* of the Planets; but he was not able, from want of data, to explain the planetary *irregularities* by means of eccentrics. The whole mass of good observations of the planets which he received from preceding ages, did not contain so many, says Ptolemy, as those which he has transmitted to us of his own. "Hence[5] it was," he adds,

[5] Synt. ix. 2.

"that while he laboured, in the most assiduous manner, to represent the motions of the sun and moon by means of equable circular motions; with respect to the planets, so far as his works show, he did not even make the attempt, but merely put the extant observations in order, added to them himself more than the whole of what he received from preceding ages, and showed the insufficiency of the hypothesis current among astronomers to explain the phenomena." It appears, that preceding mathematicians had already pretended to construct "a Perpetual Canon," that is, Tables which should give the places of the planets at any future time; but these, being constructed without regard to the eccentricity of the orbits, must have been very erroneous.

Ptolemy declares, with great reason, that Hipparchus showed his usual love of truth, and his right sense of the responsibility of his task, in leaving this part of it to future ages. The Theories of the Sun and Moon, which we have already described, constitute him a great astronomical discoverer, and justify the reputation he has always possessed. There is, indeed, no philosopher who is so uniformly spoken of in terms of admiration. Ptolemy, to whom we owe our principal knowledge of him, perpetually couples with his name epithets of praise: he is not only an excellent and careful observer, but "a[6] most truth-loving and labour-loving person,"

[6] Synt. ix. 2.

one who had shown extraordinary sagacity and remarkable desire of truth in every part of science. Pliny, after mentioning him and Thales, breaks out into one of his passages of declamatory vehemence; "Great men! elevated above the common standard of human nature, by discovering the laws which celestial occurrences obey, and by freeing the wretched mind of man from the fears which eclipses inspired.—Hail to you and to your genius, interpreters of heaven, worthy recipients of the laws of the universe, authors of principles which connect gods and men!" Modern writers have spoken of Hipparchus with the same admiration; and even the exact but severe historian of astronomy, Delambre, who bestows his praise so sparingly, and his sarcasm so generally;—who says[7] that it is unfortunate for the memory of Aristarchus that his work has come to us entire, and who cannot refer[8] to the statement of an eclipse rightly predicted by Halicon of Cyzicus without adding, that if the story be true, Halicon was more lucky than prudent;—loses all his bitterness when he comes to Hipparchus[9]. "In Hipparchus," says he, "we find one of the most extraordinary men of antiquity; the *very greatest*, in the·sciences which require a combination of observation with geometry." Delambre adds, apparently in the wish to reconcile this eulogium with the depreciating manner in which he habitually speaks of all astronomers whose observations

[7] *Astronomie Ancienne,* i. 75.　　[8] i. 17.　　[9] i. 186.

are inexact, "a long period and the continued
efforts of many industrious men are requisite to
produce good instruments, but energy and assiduity
depend on the man himself."

Hipparchus was the author of other great discoveries and improvements in astronomy, besides
the establishment of the Doctrine of Eccentrics and
Epicycles; but this, being the greatest advance in
the *theory* of the celestial motions which was made
by the ancients, must be the leading subject of our
attention in the present work; our object being to
discover in what the progress of real theoretical
knowledge consists, and under what circumstances
it has gone on.

Sect. 2.—*Estimate of the Value of the Theory of Eccentrics and Epicycles.*

IT may be useful here to explain the value of the
theoretical step which Hipparchus thus made; and
the more so, as there are, perhaps, opinions in
popular circulation, which might lead men to think
lightly of the merit of introducing or establishing
the Doctrine of Epicycles. For, in the first place,
this doctrine is now acknowledged to be false; and
some of the greatest men in the more modern history of astronomy owe the brightest part of their
fame to their having been instrumental in over-
turning this hypothesis. And, moreover, in the
next place, the theory is not only false, but ex-

tremely perplexed and entangled, so that it is usually looked upon as a mass of arbitrary and absurd complication. Most persons are familiar with passages in which it is thus spoken of[10].

> . . . . . He his fabric of the heavens
> Hath left to their disputes, perhaps to move
> His laughter at their quaint opinions wide;
> Hereafter when they come to model heaven
> And calculate the stars, how will they wield
> The mighty frame! how build, unbuild, contrive,
> To save appearances! how gird the sphere
> With centric and eccentric scribbled o'er,
> Cycle in epicycle, orb in orb!

And every one will recollect the celebrated saying of Alphonso X., king of Castile[11], when this complex system was explained to him; that "if God had consulted him at the creation, the universe should have been on a better and simpler plan." In addition to this, the system is represented as involving an extravagant conception of the nature of the orbs which it introduces;—that they are crystalline spheres, and that the vast spaces which intervene between the celestial luminaries are a solid mass, formed by the fitting together of many masses perpetually in motion; an imagination which is presumed to be incredible and monstrous.

We must endeavour to correct or remove these prejudices, not only in order that we may do justice to the Hipparchian, or, as it is usually called, Ptolemaic system of astronomy, and to its founder; but

---

[10] *Paradise Lost,* viii.   [11] A. D. 1252.

VOL. I.   O

for another reason, much more important to the purpose of this work; namely, that we may see how theories may be highly estimable, though they contain false representations of the real state of things, and may be extremely useful, though they involve unnecessary complexity. In the advance of knowledge, the value of the true part of a theory may much outweigh the accompanying errour, and the use of a rule may be little impaired by its want of simplicity. The first steps of our progress do not lose their importance because they are not the last; and the outset of the journey may require no less vigour and activity than its close.

That which is true in the Hipparchian theory, and which no succeeding discoveries have deprived of its value, is the *Resolution* of the apparent motions of the heavenly bodies into an assemblage of circular motions. The test of the truth and reality of this Resolution is, that it leads to the construction of theoretical Tables of the motions of the luminaries, by which their places are given at any time, agreeing nearly with their places as actually observed. The assumption that these circular motions, thus introduced, are all exactly uniform, is the fundamental principle of the whole process. This assumption is, it may be said, false; and we have seen how fantastic some of the arguments were, which were originally urged in its favour. But *some* assumption is necessary, in order that the motions, at different points of a revolution, may be somehow connected, that is, in order that we may have *any* theory of the motions; and no assumption more simple than the one now mentioned can be selected.   The merit of the theory is this;—that obtaining the amount of the eccentricity, the place of the apogee, and, it may be, other elements, from a *few* ·observations, it deduces from these, results agreeing with *all* observations, however numerous and distant.   To express an inequality by means of an ·epicycle, implies, not only that there is an inequality, but further,—that the inequality is at its greatest value at a certain known place,—diminishes in proceeding from that place by a known law,— continues its diminution for a known portion of the revolution of the luminary,—then increases again; and so on: that is, the introduction of the epicycle represents the inequality of motion, as completely as it can be represented with respect to its *quantity*.

We may further illustrate this, by remarking that such a Resolution of the unequal motions of the heavenly bodies into equable circular motions, is, in fact, equivalent to the most recent and improved processes by which modern astronomers deal with such motions.   Their universal method is to resolve all unequal motions into a series of *terms*, or expressions of partial motions; and these terms involve *sines* and *cosines*, that is, certain technical modes of measuring circular motion, the circular motion having some constant relation to the time. And thus the problem of the resolution of the celestial motions into equable circular ones, which was propounded above two thousand years ago in the school of Plato, is still the great object of the study of modern astronomers, whether ob-servers or calculators.

That Hipparchus should have succeeded in the first great steps of this resolution for the sun and moon, and should have seen its applicability in other cases, is a circumstance which gives him one of the most distinguished places in the roll of great astronomers. As to the charges or the sneers against the complexity of his system, to which we have referred, it is easy to see that they are of no force. As a system of *calculation*, his is not only good, but, as we have just said, in many cases no better has yet been discovered. If, when the actual motions of the heavens are calculated in the best possible way, the process is complex and difficult, and if we are discontented at this, nature, and not the astronomer, must be the object of our dis-pleasure. This plea of the astronomers must be allowed to be reasonable. " We must not be re-pelled," says Ptolemy[12], " by the complexity of the hypotheses, but explain the phenomena as well as we can. If the hypotheses satisfy each apparent inequality separately, the combination of them will represent the truth; and why should it appear wonderful to any that such a complexity should

[12] Synt. xiii. 2.

exist in the heavens, when we know nothing of their nature which entitles us to suppose that any inconsistency will result?"

But it may be said, we now know that the motions are more simple than they were thus represented, and that the theory of epicycles was false, as a conception of the real construction of the heavens. And to this we may reply, that it does not appear that the best astronomers of antiquity conceived the cycles and epicycles to have a material existence. Though the dogmatic philosophers, as the Aristotelians, appear to have taught that the celestial spheres were real solid bodies, they are spoken of by Ptolemy as imaginary[13]; and it is clear, from his proof of the identity of the results of the hypothesis of an eccentric and an epicycle, that they are intended to pass for no more than geometrical conceptions, in which view they are true representations of the apparent motions.

It is true, that the real motions of the heavenly bodies are simpler than the apparent motions; and that we, who are in the habit of representing to our minds their real arrangement, become impatient of the seeming confusion and disorder of the ancient hypotheses. But this real arrangement never could have been detected by philosophers, if the apparent motions had not been strictly examined and successfully analyzed. How far the connexion between the facts and the true theory is from being obvious

[13] Synt. iii. 3.

or easily traced, any one may satisfy himself by
endeavouring, from a general conception of the
moon's real motions, to discover the rules which
regulate the occurrences of eclipses; or even to
explain to a learner, of what nature the apparent
motions of the moon among the stars will be.

The unquestionable evidence of the merit and
value of the theory of epicycles is to be found in
this circumstance;—that it served to embody all
the most exact knowledge then extant, to direct
astronomers to the proper methods of making it
more exact and complete, to point out new objects
of attention and research; and that, after doing this
at first, it was also able to take in, and preserve, all
the new results of the active and persevering labours of a long series of Greek, Latin, Arabian, and
modern European astronomers, till a new theory
arose which could discharge this office. It may,
perhaps, surprise some readers to be told, that the
author of this next *great* step in astronomical
theory, Copernicus, adopted the theory of epicycles;
that is, he employed that which we have spoken of
as its really valuable characteristic. "We[14] must
confess," he says, "that the celestial motions are
circular, or compounded of several circles, since
their inequalities observe a fixed law and recur in
value at certain intervals, which could not be, except they were circular; for a circle alone can make
that which has been, recur again."

[14] Copernicus. De Rev. l. i. c. 4.

In this sense, therefore, the Hipparchian theory was a real and indestructible truth, which was not rejected, and replaced by different truths, but was adopted and incorporated into every succeeding astronomical theory; and which can never cease to be one of the most important and fundamental parts of our astronomical knowledge.

A moment's reflection will show that, in the events just spoken of, the introduction and establishment of the theory of epicycles, those characteristics were strictly exemplified, which we have asserted to be the conditions of every real advance in progressive science; namely, the application of distinct and appropriate Ideas to a real series of Facts. The distinctness of the geometrical conceptions which enabled Hipparchus to assign the orbits of the sun and moon, requires no illustration; and we have just explained how these ideas combined into a connected whole the various motions and places of those luminaries. To make this step in astronomy, required diligence and care exerted in collecting observations, and mathematical clearness and steadiness of view exercised in seeing and showing that the theory was a successful analysis of them.

Sect. 3.—*Discovery of the Precession of the Equinoxes.*

THE same qualities which we trace in the researches of Hipparchus already examined,—diligence in collecting observations, and clearness of idea in representing them,—appear also in other discoveries of his, which we must not pass unnoticed. The Precession of the Equinoxes, in particular, is one of the most important of these discoveries.

The circumstance here brought into notice was a Change of Longitude of the Fixed Stars. The longitudes of the heavenly bodies, being measured from the point where the sun's annual path cuts the equator, will change if that path changes. Whether this happens, however, is not very easy to decide; for the sun's path among the stars is made out, not by merely looking at the heavens, but by a series of inferences from other observable facts. Hipparchus used for this purpose eclipses of the moon; for these, being exactly opposite to the sun, afford data in marking out his path. By comparing the eclipses of his own time with those observed at an earlier period by Timocharis, he found that the bright star, Spica Virginis, was six degrees behind the equinoctial point in his own time, and had been eight degrees behind the same point at an earlier epoch. The suspicion was thus suggested, that the longitudes of all the stars increase perpetually; but Hipparchus had too truly philosophical a spirit to take this for granted. He examined the places of Regulus, and those of other stars, as he had done those of Spica; and he found, in all these instances, a change of place which could be explained by a certain alteration of position in the circles to which the stars are referred, which alteration is described as the Precession of the Equinoxes.

The distinctness with which Hipparchus conceived this change of relation of the heavens, is manifested by the question which, as we are told by Ptolemy, he examined and decided;—that this motion of the heavens takes place about the poles of the ecliptic, and not about those of the equator. The care with which he collected this motion from the stars themselves, may be judged of from this, that having made his first observations for this purpose on Spica and Regulus, zodiacal stars, his first suspicion was that the stars of the zodiac alone changed their longitude, which suspicion he disproved by the examination of other stars. By his processes, the idea of the nature of the motion, and the evidence of its existence, the two conditions of a discovery, were fully brought into view. The scale of the facts which Hipparchus was thus able to reduce to law, may be in some measure judged of, by recollecting that the precession, from his time to ours, has only carried the stars through one sign of the zodiac; and that, to complete one revolution of the sky by the motion thus discovered, would require a period of 25,000 years. Thus this discovery connected the various aspects of the heavens at the most remote periods of human history; and, accordingly, the novel and ingenious views which Newton published in his chronology, are founded on this single astronomical fact, of the Precession of the Equinoxes.

The two discoveries which have been described,

the mode of constructing Solar and Lunar Tables, and the Precession, were advances of the greatest importance in astronomy, not only in themselves, but in the new objects and undertakings which they suggested to astronomers. The one detected a constant law and order in the midst of perpetual change and apparent disorder; the other disclosed mutation and movement perpetually operating where everything had been supposed fixed and stationary. Such discoveries were well adapted to call up many questionings in the minds of speculative men; for, after this, nothing could be supposed constant till it had been ascertained to be so by close examination; and no apparent complexity or confusion could justify the philosopher in turning away in despair from the task of simplification. To answer the inquiries thus suggested, new methods of observing the facts were requisite, more exact and uniform than those hitherto employed. Moreover the discoveries which were made, and others which could not fail to follow in their train, led to many consequences, required to be reasoned upon, systematized, completed, enlarged. In short, the *Epoch of Induction* led, as we have stated that such epochs must always lead, to a *Period of Developement, of Verification, Application, and Extension.*

CHAPTER IV.

SEQUEL TO THE INDUCTIVE EPOCH OF HIPPARCHUS.

Sect. 1.—*Researches which verified the Theory.*

THE discovery of the leading Laws of the Solar and Lunar Motions, and the detection of the Precession, may be considered as the great positive steps in the Hipparchian astronomy;—the parent discoveries, from which many minor improvements proceeded. The task of pursuing the collateral and consequent researches which now offered themselves,—of bringing the other parts of astronomy up to the level of its most improved portions,—was prosecuted by a succession of zealous observers and calculators, first, in the school of Alexandria, and afterwards in other parts of the world. We must notice the various labours of this series of astronomers; but we shall do so very briefly; for the ulterior developement of doctrines once established, is not so important an object of contemplation for our present purpose, as the first conception and proof of those fundamental truths on which systematic doctrines are founded. Yet Periods of Verification, as well as Epochs of Induction, deserve to be attended to; and they can nowhere be studied with so much advantage as in the history of astronomy.

In truth, however, Hipparchus did not leave to his successors the task of pursuing into detail those views of the heavens to which his discoveries led him. He examined with scrupulous care almost every part of the subject. We must briefly mention some of the principal points which were thus settled by him.

The verification of the laws of the changes which he assigned to the skies, implied that the condition of the heavens was constant, except so far as it was affected by those changes. Thus, the doctrine that the changes of position of the stars were rightly represented by the precession of the equinoxes, supposed that the stars were fixed with regard to each other; and the doctrine that the unequal number of days, in certain subdivisions of months and years, was adequately explained by the theory of epicycles, assumed that years and days were always of constant lengths. But Hipparchus was not content with assuming these bases of his theory, he endeavoured to prove them.

1. *Fixity of the Stars.*—The question necessarily arose after the discovery of the precession, even if such a question had never suggested itself before, whether the stars which were called *fixed*, and to which the motions of the other luminaries are referred, do really retain constantly the same relative position. In order to determine this funda-

mental question, Hipparchus undertook to construct a *Map* of the heavens; for though the result of his survey was expressed in words, we may give this name to his Catalogue of the positions of the most conspicuous stars. These positions are described by means of *alineations;* that is, three or more such stars are selected as can be touched by an apparent straight line drawn in the heavens. Thus Hipparchus observed that the southern claw of Cancer, the bright star in the same constellation which precedes the head of the Hydra, and the bright star Procyon, were nearly in the same line. Ptolemy quotes this and many other of the configurations which Hipparchus had noted, in order to show that the positions of the stars had not changed in the intermediate time; a truth which the catalogue of Hipparchus thus gave astronomers the means of ascertaining. It contained 1080 stars.

The construction of this catalogue of the stars by Hipparchus is an event of great celebrity in the history of astronomy. Pliny[1], who speaks of it with admiration as a wonderful and superhuman task ("ausus rem etiam Deo improbam, annumerare posteris stellas") asserts the undertaking to have been suggested by a remarkable astronomical event, the appearance of a new star; "novam stellam et aliam in ævo suo genitam deprehendit; ejusque motu, qua die fulsit, ad dubitationem est adductus anne hoc sæpius fieret, moverenturque et eæ quas puta-

---

[1] *Hist. Nat.* Lib. ii. (xxvi.)

mus affixas." There is nothing inherently impro- bable in this tradition, but we may observe, with Delambre[2], that we are not informed whether this new star remained in the sky, or soon disappeared again. Ptolemy makes no mention of the star or the story; and his catalogue contains no *bright* star which is not found in the "Catasterisms" of Eratos- thenes. These Catasterisms were an enumeration of 475 of the principal stars, according to the con- stellations in which they are; and were published about sixty years before Hipparchus.

2. *Constant Length of Years.*—Hipparchus also attempted to ascertain whether successive years are all of the same length; and though, with his scrupulous love of accuracy[3], he does not ap- pear to have thought himself justified in asserting that the years were always exactly equal, he showed, both by observations of the time when the sun passed the equinoxes, and by eclipses, that the difference of successive years, if there were any difference, must be extremely slight. The obser- vations of succeeding astronomers, and especially of Ptolemy, confirmed this opinion, and proved, with certainty, that there is no progressive increase or diminution in the duration of the year.

3. *Constant Length of Days. Equation of Time.*—The equality of days was more difficult to ascertain than that of years; for the year is mea- sured, as on a natural scale, by the number of

---

[2] A. A. i. 290.   [3] Ptolem. Synt. iii. 2.

days which it contains; but the day can be subdivided into hours only by artificial means; and
the mechanical skill of the ancients did not enable
them to attain any considerable accuracy in the
measure of such portions of time; though clep-
sydras and similar instruments were used by astronomers. The equality of days could only be proved,
therefore, by the consequences of such a supposition; and in this manner it appears to have been
assumed, as the fact really is, that the apparent
revolution of the stars is accurately uniform, never
becoming either quicker or slower. It followed as
a consequence of this, that the solar days (or rather
the *nycthemers*, compounded of a night and a day,)
would be unequal, in consequence of the sun's
unequal motion, thus giving rise to what we now
call the *Equation of Time*,—the interval by which
the time, as marked on a dial, is before or after
the time, as indicated by the accurate time-pieces
which modern skill can produce. This inequality
was fully taken account of by the ancient astronomers; and they thus in fact assumed the equality
of the sidereal days.

Sect. 2.—*Researches which did not verify the Theory.*

SOME of the researches of Hipparchus and his followers fell upon the weak parts of his theory;
and if the observations had been sufficiently exact,
must have led to its being corrected or rejected.

Among these we may notice the researches which were made concerning the *Parallax* of the heavenly bodies, that is, their apparent displacement by the alteration of position of the observer from one part of the earth's surface to the other. This subject is treated of at length by Ptolemy; and there can be no doubt that it was well examined by Hipparchus, who invented a *parallatic instrument* for that purpose. The idea of parallax, as a geometrical possibility, was indeed too obvious to be overlooked by geometers at any time; and when the doctrine of the sphere was established, it must have appeared strange to the student, that every place on the earth's surface might alike be considered as the center of the celestial motions. But if this was true with respect to the motions of the fixed stars, was it also true with regard to those of the sun and moon? The displacement of the sun by parallax is so small that the best observers among the ancients could never be sure of its existence; but with respect to the moon, the case is different. She may be displaced by this cause to the amount of twice her own breadth, a quantity easily noticed by the rudest process of instrumental observation. The law of the displacement thus produced is easily obtained by theory, the globular form of the earth being supposed known; but the amount of the displacement depends upon the distance of the moon from the earth, and requires at least one good observation to determine it. Ptolemy has given a table of the effects of parallax, calculated according to the apparent altitude of the moon, assuming certain supposed distances; these distances, however, do not follow the real law of the moon's distances, in consequence of their being founded upon the Hypothesis of the Eccentric and Epicycle.

In fact this Hypothesis, though a very close representation of the truth, so far as the *positions* of the luminaries are concerned, fails altogether when we apply it to their *distances*. The radius of the epicycle, or the eccentricity of the eccentric, are determined so as to satisfy the observations of the apparent motions of the bodies : but, inasmuch as the hypothetical motions are different altogether from the real motions, the Hypothesis does not, at the same time, satisfy the observations of the distances of the bodies, if we are able to make any such observations.

Parallax is one method by which the distances of the moon, at different times, may be compared ; her Apparent Diameters afford another method. Neither of these modes, however, is easily capable of such accuracy as to overturn at once the Hypothesis of epicycles; and, accordingly, the Hypothesis continued to be entertained in spite of such measures ; the measures being, indeed, in some degree falsified in consequence of the reigning opinion. In fact, however, the imperfection of the methods of measuring parallax and magnitude, which were in use at this period, was such, their results could not lead to any degree of conviction deserving to be set in opposition to a theory which was so satisfactory with regard to the more certain observations.

The Eccentricity, or the Radius of the Epicycle, which would satisfy the inequality of the *motions* of the moon, would, in fact, double the inequality of the *distances*. The Eccentricity of the moon's orbit is determined by Ptolemy as $\frac{1}{12}$ of the radius of the orbit; but its real amount is only half as great; this difference is a necessary consequence of the supposition of uniform circular motions, on which the Epicyclic Hypothesis proceeds.

We see, therefore, that this part of the Hipparchian theory carries in itself the germ of its own destruction. As soon as the art of celestial measurement was so far perfected, that astronomers could be sure of the apparent diameter of the moon within $\frac{1}{30}$ or $\frac{1}{40}$ of the whole, the inconsistency of the theory with itself would become manifest. We shall see, hereafter, the way in which this inconsistency operated; in reality, a very long period elapsed before the methods of observing were sufficiently good to bring it clearly into view.

Sect. 3.—Methods of Observation of the Greek Astronomers.

WE must now say a word concerning the Methods above spoken of. Since one of the most important tasks of a period of verification is to ascertain with accuracy the magnitude of the quantities which enter, as elements, into the theory which occupies men during the period ; the improvement of instruments, and the methods of observing and experimenting, are principal features in such periods. We shall, therefore, mention some of the 'facts which bear upon this point.

The estimation of distances among the stars by the eye, is an extremely inexact process. In some of the ancient observations, however, this appears to have been the method employed : and stars are described as being a *cubit* or *two cubits* from other stars. We may form some notion of the scale of this kind of measurement, from what Cleomedes remarks[4], that the sun appears to be about a foot broad ; an opinion which he confutes at length.

' A method of determining the positions of the stars, susceptible of a little more exactness than the former, is the use of *alineations*, already noticed in speaking of Hipparchus's catalogue. Thus, a straight line passing through two stars of the Great Bear passes also through the pole-star : this is, indeed, even now a method usually employed to enable us readily to fix on the pole-star ; and the two stars, β and α of Ursa Major, are hence often called " the pointers."

But nothing like accurate measurements of any portions of the sky were obtained, till astronomers

[4] Del. A. A. i. 222.

P 2

adopted the method of making visual coincidences of the objects with the instruments, either by means of *shadows* or of *sights*.

Probably the oldest and most obvious measurements of the positions of the heavenly bodies were those in which the elevation of the sun was determined by comparing the length of the shadow of an upright staff or *gnomon*, with the length of the staff itself. It appears[5], from a memoir of Gautil, first printed in the Connaissance des Temps for 1809, that, at the lower town of Loyang, now called Hon-anfou, Tchon-kong found the length of the shadow of the gnomon, at the summer solstice, equal to one foot and a half, the gnomon itself being eight feet in length. This was about 1100 B.C. The Greeks, at an early period, used the same method. Strabo says[6] that "Byzantium and Marseilles are on the same parallel of latitude, because the shadows at those places have the same proportion to the gnomon, according to the statement of Hipparchus, who follows Pytheas."

But the relations of position which astronomy considers, are, for the most part, angular distances; and these are most simply expressed by the intercepted portion of a circumference described about the angular point. The use of the gnomon might lead to the determination of the angle by the graphical methods of geometry; but the numerical expression of the circumference required some pro-

[5] Lib. U. K. *Hist. Ast.* p. 5.   [6] Del. A. A. i. 257.

gress in trigonometry; for instance, a table of the tangents of angles.

Instruments were soon invented for measuring angles, by means of circles, which had a border, or *limb*, divided into equal parts. The whole circumference was divided into 360 *degrees*: perhaps because the circles, first so divided, were those which represented the sun's annual path; one such degree would be the sun's daily advance, more nearly than any other convenient aliquot part which could be taken. The position of the sun was determined by means of the shadow of one part of the instrument upon the other. The most ancient instrument of this kind appears to be the *Hemisphere of Berosus*. A hollow hemisphere was placed with its rim horizontal, and a style was erected in such a manner that the extremity of the style was exactly at the center of the sphere. The shadow of this extremity, on the concave surface, had the same position with regard to the lowest point of the sphere which the sun had with regard to the highest point of the heavens. But this instrument was in fact used rather for dividing the day into portions of time than for determining position.

Eratosthenes[7] observed the amount of the obliquity of the sun's path to the equator; we are not informed what instruments he used for this purpose: but he is said to have obtained, from the

[7] Delambre, A. A. i. 86.

munificence of Ptolemy Euergetes, two *Armils,* or instruments composed of circles, which were placed in the portico at Alexandria, and long used for observations.   If a circular rim were placed so as to coincide with the plane of the equator, the inner concave edge would be enlightened by the sun's rays which came under the front edge, when the sun was south of the equator, and by the rays which came over the front edge, when the sun was north of the equator: the moment of the transition would be the time of the equinox.   Such an instrument appears to be referred to by Hipparchus, as quoted by Ptolemy[8].   " The circle of copper, which stands at Alexandria in what is called the Square Porch, appears to mark, as the day of the equinox, that on which the concave surface begins to be enlightened from the other side."   Such an instrument was called an *equinoctial armil.*

A *solstitial armil* is described by Ptolemy, consisting of two circular rims, one sliding round within the other, and the inner one furnished with two pegs standing out from its surface at right angles, and diametrically opposite to each other. These circles being fixed in the plane of the meridian, and the inner one turned, till, at noon, the shadow of the peg in front falls upon the peg behind, the position of the sun at noon would be determined by the degrees on the outer circle.

In calculation, the degree was conceived to

[8] Ptol. Synt. iii. 2.

be divided into 60 *minutes*, the minute into 60 *seconds*, and so on.   But in practice it was impossible to divide the limb of the instrument into parts so small.   The armils of Alexandria were divided into no parts smaller than sixths of degrees, or divisions of 10 minutes.

The angles, observed by means of these divisions, were expressed as a fraction of the circumference.   Thus Eratosthenes stated the interval between the tropics to be $\frac{11}{83}$ of the circumference[9].

It was soon remarked that the whole circumference of the circle was not wanted for such observations.   Ptolemy[10] says, that he found it more convenient to observe altitudes by means of a square flat piece of stone or wood, with a *quadrant* of a circle described on one of its flat faces, about a center near one of the angles.   A peg was placed at the center, and one of the extreme radii of the quadrant being perpendicular to the horizon, the elevation of the sun above the horizon was determined by observing the point of the arc of the quadrant on which the shadow of the peg fell.

As the necessity of accuracy in the observations was more and more felt, various adjustments of such instruments were practised.   The instruments were placed in the meridian by means of *a meridian*

---

[9] Delambre, A. A. i. 87.   It is probable that his observation gave him $47\frac{2}{3}$ degrees.   The fraction $\frac{47\frac{3}{4}}{360} = \frac{143}{1080} = \frac{11 \cdot 13}{1080} = \frac{11}{83\frac{1}{13}}$, which is very nearly $\frac{11}{83}$.

[10] Synt. i. 1.

line drawn by astronomical methods on the floor on which they stood. The plane of the instrument was made vertical by means of a plumb-line: the bounding radius, from which angles were measured, was also adjusted by the *plumb-line*[11].

In this manner, the places of the sun and of the moon could be observed by means of the shadows which they cast. In order to observe the stars[12], the observer looked along the face of the circle of the armil, so as to see its two edges apparently brought together, and the star apparently touching them[13].

It was afterwards found important to ascertain the position of the sun with regard to the ecliptic: and, for this purpose, an instrument, called an *astrolabe*, was invented, of which we have a description in Ptolemy[14]. This also consisted of circular rims, moveable within one another, or about poles; and contained circles which were to be brought into the position of the ecliptic, and of a plane passing through the sun and the poles of the ecliptic. The position of the moon with regard to the ecliptic, and its position in longitude with

[11] The curvature of the plane of the circle, by warping, was noticed. *Ptol.* iii. 2. p. 155, observes that his equatorial circle was illuminated on the hollow side twice in the same day. (He did not know that this might arise from refraction.)

[12] Delamb. A. A. i. 185.

[13] Ptol. Synt. i. 1. ῞Ωσπερ κεκολλημένος ἀμφοτέραις αὐτῶν ταῖς ἐπιφανέιαις ὁ ἀστὴρ ἐν τῷ δι᾽ αὐτῶν ἐπιπέδῳ διοπτεύηται.

[14] Synt. v. 1.

regard to the sun or a star, were thus determined.

· The astrolabe continued long in use, but not so long as the quadrant described by Ptolemy; this in a larger form, is the *mural quadrant*, which has been used up to the most recent times.

It may be considered surprising[15], that Hipparchus, after having observed, for some time, right ascensions and declinations, quitted equatorial armils for the astrolabe, which immediately refers the stars to the ecliptic. He probably did this because, after the discovery of precession, he found the latitudes of the stars constant, and wanted to ascertain their motion in longitude.

To the above instruments, may be added the *dioptra* and the *parallactic instrument* of Hipparchus, and Ptolemy. In the latter, the distance of a star from the zenith was observed by looking through two sights fixed in a rule, this being annexed to another rule, which was kept in a vertical position by a plumb-line; and the angle between the two rules was measured.

The following example of an observation, taken from Ptolemy, may serve to show the form in which the results of the instruments, just described, were usually stated[16].

"In the 2nd year of Antoninus, the 9th day of Pharmouthi, the sun being near setting, the last division of Taurus being on the meridian (that is,

---

[15] Del. A. A. 181.   [16] Del. A. A. ii. 248.

5½ equinoctial hours after noon), the moon was in 3 degrees of Pisces, by her distance from the sun (which was 92 degrees, 8 minutes); and half an hour after, the sun being set, and the quarter of Gemini on the meridian, Regulus·appeared, by the other circle of the astrolabe, 57½ degrees more forwards than the moon in longitude." From these data the longitude of Regulus is calculated.

From what has been said respecting the observations of the Alexandrian astronomers, it will have been seen that their instrumental observations could not be depended on for any close accuracy. This defect, after the general reception of the Hipparchian theory, operated very unfavourably on the progress of the science. If they could have traced the moon's place distinctly from day to day, they must soon have discovered all the inequalities which were known to Tycho Brahe; and if they could have measured her parallax or her diameter with any considerable accuracy, they must have obtained a confutation of the epicycloidal form of her orbit. By the badness of their observations, and the imperfect agreement of these with calculation, they not only were prevented making such steps, but were led to receive the theory with a servile assent and an indistinct apprehension, instead of that rational conviction and intuitive clearness which would have given a progressive impulse to their knowledge.

Sect. 4.—Period from Hipparchus to Ptolemy.

WE have now to speak of the cultivators of astronomy from the time of Hipparchus to that of Ptolemy, the next great name which occurs in the history of this science; though even he holds place only among those who verified, developed, and extended the theory of Hipparchus. The astronomers who lived in the intermediate time, indeed, did little, even in this way; though it might have been supposed that their studies were carried on under considerable advantages, inasmuch as they all enjoyed the liberal patronage of the kings of Egypt[17]. The "divine school of Alexandria," as it is called by Synesius, in the fourth century, appears to have produced few persons capable of carrying forwards, or even of verifying, the labours of its great astronomical teacher. The mathematicians of the school wrote much, and apparently they observed sometimes; but their observations are of little value: and their books are expositions of the theory and its geometrical consequences, without any attempt to compare it with observation. For instance, it does not appear that any one verified the remarkable discovery of the precession, till the time of Ptolemy, 250 years after; nor does the statement of this motion of the heavens appear in the treatises of the intermediate writers; nor does Ptolemy quote a single observation of any person

[17] Delamb. A. A. ii. 240.

made in this long interval of time; while his references to those of Hipparchus are perpetual.; and to those of Aristyllus and Timocharis, and of others, as Conon, who preceded Hipparchus, are not unfrequent.

This Alexandrian period, so inactive and barren in the history of science, was prosperous, civilized, and literary; and many of the works which belong to it are come down to us, though those of Hipparchus are lost. We have the "Uranologion" of Geminus[18], a systematic treatise on Astronomy, expounding correctly the Hipparchian Theories and their consequences, and containing a good account of the use of the various cycles, which ended in the adoption of the Calippic period. We have likewise "The Circular Theory of the Celestial Bodies" of Cleomedes[19], of which the principal part is a developement of the doctrine of the sphere, including the consequences of the globular form of the earth. We have also another work on "Spherics" by Theodosius of Bithynia[20], which contains some of the most important propositions of the subject, and has been used as a book of instruction even in modern times. Another writer on the same subject is Menelaus, who lived somewhat later, and whose Three Books on Spherics still remain.

One of the most important kinds of deduction from a geometrical theory, such as that of the

[18] B. C. 70.   [19] B. C. 60.   [20] B. C. 50.

doctrine of the sphere, or that of epicycles, is the calculation of its numerical results in particular cases. With regard to the latter theory, this was done in the construction of Solar and Lunar Tables, as we have already seen; and this process required the formation of a *Trigonometry*, or system of rules for calculating the relations between the sides and angles of triangles. Such a science had been formed by Hipparchus, who appears to be the author of every great step in ancient astronomy[21]. He wrote a work in twelve books, "On the Construction of the Tables of Chords of Arcs;" such a table being the means by which the Greeks solved their triangles. The Doctrine of the Sphere required, in like manner, a *Spherical Trigonometry*, in order to enable mathematicians to calculate its results; and this branch of science also appears to have been formed by Hipparchus[22], who gives results that imply the possession of such a method. Hypsicles, who was a contemporary of Ptolemy, also made some attempts at the solution of such problems: but it is extraordinary that the writers whom we have mentioned as coming after Hipparchus, namely, Theodosius, Cleomedes, and Menelaus, do not even mention the calculation of triangles[23], either plane or spherical; though the latter writer[24] is said to have written on "the Table of Chords," a work which is now lost.

[21] Delamb. A. A. ii. 37.   [22] A. A. i. 117.
[23] A. A. i. 249.   [24] A. A. ii. 37.

We shall see, hereafter, how prevalent a disposition in literary ages is that which induces authors to become commentators. This tendency showed itself at an early period in the school of Alexandria. Aratus[25], who lived 270 B.C. at the court of Antigonus, king of Macedonia, described the celestial constellations in two poems, entitled "Phænomena," and "Prognostics." These poems were little more than a versification of the treatise of Eudoxus on the acronycal and heliacal risings and settings of the stars. The work was the subject of a comment by Hipparchus, who perhaps found this the easiest way of giving connexion and circulation to his knowledge. Three Latin translations of this poem gave the Romans the means of becoming acquainted with it: the first is by Cicero, of which we have numerous fragments extant[26]; Germanicus Cæsar, one of the sons-in-law of Augustus, also translated the poem, and this translation remains almost entire. Finally, we have a complete translation by Avienus[27]. The "Astronomica" of Manilius, the "Poeticon Astronomicon" of Hyginus, both belonging to the time of Augustus, are, like the work of Aratus, poems which combine mythological ornament with, elementary astronomical exposition; but have no value in the

[25] A. A. i. 74.
[26] Two copies of this translation, illustrated by drawings of different ages, one set Roman, and the other Saxon, according to Mr. Ottley, are described in the *Archæologia*, vol. xviii.
[27] Mont. i. 221.

history of science. We may pass nearly the same judgment upon the explanations and declamations of Cicero, Seneca, and Pliny, for they do not apprize us of any additions to astronomical knowledge; and they do not always indicate a very clear apprehension of the doctrines which the writers adopt.

Perhaps the most remarkable feature in the two last-named writers, is the declamatory expression of their admiration for the discoverers of physical knowledge; and in one of them, Seneca, the persuasion of a boundless progress in science to which man was destined. Though this belief was no more than a vague and arbitrary conjecture, it suggested other conjectures in detail, some of which, having been verified, have attracted much notice. For instance, in speaking of comets[28], Seneca says, "The time will come when those things which are now hidden shall be brought to light by time and persevering diligence. Our posterity will wonder that we should be ignorant of what is so obvious." "The motions of the planets," he adds, "complex and seemingly confused, have been reduced to rule; and some one will come hereafter, who will reveal to us the paths of comets." Such convictions and conjectures are not to be admired for their wisdom; for Seneca was led rather by enthusiasm, than by any solid reasons, to entertain this opinion; nor, again, are they to be considered as merely lucky guesses, implying

[28] Seneca. Qu. N. vii. 25.

no merit: they are remarkable as showing how
the persuasion of the universality of law, and the
belief of the probability of its discovery by man,
grow up in men's minds, when speculative knowledge becomes a prominent object of attention.

An important practical application of astronomical knowledge was made by Julius Cæsar, in his
correction of the calendar, which we have already
noticed: and this was strictly due to the Alexandrian School: Sosigenes, an astronomer belonging
to that school, came from Egypt to Rome for the
purpose.

Sect. 5.—*Measures of the Earth.*

THERE were, as we have said, few attempts made,
at the period of which we are speaking, to improve
the accuracy of any of the determinations of the
early Alexandrian astronomers.   One question naturally excited much attention at all times, the
magnitude of the earth, its figure being universally
acknowledged to be a globe.   The Chaldeans, at
an earlier period, had asserted that a man, walking
without stopping, might go round the circuit of
the earth in a year; but this might be a mere
fancy, or a mere guess.   The attempt of Eratosthenes to decide this question went upon principles
entirely correct.   Syene was situated on the tropic;
for there, on the day of the solstice, at noon, objects cast no shadow; and a well was enlightened
to the bottom by the sun's rays.   At Alexandria,
on the same day, the sun was, at noon, distant

from the zenith by a fiftieth part of the circumference. These two cities were north and south from each other : and the distance had been determined, by the royal overseers of the roads, to be 5000 stadia. This gave a circumference of 250,000 stadia to the earth, and a radius of about 40,000. Aristotle[29] says that the mathematicians make the circumference 400,000 stadia. Hipparchus conceived that the measure of Eratosthenes ought to be increased by about one tenth[30]. Posidonius, the friend of Cicero, made another attempt of the same kind. At Rhodes, the star Canopus but just appeared above the horizon : at Alexandria, the same star rose to an altitude of $\frac{1}{48}$th of the circumference ; the direct distance on the meridian was 5000 stadia, which gave 240,000 for the whole circuit. We cannot look upon these measures as very precise ; the stadium employed is not certainly known ; and no peculiar care appears to have been bestowed on the measure of the direct distance.

When the Arabians, in the ninth century, came to be the principal cultivators of astronomy, they repeated this observation in a manner more suited to its real importance and capacity of exactness. Under the Caliph Almamon[31], the vast plain of Singiar, in Mesopotamia, was the scene of this undertaking. The Arabian astronomers there divided themselves into two bands, one under the direction

[29] De Cœlo. ii. ad fin.   [30] Plin. ii. (cviii.)
[31] Montu. i. 357.

of Chalid ben Abdolmalic, and the other having at its head Alis ben Isa. These two parties proceeded, the one north, the other south, determining the distance by the actual application of their measuring-rods to the ground, till each was found, by astronomical observation, to be a degree from the place at which they started. It then appeared that these terrestrial degrees were respectively 56 miles, and 56 miles and two thirds, the mile being 4000 cubits. In order to remove all doubt concerning the scale of this measure, we are informed that the cubit is that called the black cubit, which consists of 27 inches, each inch being the thickness of six grains of barley.

Sect. 6.—Ptolemy's Discovery of Evection.

BY referring, in this place, to the last-mentioned measure of the earth, we include the labours of the Arabian as well as the Alexandrian astronomers, in the period of mere detail, which forms the sequel to the great astronomical revolution of the Hipparchian epoch. And this period of verification is rightly extended to those later times; not merely because astronomers were then still employed in determining the magnitude of the earth, and the amount of other elements of the theory; for these are some of their employments to the present day; but because no great intervening discovery marks a new epoch, and begins a new period;—because no great revolution in the theory added to the objects of investigation, or presented them in a new point of view. This being the case, it will be more instructive for our purpose to consider the general character and broad intellectual features of this period, than to offer a useless catalogue of obscure and worthless writers, and of opinions either borrowed or unsound. But before we do this, there is one writer whom we cannot leave undistinguished in the crowd; since his name is more celebrated even than that of Hipparchus; his works contain ninety-nine hundredths of what we know of the Greek astronomy; and though he was not the author of a new theory, he made some very remarkable steps in the verification, correction, and extension of the theory which he received. I speak of Ptolemy, whose work, "The Mathematical Construction" (of the heavens), contains a complete exposition of the state of astronomy in his time, the reigns of Adrian and Antonine. This book is familiarly known to us by a term which contains the record of our having received our first knowledge of it from the Arabic writers. The "*Megiste* Syntaxis," or Great Construction, gave rise, among them, to the title *Al Magisti*, or *Almagest*, by which the work is commonly described. As a mathematical exposition of the Theory of Epicycles and Eccentrics, of the observations and calculations which were employed in order to apply this theory to the sun, moon, and planets, and of the other calculations which are requisite, in order to deduce the consequences of this theory, the work is a splendid and lasting monument of diligence, skill and judgment. Indeed, all the other astronomical works of the ancients hardly add anything whatever to the information we obtain from the Almagest; and the knowledge which the student possesses of the ancient astronomy must depend mainly upon his acquaintance with Ptolemy. Among other merits, Ptolemy has that of giving us a very copious account of the manner in which Hipparchus established the main points of his theories; an account the more agreeable, in consequence of the admiration and enthusiasm with which this author everywhere speaks of the great master of the astronomical school.

In our present survey of the writings of Ptolemy, we are concerned less with his exposition of what had been done before him, than with his own original labours. In most of the branches of the subject, he gave additional exactness to what Hipparchus had done; but our main business, at present, is with those parts of the Almagest which contain new steps in the application of the Hipparchian hypothesis. There are two such cases, both very remarkable,—that of the moon's *Evection*, and that of the *Planetary Motions*.

The law of the moon's anomaly, that is, of the leading and obvious inequality of her motion, could be represented, as we have seen, either by an eccentric or an epicycle; and the amount of this inequality had been collected by observations of eclipses. But though the hypothesis of an epicycle, for instance, would bring the moon to her proper place, so far as eclipses could show it, that is, at new and full moon, this hypothesis did not rightly represent her motions at other points of her course. This appeared, when Ptolemy set about measuring her distances from the sun at different times. "These," he[32] says, sometimes agreed, and sometimes disagreed." But by further attention to the facts, a rule was detected in these differences. "As my knowledge became more complete and more connected, so as to show the order of this new inequality, I perceived that this difference was small, or nothing, at new and full moon; and that at both the *dichotomies* (when the moon is half illuminated,) it was small, or nothing, if the moon was at the apogee or perigee of the epicycle, and was greatest when she was in the middle of the interval, and therefore when the first inequality was greatest also." He then adds some further remarks on the circumstances according to which the moon's place, as affected by this new inequality, is before or behind the place, as given by the epicyclical hypothesis.

Such is the announcement of the celebrated discovery of the moon's second inequality, afterwards called (by Bullialdus) the *Evection*. Ptolemy

[32] Synt. v. 2.

soon proceeded to represent this inequality by a combination of circular motions, uniting, for this purpose, the hypothesis of an epicycle, already employed to explain the first inequality, with the hypothesis of an eccentric, in the circumference of which the center of the epicycle was supposed to move. The mode of combining these was somewhat complex; more complex we may, perhaps, say, than was absolutely requisite[33]; the apogee of the eccentric moved backwards, or contrary to the order of the signs, and the center of the epicycle moved forwards nearly twice as fast upon the circumference of the eccentric, so as to reach a place nearly, but not exactly, the same, as if it had moved in a concentric instead of an eccentric path. Thus the center of the epicycle went twice round the eccentric in the course of one month: and in this manner it satisfied the condition that it should vanish at new and full moon, and be greatest when the moon was in the quarters of her monthly course (G).

The discovery of the Evection, and the reduction of it to the epicyclical theory, was, for several reasons, an important step in astronomy; some of these reasons may be stated.

1.   It obviously suggested, or confirmed, the

---

[33] If Ptolemy had used the hypothesis of an eccentric instead of an epicycle for the first inequality of the moon, an epicycle would have represented the second inequality more simply than his method did.

suspicion that the motions of the heavenly bodies might be subject to *many* inequalities;—that when one set of anomalies had been discovered and reduced to rule, another set might come into view;—that the discovery of a rule was a step to the discovery of deviations from the rule, which would require to be expressed in other rules;—that in the application of theory to observation, we find, not only the *stated phenomena*, for which the theory does account, but also *residual phenomena*, which remain unaccounted for, and stand out beyond the calculation;—that thus nature is not simple and regular, by conforming to the simplicity and regularity of our hypotheses, but leads us forwards to apparent complexity, and to an accumulation of rules and relations. A fact like the Evection, explained by an Hypothesis like Ptolemy's, tended altogether to discourage any disposition to guess at the laws of nature from mere ideal views, or from a few phenomena.

2. The discovery of Evection had an importance which did not come into view till long afterwards, in being the first of a numerous series of inequalities of the moon, which result from the *Disturbing Force* of the sun. These inequalities were successively discovered; and led finally to the establishment of the law of universal gravitation. The moon's first inequality arises from a different cause;—from the same cause as the inequality of the sun's motion;—from the motion

in an ellipse, so far as the central attraction is undisturbed by any other. This first inequality is called the Elliptic Inequality, or, more usually, the *Equation of the Center* (H). All the planets have such inequalities, but the Evection is peculiar to the moon. The discovery of other inequalities of the moon's motion, the Variation and Annual Equation, made an immediate sequel in the order of the subject to the discoveries of Ptolemy, although separated by a long interval of time; for these discoveries were only made by Tycho Brahe in the sixteenth century. The imperfection of astronomical instruments was the great cause of this long delay.

3. The Epicyclical Hypothesis was found capable of accommodating itself to such new discoveries. These new inequalities could be represented by new combinations of eccentrics and epicycles: all the real and imaginary discoveries of astronomers, up to Copernicus, were actually embodied in these hypotheses; Copernicus, as we have said, did not reject such hypotheses; the lunar inequalities which Tycho detected might have been similarly exhibited; and even Newton[34] represents the motion of the moon's apogee by means of an epicycle. As a mode of expressing the law of the irregularity, and of calculating its results in particular cases, the epicyclical theory was capable of continuing to render great

---

[34] *Principia*, lib. iii. prop. xxxv.

service to astronomy, however extensive the progress of the science might be. It was, in fact,
as we have already said, the modern process of
representing the motion by means of a series of
circular functions.

4. But though the doctrine of eccentrics and
epicycles was thus admissible as an Hypothesis,
and convenient as a means of expressing the laws
of the heavenly motions, the successive occasions
on which it was called into use, gave no countenance
to it as a Theory; that is, as a true view of the
nature of these motions, and their causes. By
the steps of the progress of this Hypothesis, it
became more and more complex, instead of becoming more simple, which, as we shall see, was
the course of the true Theory. The notions concerning the position and connexion of the heavenly
bodies, which were suggested by one set of phenomena, were not confirmed by the indications of
another set of phenomena; for instance, those
relations of the epicycles which were adopted to
account for the Motions of the heavenly bodies, were
not found to fall in with the consequences of their
apparent Diameters and Parallaxes. In reality, as
we have said, if the relative distances of the sun
and moon at different times could have been accurately determined, the Theory of Epicycles must
have been forthwith overturned. The insecurity of
such measurements alone maintained the theory to
later times (1).

Sect. 7.—Conclusion of the History of Greek Astronomy.

I MIGHT now proceed to give an account of Ptolemy's other great step, the determination of the Planetary Orbits; but as this, though in itself very curious, would not illustrate any point beyond those already noticed, I shall refer to it very briefly. The planets all move in ellipses about the sun, as the moon moves ·about the earth; and as the sun apparently moves about the earth. They will therefore each have an Elliptic Inequality or Equation of the ˙ center, for the same reason that the sun and moon have such inequalities. And this inequality may be represented, in the cases of the planets, just as in the other two, by means of an eccentric; the epicycle, it will be re-collected, had already been used in order to repre-sent the more obvious changes of the planetary motions. To determine the amount of the Eccen-tricities and the places of the Apogees of the planetary orbits, was the task which Ptolemy un-dertook; Hipparchus, as we have seen, having been destitute of the observations which such a process required. The determination of the Eccentricities in these cases involved some pecu-liarities which might not at first sight occur to the reader. The elliptical motion of the planets takes place about the sun; but Ptolemy considered their movements as altogether independent of the sun, and referred them to the earth alone; and thus the apparent eccentricities which he had to account for, were the compound result of the Eccentricity of the Earth's orbit, and of the proper Eccentricity of the orbit of the Planet. He explained this result by the received mechanism of an eccentric *Deferent*, carrying an Epicycle; but the motion in the Deferent is uniform, not about the center of the circle, but about another point, the *Equant*. Without going further into detail, it may be sufficient to state that, by a combination of Eccentrics and Epicycles, he did account for the leading features of these motions; and by using his own observations, compared with more ancient ones, (for instance, those of Timocharis for Venus,) he was able to determine the Dimensions and Positions of the Orbits (J).

I shall here close my account of the astronomical progress of the Greek School. My purpose is only to illustrate the principles on which the progress of science depends, and therefore I have not at all pretended to touch upon every part of the subject. Some portions of the ancient theories, as for instance, the mode of accounting for the motions of the moon and planets in latitude, are sufficiently analogous to what has been explained, not to require any more especial notice. Other parts of the Greek astronomical knowledge, as, for instance, their acquaintance with refraction, did not assume any clear or definite form, and can only be considered as the prelude to modern discoveries on the same subject. And before we can with propriety pass on to these, there is a long and remarkable, though unproductive interval, of which some account must be given.

Sect. 8.—*Arabian Astronomy.*

THE interval to which I have just alluded may be considered as extending from Ptolemy to Copernicus; we have no advance in Greek astronomy after the former; no signs of a revival of the power of discovery till the latter. During this interval of 1350 years[35], the principal cultivators of astronomy were the Arabians, who adopted this science from the Greeks whom they conquered, and from whom the conquerors of western Europe again received back their treasure, when the love of science and the capacity for it had been awakened in their minds. In the intervening time, the precious deposit had undergone little change. The Arab astronomer had been the scrupulous but unprofitable servant, who kept his talent without apparent danger of loss, but also without prospect of increase. There is little in Arabic literature which bears upon the *progress* of astronomy; but as the little that there is must be considered as a sequel to the Greek science, I shall

---

[35] Ptolemy died about A. D. 150. Copernicus was living A. D. 1500.

notice one or two points before I treat of the stationary period in general.

When the sceptre of western Asia had passed into the hands of the Abasside caliphs[36], Bagdad, "the city of peace," rose to splendour and refinement, and became the metropolis of science under the successors of Almansor the Victorious, as Alexandria had been under the successors of Alexander the Great. Astronomy attracted peculiarly the favour of the powerful as well as the learned; and almost all the culture which was bestowed upon the science, appears to have had its source in the patronage, often also in the personal studies, of Saracen princes. Under such encouragement, much was done, in those scientific labours which money and rank can command. Translations of Greek works were made, large instruments were erected, observers were maintained; and accordingly as observation showed the defects and imperfection of the extant tables of the celestial motions, new ones were constructed. Thus under Almansor, the Grecian works of science were collected from all quarters, and many of them translated into Arabic[37]. The translation of the "Megiste Syntaxis" of Ptolemy, which thus became the Almagest, is ascribed to Isaac ben Homain in this reign.

The greatest of the Arabian astronomers comes half a century later. This is Albategnius, as he is commonly called; or more exactly, Muhammed

[46] Gibbon, x. 31.   [37] Id. x. 36.

ben Geber Albatani, the last appellation indicating that he was born at Batan, a city of Mesopotamia[38]. He was a Syrian prince, whose residence was at Aracte or Racha in Mesopotamia; a part of his observations were made at Antioch. His work still remains to us in Latin. "After having read," he says, "the Syntaxis of Ptolemy, and learnt the methods of calculation employed by the Greeks, his observations led him to conceive that some improvements might be made in their results. He found it necessary to add to Ptolemy's observations, as Ptolemy had added to those of Abrachis" (Hipparchus). He then published Tables of the motions of the sun, moon, and planets, which long maintained a high reputation.

These, however, did not prevent the publication of others. Under the Caliph Hakem (about A.D. 1000,) Ebon Iounis published Tables of the Sun, Moon, and Planets, which were hence called the *Hakemite* Tables. Not long after, Arzachel of Toledo published the *Toletan* Tables. In the 13th century, Nasir Eddin published Tables of the Stars, dedicated to Ilchan, a Tartar prince, and hence termed the *Ilchanic* Tables. Two centuries later, Ulugh Beigh, the grandson of Tamerlane, and prince of the countries beyond the Oxus, was a zealous practical astronomer; and his Tables, which were published in Europe by Hyde in 1665, are referred to as important authority by modern astronomers.

[38] Del., *Astronomie du Moyen Age*, 4.

The series of Astronomical Tables which we have thus noticed, in which, however, many are omitted, leads us to the *Alphonsine* tables, which were put forth in 1488, and in succeeding years, under the auspices of Alphonso, king of Castile; and thus brings us to the verge of modern astronomy.

For all these Tables, the Ptolemaic hypotheses were employed; and, for the most part, without alteration. The Arabs sometimes felt the extreme complexity and difficulty of the doctrine which they studied; but their minds did not possess that kind of invention and energy by which the philosophers of Europe, at a later period, won their way into a simpler and better system.

Thus Alpetragius states, in the outset of his "Planetarum Theorica," that he was at first astonished and stupified with this complexity, but that afterwards "God was pleased to open to him the occult secret in the theory of his orbs, and to make known to him the truth of their essence, and the rectitude of the quality of their motion." His system consists, according to Delambre[39], in attributing to the planets a spiral motion from east to west, an idea already refuted by Ptolemy. Geber of Seville criticizes Ptolemy very severely[40], but without introducing any essential alteration into his system. The Arabian observations are in many cases valuable; both because they were made with more skill and with better instruments than those

[39] Delambre, M. A. p. 7.   [40] M. A. p. 180, &c.

of the Greeks; and also because they illustrate
the permanence or variability of important elements, such as the obliquity of the ecliptic and the
inclination of the moon's orbit.

We must, however, notice one or two peculiar
Arabian doctrines. The most important of these
is the discovery of the Motion of the Sun's Apogee
by Albategnius. He found the Apogee to be in
longitude 82 degrees; Ptolemy had placed it in
longitude 65 degrees. The difference of 17 degrees
was beyond all limit of probable errour of calculation, though the process is not capable of great
precision; and the inference of the Motion of the
Apogee was so obvious, that we cannot agree with
Delambre, in doubting or extenuating the claim
of Albategnius to this discovery, on the ground
of his not having expressly stated it.

In detecting this motion, the Arabian astronomers reasoned rightly from facts well observed;
they were not always so fortunate. Arzachel, in
the 11th century, found the apogee of the sun to
be less advanced than Albategnius had found it,
by some degrees; he inferred that it had receded in
the intermediate time; but we now know, from an
acquaintance with its real rate of moving, that the
true inference would have been, that Albategnius,
whose method was less trustworthy than that of
Arzachel, had made an errour to the amount of the
difference thus arising. A curious, but utterly false
hypothesis was founded on observations thus erro-

neously appreciated; namely, the *Trepidation of the fixed stars.* Arzachel conceived that a uniform Precession of the equinoctial points would not account for the apparent changes of position of the stars, and that for this purpose, it was necessary to conceive two circles of about 8 degrees radius described round the equinoctial points of the immoveable sphere, and to suppose the first points of Aries and Libra to describe the circumferences of these circles in about 800 years. This would produce, at one time a progression, and at another a regression, of the apparent equinoxes, and would moreover change the latitudes of the stars. Such a motion is entirely visionary; but the doctrine made a sect among astronomers, and was adopted in the first edition of the Alphonsine Tables, though afterwards rejected.

. An important exception to the general unprogressive character of Arabian science has been pointed out recently by M. Sedillot[41]. It appears that Mohammed-Aboul Wefa-al-Bouzdjani, an Arabian astronomer of the tenth century, who resided at Cairo, and observed at Bagdad in 975, discovered a third inequality of the moon, in addition to the two expounded by Ptolemy, the Equation of the Center, and the Evection. This third inequality, the *Variation,* is usually supposed to have been discovered by Tycho Brahe, six centuries

[41] Sedillot, Nouvelles Rech. sur l'Hist. de l'Astron. chez les Arabes. *Nouveau Journal Asiatique.* 1836.

later. It is an inequality of the moon's motion, in virtue of which she moves quickest when she is at new or full, and slowest at the first and third quarter; in consequence of this, from the first quarter to the full, she is behind her *mean* place; at the full, she does not differ from her mean place; from the full to the third quarter, she is before her true place; and so on; and the greatest effect of the inequality is in the *octants*, or points half-way between the four quarters. In an Almagest of Aboul Wefa, a part of which exists in the Royal Library at Paris, after describing the two inequalities of the moon, he has a Section ix., "Of the Third Anomaly of the Moon called *Muhazal* or *Prosneusis*." He there says, that taking cases when the moon was in apogee or perigee, and when, consequently, the effect of the two first inequalities vanishes, he found, *by observation of the moon*, when she was nearly *in trine* and *in sextile* with the sun, that she was a degree and a quarter from her calculated place. "And hence," he adds, "I perceived that this anomaly exists independently of the two first: and this can only take place by a declination of the diameter of the epicycle with respect to the center of the zodiac."

We may remark that we have here this inequality of the moon made out in a really philosophical manner; a residual quantity in the moon's longitude being detected by observation, and the cases in which it occurs selected and grouped by an inductive effort of the mind. The advance is not great; for Aboul Wefa appears only to have detected the existence, and not to have fixed the law or the exact quantity of the inequality; but still it places the scientific capacity of the Arabs in a more favourable point of view than any circumstance with which we were previously acquainted.

But this discovery of Aboul Wefa appears to have excited no notice among his contemporaries and followers; at least it had been long quite forgotten when Tycho Brahe rediscovered the same lunar inequality. We can hardly help looking upon this circumstance as an evidence of a servility of intellect belonging to the Arabian period. The learned Arabians were so little in the habit of considering science as progressive, and looking with pride and confidence at examples of its progress, that they had not the courage to believe in a discovery which they themselves had made, and were dragged back by the chain of authority, even when they had advanced beyond their Greek masters.

As the Arabians took the whole of their theory (with such slight exceptions as we have been noticing) from the Greeks, they took from them also the mathematical processes by which the consequences of the theory were obtained. Arithmetic and Trigonometry, two main branches of these processes, received considerable improvements at their hands. In the former, especially, they rendered a service to the world which it is difficult to estimate too highly, in abolishing the cumbrous Sexagesimal Arithmetic of the Greeks, and introducing the notation by means of the digits 1, 2, 3, 4, 5, 6, 7, 8, 9, 0, which we now employ[12]. These numerals appear to be of Indian origin, as is acknowledged by the Arabs themselves; and thus form no exception to the sterility of the Arabian genius as to great scientific inventions. Another improvement, of a subordinate kind, but of great utility, was Arabian, being made by Albategnius. He introduced into calculation the *sine*, or half-chord of the double arc, instead of the chord of the arc itself, which had been employed by the Greek astronomers. There have been various conjectures concerning the origin of the word *sine;* the most probable appears to be that *sinus* is the Latin translation of the Arabic word *gib*, which signifies a fold, the two halves of the chord being conceived to be folded together.

The great obligation which Science owes to the Arabians, is to have preserved it during a period of darkness and desolation, so that Europe might receive it back again when the evil days were past. We shall see hereafter how differently the European intellect dealt with this hereditary treasure when once recovered.

[12] Mont. i. 376.

Before quitting the subject, we may observe that Astronomy brought back, from her sojourn among the Arabs, a few terms which may still be perceived in her phraseology.   Such are the *zenith*, and the opposite imaginary point, the *nadir ;*— the circles of the sphere termed *almacantars* and *azimuth* circles.   The *alidad* of an instrument is its index, which possesses an angular motion. Some of the stars still retain their Arabic names; *Aldebaran, Rigel, Fomalhaut;* many others were known by such appellations a little while ago.   Perhaps the word *almanac* is the most familiar vestige of the Arabian period of astronomy[43].

[43] It is foreign to my purpose to note any efforts of the intellectual faculties among other nations, which may have taken place independently of the great system of progressive European culture, from which all our existing science is derived.   Otherwise I might speak of the astronomy of some of the Orientals, for example, the Chinese, who are said, by Montucla (i. 465) to have discovered the first equation of the moon, and the proper motion of the fixed stars (the Precession), in the third century of our era.   The Greeks had made these discoveries 500 years earlier.

NOTES TO BOOK III.

(G.) p. 230. I WILL insert here the explanation which my German translator, the late distinguished astronomer Littrow, has given of this point. The Rule of this Inequality, the Evection, may be most simply expressed thus. If a denote the excess of the Moon's Longitude over the Sun's, and b the Anomaly of the moon reckoned from her Perigee, the Evection is equal to $1^\circ.3.\sin(2a-b)$. At New and Full Moon, a is 0 or 180°, and thus the Evection is $-1^\circ.3.\sin b$. At both quarters, or dichotomies, a is 90° or 270°, and consequently the Evection is $+1^\circ.3.\sin b$. The Moon's Elliptical Equation of the center is at all points of her orbit equal to $6^\circ.3.\sin b$. The Greek Astronomers before Ptolemy observed the moon only at the time of eclipses; and hence they necessarily found for the sum of these two greatest inequalities of the moon's motion the quantity $6^\circ.3.\sin b - 1^\circ.3.\sin b$, or $5^\circ.\sin b$: and as they took this for the moon's equation of the center, which depends upon the excentricity of the moon's orbit, we obtain from this too small equation of the center, an excentricity also smaller than the truth. Ptolemy, who first observed the moon in her quarters, found for the sum of those Inequalities at those points the quantity $6^\circ.3.\sin b + 1^\circ.3.\sin b$, or $7^\circ.6.\sin b$; and thus made the excentricity of the moon as much too great at the quarters as the observers of eclipses had made it too small. He hence concluded that the excentricity of the Moon's orbit is variable, which is not the case.

(H.) p. 232. The Equation of the Center is the difference between the place of the Planet in its elliptical orbit, and that place which a Planet would have, which revolved uniformly round the Sun as a center in a circular orbit in the same time. An imaginary Planet moving in the manner last described, is called the *mean* Planet, while the actual Planet which moves in the ellipse is called the *true* Planet. The Longitude of the mean Planet at a given time is easily found, because its motion is uniform. By adding to it the Equation of the Center, we find the Longitude of the true Planet, and thus, its place in its orbit.—*Littrow's Note.*

I may add that the word *Equation*, used in such cases, denotes in general a quantity which must be added to or subtracted from a mean quantity, to make it *equal* to the true quantity: or rather, a quantity which must be added to or subtracted from a variably increasing quantity, to make it increase *equably*.

(I.) p. 233. The alteration of the apparent diameter of the moon is so great that it cannot escape us, even with very moderate instruments. This apparent diameter contains, when the moon is nearest the earth, 2010 seconds, when she is farthest off, 1762 seconds; that is, 248 seconds; or 4 minutes 8 seconds, less than in the former case. [The two quantities are in the proportion of 8 to 7, nearly].—*Littrow's Note.*

(J.) p. 235. Ptolemy determined the Radius and the Periodic Time of his two circles for each Planet in the following manner: For the *inferior* Planets, that is, Mercury and Venus, he took the Radius of the Deferent equal to the Radius of the Earth's orbit, and the Radius of the Epicycle equal to that of the Planet's orbit. For these Planets, according to his assumption, the Periodic Time of the Planet in its Epicycle was to the Periodic Time of the Epicyclical Center on the Deferent, as the *synodical* Revolution of the Planet to the *tropical* Revolution of the Earth above the Sun. For the three *superior* Planets, Mars, Jupiter, and Saturn, the Radius of the Deferent was equal to the Radius of the Planet's orbit, and the Radius of the Epicycle was equal to the Radius of the Earth's orbit; the Periodic Time of the Planet in its Epicycle was to the Periodic Time of the Epicyclical Center on the Deferent, as the *synodical* Revolution of the Planet to the *tropical* Revolution of the same Planet.

Ptolemy might obviously have made the geometrical motions of *all* the Planets correspond with the observations by one of these two modes of construction ; but he appears to have adopted this double form of the theory, in order that in the inferior, as well as in the superior Planets, he might give the smaller of the two Radii to the Epicycle : that is, in order that he might make the smaller circle move round the larger, not *vice versâ*.— *Littrow's Note.*

BOOK IV.

HISTORY

OF

PHYSICAL SCIENCE IN THE MIDDLE AGES;

OR,

VIEW OF THE STATIONARY PERIOD OF
INDUCTIVE SCIENCE.

In vain, in vain! the all-composing hour
Resistless falls . . . .

.   .   .   .

As one by one, at dread Medea's strain,
The sickening stars fade off th' ethereal plain;
As Argus' eyes, by Hermes' wand opprest,
Closed one by one to everlasting rest;
Thus at her felt approach and secret might,
Art after art goes out, and all is night.
See skulking Truth to her old cavern fled,
Mountains of casuistry heaped on her head;
Philosophy, that reached the heavens before,
Shrinks to her hidden cause, and is no more.
Physic of Metaphysic begs defence,
And Metaphysic calls for aid to Sense:
See Mystery to Mathematics fly!
In vain! they gaze, turn giddy, rave, and die.

Dunciad, B. iv.

INTRODUCTION.

WE have now to consider more especially a long and barren period, which intervened between the scientific activity of ancient Greece, and that of modern Europe; and which we may, therefore, call the Stationary Period of Science. It would be to no purpose to enumerate the various forms in which, during these times, men reproduced the discoveries of the inventive ages: or to trace in them the small successes of Art, void of any principle of genuine Philosophy. Our object requires rather that we should point out the general and distinguishing features of the intellect and habits of those times. We must endeavour to delineate the character of the Stationary Period, and, as far as possible, to analyze its defects and errours; and thus obtain some knowledge of the causes of its barrenness and darkness.

We have already stated, that real scientific progress requires distinct general Ideas, applied to many special and certain Facts. In the period of which we now have to speak, men's Ideas were obscured, their disposition to bring their general views into accordance with Facts was enfeebled. They were thus led to employ themselves unprofitably, among indistinct and unreal notions. And the evil of these tendencies was further inflamed, by moral peculiarities in the character of those times ;—by an abjectness of thought on the one hand, which could not help looking towards some intellectual superior, and by an impatience of dissent on the other.   To this must be added an enthusiastic temper, which, when introduced into speculation, tends to subject the mind's operations to ideas altogether distorted and delusive.

These characteristics of the stationary period, its obscurity of thought, its servility, its intolerant disposition, and its enthusiastic temper, will be treated of in the four following chapters, on the Indistinctness of Ideas, the Commentatorial Spirit, the Dogmatism, and the Mysticism of the Middle Ages.

CHAPTER I.

On the Indistinctness of Ideas of the Middle Ages.

THAT firm and entire possession of certain clear and distinct general ideas which is necessary to sound science, was the character of the minds of those among the ancients who created the several sciences which arose among them. It was indispensable, that such inventors should have a luminous and steadfast apprehension of certain general relations, such as those of space and number, order and cause; and should be able to apply these ·notions with perfect readiness and precision to special facts and cases. It is necessary that such scientific notions should be more definite and precise than those which common language conveys; and in this state of unusual clearness, they must be so familiar to the philosopher, that they are the language in which he thinks. The discoverer is thus led to doctrines which other men adopt and follow out, in proportion as they seize the fundamental ideas, and become acquainted with the leading facts. Thus Hipparchus, conceiving clearly the motions and combinations of motion which enter into his theory, saw that the relative lengths of the seasons were sufficient data for determining the form of the sun's orbit; thus Archimedes, possessing a steady notion of mechanical pressure, was able, not only to deduce the properties of the lever and of the center of gravity, but also to see the truth of those principles respecting the distribution of pressure in fluids, on which the science of hydrostatics depends.

With the progress of such distinct ideas, the inductive sciences rise and flourish; with the decay and loss of such distinct ideas, these sciences become stationary, languid, and retrograde. When men merely repeat the terms of science, without attaching to them any clear conceptions;—when their apprehensions become vague and dim;—when they assent to scientific doctrines as a matter of tradition, rather than of conviction, on trust rather than on sight; —when science is considered as a collection of opinions, rather than a record of laws by which the universe is really governed;—it must inevitably happen, that men will lose their hold on the knowledge which the great discoverers who preceded them have brought to light. They are not able to push forwards the truths on which they lay so feeble and irresolute a hand; probably they cannot even prevent their sliding back towards the obscurity from which they had been drawn, or from being lost altogether. Such indistinctness and vacillation of thought appear to have prevailed in the stationary period, and to be, in fact, intimately connected with its stationary character. I shall point out some indications of the intellectual peculiarity of which I speak.

1. *Collections of Opinions.*—The fact, that mere Collections of the opinions of physical philosophers came to hold a prominent place in literature, already indicated a tendency to an indistinct and wandering apprehension of such opinions. I speak of such works as Plutarch's five Books " on the Opinions of Philosophers," or the physical opinions which Diogenes Laërtius gives in his " Lives of the Philosophers." At an earlier period still, books of this kind appear ; as for instance, a large portion of Pliny's Natural History, a work which has very appropriately been called the·Encyclopædia of Antiquity ; even Aristotle himself is much in the habit of enumerating the opinions of those who had preceded him. To present such statements as an important part of physical philosophy, shows an erroneous and loose apprehension of its nature. For the only proof of which its doctrines admit, is the possibility of applying the general theory to each particular case : the authority of great men, which in moral and practical matters may or must have its weight, is here of no force ; and the technical precision of ideas which the terms of a sound physical theory usually demand, renders a mere statement of the doctrines very imperfectly intelligible to readers familiar with common notions only. To dwell upon such collections of opinions, therefore, both

implies, and produces, in writers and readers, an obscure and inadequate apprehension of the full meaning of the doctrines thus collected; supposing there be among them any which really possess such a clearness, solidity, and reality, as to make them important in the history of science. Such diversities of opinion convey no truth; such a multiplicity of statements of what has been *said*, in no degree teaches us what *is;* such accumulations of indistinct notions, however vast and varied, do not make up one distinct idea. On the contrary, the habit of dwelling upon the verbal expressions of the views of other persons, and of being content with such an apprehension of doctrines as a transient notice can give us, is fatal to firm and clear thought: it indicates wavering and feeble conceptions, which are inconsistent with sound physical speculation.

We may, therefore, consider the prevalence of Collections of the kind just referred to, as indicating a deficiency of philosophical talent in the ages now under review. As evidence of the same character, we may add the long train of publishers of Abstracts, Epitomes, Bibliographical Notices, and similar writers. All such writers are worthless for all purposes of *science*, and their labours may be considered as dead works; they have in them no principle of philosophical vitality; they draw their origin and nutriment from the death of true physical knowledge; and resemble the swarms of insects that are born from the perishing carcass of some nobler animal.

2. *Indistinctness of Ideas in Mechanics.*—But the indistinctness of thought which is so fatal a feature in the intellect of the stationary period, may be traced more directly in the works, even of the best authors, of those times. We find that they did not retain steadily the ideas on which the scientific success of the previous period had depended. For instance, it is a remarkable circumstance in the history of the science of Mechanics, that it did not make any advance from the time of Archimedes to that of Stevinus and Galileo. Archimedes had established the doctrine of the lever; several persons tried, in the intermediate time, to prove the property of the inclined plane, and none of them succeeded. But let us look to the attempts; for example, that of Pappus, in the eighth Book of his Mathematical Collections, and we may see the reason of the failure. His Problem shows, in the very terms in which it is propounded, the want of a clear apprehension of the subject. " Having given the power which will draw a given weight along a horizontal plane, to find the additional power which will draw the same weight along a given inclined plane." This is proposed without previously defining how Powers, producing such effects, are to be measured; and as if the speed with which the body were drawn, and the nature of the surface of the plane, were of no consequence.

The proper elementary Problem is, To find, the force which will *support* a body on a smooth inclined plane; and no doubt the solution of Pappus has more reference to this problem than to his own. His reasoning is, however, totally at variance with mechanical ideas on any view of the problem. He supposes the weight to be formed into a sphere; and this sphere being placed in contact with the inclined plane, he assumes that the effect will be the same as if the weight were supported on a horizontal lever, the fulcrum being the point of contact of the sphere with the plane, and the power acting at the circumference of the sphere. Such an assumption implies an entire absence of those distinct ideas of force and mechanical pressure, on which our perception of the identity or difference of different modes of action must depend;—of those ideas by the help of which Archimedes had been able to demonstrate the properties of the lever, and Stevinus afterwards discovered the true solution of the problem of the inclined plane. The motive to Pappus's assumption was probably no more than this; —he perceived that the additional power, which he thus obtained, vanished when the plane became horizontal, and increased as the inclination became greater. Thus his views were vague; he had no clear conception of mechanical action, and he tried a geometrical conjecture. This is not the way to real knowledge.

Pappus (who lived about A.D. 400) was one

of the best mathematicians of the Alexandrian school; and, on subjects where his ideas were so indistinct, it is not likely that any much clearer were to be found in the minds of his contemporaries. Accordingly, on all subjects of speculative mechanics, there appears to have been an entire confusion and obscurity of thought till modern times. Men's minds were busy in endeavouring to systematize the distinctions and subtleties of the Aristotelian school, concerning Motion and Power; and, being, thus employed among doctrines in which there was involved no definite meaning capable of real exemplification, they, of course, could not acquire sound physical knowledge. We have already seen that the physical opinions of Aristotle, even as they came from him, had no proper scientific precision. His followers, in their endeavours to perfect and develop his statements, never attempted to introduce clearer ideas than those of their master; and as they never referred, in any steady manner, to facts, the vagueness of their notions was not corrected by any collision with observation. The physical doctrines which they extracted from Aristotle were, in the course of time, built up into a regular system; and though these doctrines could not be followed into a practical application without introducing distinctions and changes, such as deprived the terms of all steady signification, the dogmas continued to be repeated, till the world was persuaded that they were self-evident; and when, at a later period, experimental philosophers, such as Galileo and Boyle, ventured to contradict these current maxims, their new principles sounded in men's ears as strange as they now sound familiar. Thus Boyle promulgated his opinions on the mechanics of fluids, as " Hydrostatical *Paradoxes*, proved and illustrated by experiments." And the opinions which he there opposes, are those which the Aristotelian philosophers habitually propounded as certain and indisputable; such, for instance, as that " in fluids the upper parts do not gravitate on the lower;" that " a lighter fluid will not gravitate on a heavier;" that " levity is a positive quality of bodies as well as gravity." So long as these assertions were left uncontested and untried, men heard and repeated them, without perceiving the incongruities which they involved: and thus they long evaded refutation, amid the vague notions and undoubting habits of the stationary period. But when the controversies of Galileo's time had made men think with more acuteness and steadiness, it was discovered that many of these doctrines were inconsistent with themselves, as well as with experiment. We have an example of the confusion of thought to which the Aristotelians were liable, in their doctrine concerning falling bodies. "Heavy bodies," said they, "must fall quicker than light ones; for weight is the cause of their fall, and the weight of the greater bodies is greater." They did not perceive that, if they considered the weight of the body as a power acting to produce motion, they must consider the body itself as offering a resistance to motion; and that the effect must depend on the proportion of the power to the resistance; in short, they had no clear idea of *accelerating force*. This defect runs through all their mechanical speculations, and renders them entirely valueless.

We may exemplify the same confusion of thought on mechanical subjects in writers of a less technical character. Thus, if men had any distinct idea of mechanical action, they could not have accepted for a moment the fable of the Echineis or Remora, a little fish which was said to be able to stop a large ship merely by sticking to it. Lucan[1] refers to this legend in a poetical manner, and notices this creature only in bringing together a collection of monstrosities; but Pliny relates the tale gravely, and moralizes upon it after his manner. "What," he cries[2], "is more violent than the sea and the winds? what, a greater work of art than a ship? Yet one little fish (the Echineis)

---

[1] Lucan is describing one of the poetical compounds introduced in incantations.

Huc quicquid fœtu genuit Natura sinistro
Miscetur: non spuma canum quibus unda timori est,
Viscera non lyncis, non duræ nodus hyænæ
Defuit, et cervi pasti serpente medullæ;
Non puppes retinens, Euro tendente rudentes
In mediis *Echineis* aquis, oculique draconum.
     Etc.   *Pharsalia*, iv. 670.

[2] Plin. Hist. N. xxxii. 1

can hold back all these when they all strḋl. ex-
same way. The winds may blow, the waves rle,
rage ; but this small creature controls their fury,
and stops a vessel, when chains and anchors would
not hold it : and this it does, not by hard labour,
but merely by adhering to it. Alas, for human
vanity! when the turretted ships which man has
built, that he may fight from castle-walls, at sea
as well as at land, are held captive and motionless
by a fish a foot and a half long. Such a fish is
said to have stopt the admiral's ship at the battle of Actium, and compelled Antony to go into
another. And in our own memory, one of these
animals held fast the ship of Caius, the emperor,
when he was sailing from Astura to Antium. The
stopping of this ship, when all the rest of the fleet
went on, caused surprize ; but this did not last
long, for some of the men jumped into the water
to look for the fish, and found it sticking to the
rudder ; they showed it to Caius, who was indig-
nant that this animal should interpose its prohi-
bition to his progress, when impelled by four
hundred rowers. It was like a slug ; and had no
power, after it was taken into the ship."

A very little advance in the power of thinking
clearly on the force which is exerted in pulling,
would have enabled the Romans to see, that the
ship and its rowers must pull the adhering fish
by the hold the oars had upon the water ; and
that, except the fish had a hold equally strong on
some external body, it could not resist this force.

perce;·· *Indistinctness of Ideas shown in Architec-*
bod·*re.*—Perhaps it may serve to illustrate still fur-
r '·ther the extent to which, under the Roman empire,
men's notions of mechanical relations became faint,
wavered, and disappeared, if we observe the change
which took place in architecture. All architecture, to possess genuine beauty, must be mecha-
nically consistent. The decorative members m ust
represent a structure which has in it a principal of
support and stability. Thus the Grecian colonnade
was a straight horizontal beam, resting on vertical
props; and the pediment imitated a frame like a
roof, where oppositely-inclined beams support each
other. These forms of building were, therefore,
proper models of art, because they implied supporting forces. But to be content with colonnades
and pediments, which, though they imitated the
forms of the Grecian ones, were destitute of their
mechanical truth, belonged to the decline of art;
and showed that men had lost the idea of force,
and retained only that of shape. Yet this was what
the architects of the empire did. Under their
hands, the pediment was severed at its vertex, and
divided into separate halves, so that it was no
longer a mechanical possibility. The entablature
no longer lay straight from pillar to pillar, but,
projecting over each column, turned back to the
wall, and adhered to it in the intervening space.
The splendid remains of Palmyra, Balbec, Petra,
exhibit endless examples of this kind of perverse

inventiveness; and show us, very instructively, how the decay of art and of science alike accompany this indistinctness of ideas which we are endeavouring to illustrate.

4. *Indistinctness of Ideas in Astronomy.*— Returning to the sciences, it may be supposed, at first sight, that, with regard to astronomy, we have not the same ground for charging the stationary period with indistinctness of ideas on that subject, since they were able to acquire and verify, and, in some measure, to apply, the doctrines previously established. And, undoubtedly, it must be confessed that men's notions of the relations of space and number are never very indistinct. It appears to be impossible for these chains of elementary perception ever to be much entangled. The later Greeks, the Arabians, and the earliest modern astronomers, must have conceived the hypotheses of the Ptolemaic system with tolerable completeness. And yet, we may assert, that, during the stationary period, men did not possess the notions, even of space and number, in that vivid and vigorous manner which enables them to discover new truths. If they had perceived distinctly that the astronomical theorist had merely to do with *relative* motions, they must have been led to see the possibility, at least, of the Copernican system; as the Greeks, at an earlier period, had already perceived it. We find no trace of this. Indeed the mode in which the Arabian mathematicians pre-

sent the solutions of their problems, does not indicate that clear apprehension of the relations of space, and that delight in the contemplation of them, which the Greek geometrical speculations imply. The Arabs are in the habit of giving conclusions without demonstrations, precepts without the investigations by which they are obtained; as if their main object were practical rather than speculative,—the calculation of results rather than the exposition of theory. Delambre[3] has been obliged to exercise great ingenuity, in order to discover the method by which Ibn Iounis proved his solution of certain difficult problems.

5. *Indistinctness of Ideas shown by Skeptics.*—The same unsteadiness of ideas which prevents men from obtaining clear views, and steady and just convictions, on special subjects, may lead them to despair of or deny the possibility of acquiring certainty at all, and may thus make them skeptics with regard to all knowledge. Such skeptics are themselves men of indistinct views, for they could not otherwise avoid assenting to the demonstrated truths of science; and, so far as they may be taken as specimens of their contemporaries, they prove that indistinct ideas prevail in the age in which they appear. In the stationary period, moreover, the indefinite speculations and unprofitable subtleties of the schools might further impel a man of bold and acute mind to this universal skep-

[3] Delamb. M. A. p. 125-8.

ticism, because they offered nothing which could fix or satisfy him. And thus the skeptical spirit may deserve our notice as indicative of the defects of a system of doctrine too feeble in demonstration to control such resistance.

The most remarkable of these philosophical skeptics is Sextus Empiricus; so called, from his belonging to that medical sect which was termed the *empirical*, in contradistinction to the *rational* and *methodical* sects. His works contain a series of treatises, directed against all the divisions of the science of his time. He has chapters against the Geometers, against the Arithmeticians, against the Astrologers, against the Musicians, as well as against Grammarians, Rhetoricians and Logicians; and, in short, as a modern writer has said, his skepticism is employed as a sort of frame-work which embraces an encyclopedical view of human knowledge. It must be stated, however, that his objections are rather to the metaphysical grounds, than to the details of the sciences; he rather denies the possibility of speculative truth in general, than the experimental truths which had been then obtained. Thus his objections to geometry and arithmetic are founded on abstract cavils concerning the nature of points, letters, unities, &c. And when he comes to speak against astrology, he says, " I am not going to consider that perfect science which rests upon geometry and arithmetic; for I have already shown the weakness of those sciences; nor that faculty of prediction (of the motions of the heavens) which belongs to the pupils of Eudoxus, and Hipparchus, and the rest, which some call Astronomy; for that is an observation of phenomena, like agriculture or navigation; but against the Art of Prediction from the time of birth, which the Chaldeans exercise." Sextus, therefore, though a skeptic by profession, was not insensible to the difference between experimental knowledge and mystical dogmas, though the former had nothing which excited his admiration.

The skepticism which denies the evidence of the truths of which the best established physical sciences consist, must necessarily involve a very indistinct apprehension of those truths; for such truths, properly exhibited, contain their own evidence, and are the best antidote to this skepticism. But an incredulity or contempt towards the asserted truths of physical science may arise also from the attention being mainly directed to the certainty and importance of religious truths. A veneration for revealed religion may thus assume the aspect of a skepticism with regard to natural knowledge. Such appears to be the case with Algazel or Algezeli, who is adduced by Degerando[4] as an example of an Arabian skeptic. He was a celebrated teacher at Bagdad in the eleventh century, and he declared himself the enemy, not only of the mixed Peripatetic and Platonic philosophy of the time, but of Aristotle himself.

[4] Degerando, *Hist. Comp. des Systèmes,* iv. 224.

His work entitled *The Destructions of the Philosophers*, is known to us by the refutation of it which Averrhoes published, under the title of *Destruction of Algazel's Destructions of the Philosophers*. It appears that he contested the fundamental principles both of the Platonic and of the Aristotelian schools, and denied the possibility of a known connexion between cause and effect; thus making a prelude, says Degerando, to the celebrated argumentation of Hume (к).

6. *Neglect of Physical Reasoning in Christendom.*—If the Arabians, who, during the ages of which we are speaking, were the most eminent cultivators of science, entertained only such comparatively feeble and servile notions of its doctrines, it will easily be supposed, that in the Christendom of that period, where physical knowledge was comparatively neglected, there was still less distinctness and vividness in the prevalent ideas on such subjects. Indeed, during a considerable period of the history of the Christian church, and by many of its principal authorities, the study of natural philosophy was not only disregarded but discommended. The great practical doctrines which were presented to men's minds, and the serious tasks, of the regulation of the will and affections, which religion impressed upon them, made inquiries of mere curiosity seem to be a reprehensible misapplication of human powers; and many of the fathers of the church revived, in a still more peremptory form, the opi-

nion of Socrates, that the only valuable philosophy is that which teaches us our moral duties and religious hopes[5]. Thus Eusebius says[6], "It is not through ignorance of the things admired by them, but through contempt of their useless labour, that we think little of these matters, turning our souls to the exercise of better things." When the thoughts were thus intentionally averted from those ideas which natural philosophy involves, the ideas inevitably became very indistinct in their minds; and they could not conceive that any other persons could find, on such subjects, grounds of clear conviction and certainty. They held the whole of their philosophy to be, as Lactantius[7] asserts it to be "empty and false." "To search," says he, "for the causes of natural things; to inquire whether the sun be as large as he seems, whether the moon is convex or concave, whether the stars are fixed in the sky or float freely in the air; of what size and of what material are the heavens; whether they be at rest or in motion; what is the magnitude of the earth; on what foundations it is suspended and balanced;—to dispute and conjecture on such matters, is just as if we chose to discuss what we think of a city in a remote country, of which we never heard but the name." It is impossible to express more forcibly that absence of any definite notions on physical subjects which led to this tone of thought.

7. *Question of Antipodes.*—With such habits

[5] Brucker, iii. 317.   [6] Præp. Ev. xv. 61.   [7] Inst. l. iii. init.

of thought, we are not to be surprized if the relations resulting from the best established theories were apprehended in an imperfect and incongruous manner. We have some remarkable examples of this; and a very notable one is the celebrated question of the existence of *Antipodes*, or persons inhabiting the opposite side of the globe of the earth, and consequently having the soles of their feet directly opposed to ours. The doctrine of the globular form of the earth results, as we have seen, by a geometrical necessity, from a clear conception of the various points of knowledge which we·obtain, bearing upon that subject. This doctrine was held distinctly by the Greeks; it was adopted by all astronomers, Arabian and European, who followed them; and· was, in fact, an inevitable part of every system of astronomy which gave a consistent and intelligible representation of phenomena. But those who did not call before their minds any distinct representation at all, and who referred the whole question to other relations than those of space, might still deny this doctrine; and they did so. The existence of inhabitants on the opposite side of the terraqueous globe, was a fact of which experience alone could teach the truth or falsehood; but the religious relations, which extend alike to all mankind, were supposed to give the Christian philosopher grounds for deciding against the possibility of such a race of men. Lactantius[a] in the fourth century, argues this

---

[a] Inst. l. iii. 23.

matter, in a way very illustrative of that impatience of such speculations, and consequent confusion of thought which we have mentioned. "Is it possible," he says, "that men can be so absurd as to believe that the crops and trees on the other side of the earth hang downwards, and that men there have their feet higher than their heads? If you ask of them how they defend these monstrosities?—how things do not fall away from the earth on that side? they reply, that the nature of things is such that heavy bodies tend towards the center, like the spokes of a wheel, while light bodies, as clouds, smoke, fire, tend from the center towards the heavens on all sides. Now I am really at a loss what to say of those who, when they have once gone wrong, steadily persevere in their folly, and defend one absurd opinion by another." It is obvious that so long as the writer refused to admit into his thoughts the fundamental conception of their theory, he must needs be at a loss what to say to their arguments, without being on that account in any degree convinced of their doctrines.

In the sixth century, indeed, in the reign of Justinian, we find a writer (Cosmas Indicopleustes[9]) who does not rest in this obscurity of representation; but in this case, the distinctness of his pictures only serves to show his want of any clear conception

[9] Montfaucon, *Collectio Nova Patrum*, t. ii. p. 113. Cosmas Indicopleustes. Christianorum Opiniones de Mundo, sive Topographia Christiana.

as to what suppositions would explain the phenomena. He describes the earth as an oblong floor,
surrounded by upright walls, and covered by a vault,
below which the heavenly bodies perform their revolutions, going round a certain high mountain,
which occupies the northern parts of the earth, and
makes night by intercepting the light of the sun.
In Augustin[10] (who flourished A.D. 400) the opinion
is treated on other grounds; and without denying
the globular form of the earth, it is asserted that
there are no inhabitants on the opposite side, because no such race is recorded by Scripture among
the descendants of Adam (L). Considerations of the
same kind operated in the well-known instance of
Virgil, bishop of Salzburg, in the eighth century.
When he was reported to Boniface, archbishop of
Mentz, as holding the existence of Antipodes, the
prelate was shocked at the assumption, as it seemed
to him, of a world of human beings, out of the reach
of the conditions of salvation; and application was
made to Pope Zachary for a censure of the holder
of this dangerous doctrine. It does not however
appear that this led to any severity; and the story
of the deposition of Virgil from his bishopric, which
is circulated by Kepler and by more modern writers,
is undoubtedly altogether false. The same scruples
continued to prevail among Christian writers to
a later period; and Tostatus[11] notes the opinion of
the rotundity of the earth as an " unsafe" doctrine,

[10] Civ. D. xvi. 9.   [11] Montfauc. Patr. t. ii.

only a few years before Columbus visited the other hemisphere.

8. *Intellectual Condition of the Religious Orders.*—It must be recollected, however, that though these were the views and tenets of many religious writers, and though they may be taken as indications of the prevalent and characteristic temper of the times of which we speak, they never were universal. Such a confusion of thought affects the minds of many persons, even in the most enlightened times ; and in what we call the Dark Ages, though clear views on such subjects might be more rare, those who gave their minds to science, entertained the true opinion of the figure of the earth. Thus Boëthius[12] (in the sixth century) urges the smallness of the globe of the earth, compared with the heavens, as a reason to repress our love of glory. This work, it will be recollected, was translated into the Anglo-Saxon by our own Alfred. It was also commented on by Bede, who, in what he says on this passage, assents to the doctrine, and shows an acquaintance with Ptolemy and his commentators, both Arabian and Greek. Gerbert, in the tenth century, went from France to Spain to study astronomy with the Arabians, and soon surpassed his masters. He is reported to have fabricated clocks, and an astrolabe of peculiar construction. Gerbert afterwards, (in the last year 'of the first thousand from the birth of Christ,)

[12] Boëthius, Cons. ii. pr. 7.

became pope, by the name of Sylvester II. Among other cultivators of the sciences, some of whom, from their proficiency, must have possessed with considerable clearness and steadiness the elementary ideas on which it depends, we may here mention, after Montucla[13], Adelbold, whose work On the Sphere was addressed to Pope Sylvester, and whose geometrical reasonings are, according to Montucla[14], vague and chimerical; Hermann Contractus, a monk of St. Gall, who, in 1050, published astronomical works; William of Hirsaugen, who followed this example in 1080; Robert of Lorraine, who was made Bishop of Hereford by William the Conqueror, in consequence of his astronomical knowledge. In the next century, Adelhard Goth, an Englishman, travelled among the Arabs for purposes of study, as Gerbert had done in the preceding age; and on his return, translated the Elements of Euclid, which he had brought from Spain or Egypt. Robert Grostête, Bishop of Lincoln, was the author of an Epitome on the Sphere; Roger Bacon, in his youth the contemporary of Robert, and of his brother Adam Marsh, praises very highly their knowledge in mathematics.

"And here," says the French historian of mathematics, whom I have followed in the preceding relation, "it is impossible not to reflect that all those men who, if they did not augment the treasure of the sciences, at least served to transmit it,

[13] Mont. i. 502.   [14] Mont. i. 503.

were monks, or had been such originally. Convents were, during these stormy ages, the asylum of sciences and letters. Without these religious men, who, in the silence of their monasteries, occupied themselves in transcribing, in studying, and in imitating the works of the ancients, well or ill, those works would have perished; perhaps not one of them would have come down to us. The thread which connects us with the Greeks and Romans would have been snapt asunder; the precious productions of ancient literature would no more exist for us, than the works, if any there were, published before the catastrophe that annihilated that highly scientific nation, which, according to Bailly, existed in remote ages in the center of Tartary, or at the roots of Caucasus. In the sciences we should have had all to create; and at the moment when the human mind should have emerged from its stupor and shaken off its slumbers, we should have been no more advanced than the Greeks were after the taking of Troy." He adds, that this consideration inspires feelings towards the religious orders very different from those which, when he wrote, were prevalent among his countrymen.

Except so far as their religious opinions interfered, it was natural that men who lived a life of quiet and study, and were necessarily in a great measure removed from the absorbing and blinding interests with which practical life occupies the

T 2

thoughts, should cultivate science more successfully than others, precisely because their ideas on speculative subjects had time and opportunity to become clear and steady. The studies which were cultivated under the name of the Seven Liberal Arts necessarily tended to favour this effect. The *Trivium*[15], indeed, which consisted of Grammar, Logic, and Rhetoric, had no direct bearing upon those ideas with which physical science is concerned; but the *Quadrivium*, Music, Arithmetic, Geometry, Astronomy, could not be pursued with any attention, without a corresponding improvement of the mind for purposes of sound knowledge[16].

9. *Popular Opinions.*—That, even in the best intellects, something was wanting to fit them for scientific progress and discovery, is obvious from the fact that science was so long absolutely stationary. And I have endeavoured to show that one part of this deficiency was the want of the requisite clearness and vigour of the fundamental scientific ideas. If these were wanting, even in the most powerful and most cultivated minds, we may easily conceive that still greater confusion and obscurity prevailed in

[15] Bruck. iii. 597.

[16] Roger Bacon, in his *Specula Mathematica*, cap. i., says, " Harum scientiarum porta et clavis est mathematica, quam sancti a principio mundi invenerunt, etc. Cujus negligentia *jam per triginta vel quadraginta annos* destruxit totum studium Latinorum." I do not know on what occasion this neglect took place.

the common class of mankind. They actually adopted the belief, however crude and inconsistent, that the form of the earth and heavens really is what at any place it appears to be; that the earth is flat, and the waters of the sky sustained above a material floor, through which in showers they descend. Yet the true doctrines of astronomy appear to have had some popular circulation. For instance, a French poem of the time of Edward the Second, called *Ymage du Monde*, contains a metrical account of the earth and heavens, according to the Ptolemaic views; and in a manuscript of this poem, preserved in the library of the University of Cambridge, there are representations, in accordance with the text, of a spherical earth, with men standing upright upon it on every side: and by way of illustrating the tendency of all things to the center, perforations of the earth, entirely through its mass, are described and depicted; and figures are exhibited dropping balls down each of these holes, so as to meet in the interior. And, as bearing upon the perplexity which attends the motions of *up* and *down*, when applied to the globular earth, and the change of the direction of gravity which would occur in passing the center, the readers of Dante will recollect the extraordinary manner in which the poet and his guide emerge from the bottom of the abyss; and the explanation which Virgil imparts to him of what he there sees. After they have crept through

the aperture in which Lucifer is placed, the poet
says,

> " Io levai gli occhi e credetti vedere
> Lucifero com' io l' avea lasciato,
> E vidile le gambe in su tenere."
>
> . . . . . " Questi come è fitto
> Si sottasopra ?" . . . .
>
> " Quando mi volsi, tu passast' il punto
> Al qual si traggon d' ogni parte i pesi."
>
> *Inferno*, xxxiv.

> . . . . . " I raised mine eyes,
> Believing that I Lucifer should see
> Where he was lately left, but saw him now
> With legs held upward." . . . .
>
> " How standeth he in posture thus reversed ?"
>
> . . . .
>
> " Thou wast on the other side so long as I
> Descended; when I turned, thou didst o'erpass
> That point to which from every part is dragged
> All heavy substance."
>
> CARY.

This is more philosophical than Milton's representation, in a more scientific age, of Uriel sliding
to the earth on a sun-beam, and sliding back again,
when the sun had sunk below the horizon.

> . . . . . . " Uriel to his charge
> Returned on that bright beam whose point now raised,
> Bore him slope downward to the sun, now fallen
> Beneath the Azores."
>
> *Par. Lost*, B. iv.

The philosophical notions of up and down are
too much at variance with the obvious suggestions
of our senses, to be held steadily and justly by

minds undisciplined in science. Perhaps it was some misunderstood statement of the curved surface of the ocean, which gave rise to the tradition of there being a part of the sea directly over the earth, from which at times an object has been known to fall, or an anchor to be let down. Even such whimsical fancies are not without instruction, and may serve to show the reader what that vagueness and obscurity of ideas is, of which I have been endeavouring to trace the prevalence in the dark ages.

We now proceed to another of the features which appears to me to mark, in a very prominent manner, the character of the stationary period.

CHAPTER II.

THE COMMENTATORIAL SPIRIT OF THE MIDDLE AGES.

WE have already noticed, that, after the first great achievements of the founders of sound speculation, in the different departments of human knowledge, had attracted the interest and admiration which those who became acquainted with them could not but give to them, there appeared a disposition among men to lean on the authority of some of these teachers;—to study the opinions of others as the only mode of forming their own;—to read nature through books;—to attend to what had been already thought and said, rather than to what really is and happens. This tendency of men's minds requires our particular consideration. Its manifestations were very important, and highly characteristic of the stationary period; it gave, in a great degree, a peculiar bias and direction to the intellectual activity of many centuries; and the kind of labour with which speculative men were occupied in consequence of this bias, took the place of that examination of realities which must be their employment, in order that real knowledge may make any decided progress.

In some subjects, indeed, as, for instance, in

the domains of morals, poetry, and the arts whose
aim is the production of beauty, this opposition
between the study of former opinion and present
reality, may not be so distinct; inasmuch as it may
be said by some, that, in these subjects, opinions
are realities; that the thoughts and feelings which
prevail in men's minds are the material upon which
we must work, the particulars from which we are
to generalize, the instruments which we are to use;
and that, therefore, to reject the study of antiquity,
or even its authority, would be to show ourselves
ignorant of the extent and mutual bearing of the
elements with which we have to deal;—would be
to cut asunder that which we ought to unite into
a vital whole. Yet even in the provinces of history and poetry, the poverty and servility of men's
minds during the middle ages, are shown by indications so strong as to be truly remarkable; for
instance, in the efforts of the antiquarians of almost
every European country to assimilate the early
history of their own state to the poet's account of
the foundation of Rome, by bringing from the sack
of Troy, Brutus to England, Bavo to Flanders, and
so on. But however this may be, our business
at present is, to trace the varying spirit of the
physical philosophy of different ages; trusting that,
hereafter, this prefatory study will enable us to
throw some light upon the other parts of philosophy. And in physics the case undoubtedly was,
that the labour of observation, which is one of

the two great elements of the progress of knowledge, was in a great measure superseded by the
collection, the analysis, the explanation, of previous
authors and opinions; experimenters were replaced
by commentators; criticism took the place of induction; and instead of great discoverers we had
learned men.

1. *Natural Bias to Authority.*—It is very evident that, in such a bias of men's studies, there is
something very natural; however strained and technical this erudition may have been, the propensities
on which it depends are very general, and are easily
seen. Deference to the authority of thoughtful and
sagacious men, a disposition which men in general
neither reject nor think they ought to reject in
practical matters, naturally clings to them, even in
speculation. It is a satisfaction to us to suppose
that there are, or have been, minds of transcendent
powers, of wide and wise views, superior to the
common errors and blindnesses of our nature. The
pleasure of admiration, and the repose of confidence, are inducements to such a belief. There are
also other reasons why we willingly believe that
there are in philosophy great teachers, so profound
and sagacious, that, in order to arrive at truth,
we have only to learn their thoughts, to understand their writings. There is a peculiar interest
which men feel in dealing with the thoughts of
their fellow-men, rather than with brute matter.
Matter feels and excites no sympathies; in seeking

for mere laws of nature, there is nothing of mental intercourse with the great spirits of the past, as there is in studying Aristotle or Plato. Moreover, a large portion of this employment is of a kind the most agreeable to most speculative minds; it consists in tracing the consequences of assumed principles: it is deductive like geometry; and the principles of the teachers being known, and being undisputed, the deduction and application of their results is an obvious, self-satisfying, and inexhaustible exercise of ingenuity.

These causes, and probably others, make criticism and commentation flourish, when invention begins to fail, oppressed and bewildered by the acquisitions it has already made; and when the vigour and hope of men's minds are enfeebled by civil and political changes. Accordingly[1], the Alexandrian school was eminently characterized by a spirit of erudition, of literary criticism, of interpretation, of imitation. These practices, which reigned first in their full vigour in the Museum, are likely to be, at all times, the leading propensities of similar academical institutions.

How natural it is to select a great writer as a paramount authority, and to ascribe to him extraordinary profundity and sagacity, we may see, in the manner in which the Greeks looked upon Homer; and the fancy which detected in his poems traces of the origin of all· arts and sciences, has,

[1] Degerando, *Hist. des Syst. de Philos.* iii. p. 134.

as we know, found favour even in modern times.
To pass over earlier instances of this feeling, we
may observe, that Strabo begins his Geography by
saying that he agrees with Hipparchus, who had
declared Homer to be the first author of our geographical knowledge : and he does not confine the
application of this assertion to the various and
curious topographical information which the Iliad
and Odyssey contain, concerning the countries surrounding the Mediterranean ; but in phrases which,
to most persons, might appear the mere play of
a poetical fancy, or a casual selection of circumstances, he finds unquestionable evidence of a
correct knowledge of general geographical truths.
Thus[2], when Homer speaks of the sun " rising from
the soft and deep-flowing ocean," of his " splendid
blaze plunging in the ocean ;" of the northern constellation

" Alone unwashen by the ocean wave ; "

and of Jupiter " who goes to the ocean to . feast
with the blameless Ethiopians ;" Strabo is satisfied
from these passages that Homer knew the dry land
to be surrounded with water : and he reasons in
like manner with respect to other points of geography.

2. *Character of Commentators.*—The spirit of
commentation, as has already been suggested, turns
to questions of taste, of metaphysics, of morals,

[2] Strabo, i. p. 5.

with far more avidity than to physics. Accordingly, critics and grammarians were peculiarly the growth of this school; and, though the commentators sometimes chose works of mathematical or physical science for their subject (as Proclus, who commented on Euclid's Geometry, and Simplicius, on Aristotle's Physics,) these commentaries were, in fact, rather metaphysical than mathematical. It does not appear that the commentators have, in any instance, illustrated the author by bringing his assertions of facts to the test of experiment. Thus, when Simplicius comments on the passage concerning a vacuum, which we formerly adduced, he notices the argument which went upon the assertion, that a vessel full of ashes would contain as much water as an empty vessel; and he mentions various opinions of different authors, but no trial of the fact. Eudemus had said, that the ashes contained something hot, as quicklime does, and that by means of this, a part of the water was evaporated; others supposed the water to be condensed, and so on[3].

The commentator's professed object is to explain, to enforce, to illustrate doctrines assumed as true. He endeavours to adapt the work on which he employs himself to the state of information and of opinion in his own time; to elucidate obscurities and technicalities; to supply steps omitted in the reasoning; but he does not seek to obtain additional truths

[3] Simplicius, p. 170.

or new generalizations. He undertakes only to give what is virtually contained in his author; to develope, but not to create. He is a cultivator of the thoughts of others: his labour is not spent on a field of his own; he ploughs but to enrich the granary of another man. Thus he does not work as a freeman, but as one in a servile condition; or rather, his is a menial, and not a productive service: his office is to adorn the appearance of his master, not to increase his wealth.

Yet though the commentator's employment is thus subordinate and dependent, he is easily led to attribute to it the greatest importance and dignity. To elucidate good books is, indeed, a useful task; and when those who undertake this work execute it well, it would be most unreasonable to find fault with them for not doing more. But the critic, long and earnestly employed on one author, may easily underrate the relative value of other kinds of mental exertion. He may ascribe too large dimensions to that which occupies the whole of his own field of vision. Thus he may come to consider such study as the highest aim, and best evidence of human genius. To understand Aristotle, or Plato, may appear to him to comprise all that is possible of profundity and acuteness. And when he has travelled over a portion of their domain, and satisfied himself that of this he too is master, he may look with complacency at the circuit he has made, and speak of it as a labour of vast effort and difficulty. We may quote, as an expression of this temper, the language of Sir Henry Savile, in concluding a course of lectures on Euclid, delivered at Oxford[4]. "By the grace of God, gentlemen hearers, I have performed my promise; I have redeemed my pledge. I have explained, according to my ability, the definitions, postulates, axioms, and *first eight propositions* of the Elements of Euclid. Here, sinking under the weight of years, I lay down my art and my instruments."

We here speak of the peculiar province of the commentator; for undoubtedly, in many instances, a commentary on a received author has been made the vehicle of conveying systems and doctrines entirely different from those of the author himself; as, for instance, when the New Platonists wrote, taking Plato for their text. The labours of learned men in the stationary period, which came under this description, belong to another class.

3. *Greek Commentators on Aristotle.*—The commentators or disciples of the great philosophers did not assume at once their servile character. At first their object was to supply and correct, as well as to explain their teacher. Thus among the earlier commentators of Aristotle, Theophrastus invented five moods of syllogism in the first figure, in addition to

---

[4] Exolvi per Dei gratiam, Domini auditores, promissum; liberavi fidem meam; explicavi pro meo modulo, definitiones, petitiones, communes sententias, et *octo priores propositiones* Elementorum Euclidis. Hic, annis fessus, cyclos artemque repono.

the four invented by Aristotle, and stated with additional accuracy the rules of hypothetical syllogisms. He also, not only collected much information concerning animals, and natural events, which Aristotle had omitted, but often differed with his master; as, for instance, concerning the saltness of the sea: this, which the Stagirite attributed to the effect of the evaporation produced by the sun's rays, was ascribed by Theophrastus to beds of salt at the bottom. Porphyry[5], who flourished in the third century, wrote a book on the *Predicables*, which was found to be so suitable a complement to the *Predicaments* or Categories of Aristotle, that it was usually prefixed to that treatise; and the two have been used as an elementary work together, up to modern times. The Predicables are the five steps which the gradations of generality and particularity introduce;—*genus, species, difference, individual, accident;*—the Categories are the ten heads under which assertions or predications may be arranged; —*substance, quantity, relation, quality, place, time, position, habit, action, passion.*

At a later period, the Aristotelian commentators became more servile, and followed the author step by step, explaining, according to their views, his expressions and doctrines; often, indeed, with extreme prolixity, expanding his clauses into sentences, and his sentences into paragraphs. Alexander Aphrodisiensis, who lived at the end of the second

---

[5] Buhle, Arist. i. 284.

century, is of this class; "sometimes useful," as one of the recent editors of Aristotle says[6]; "but by the prolixity of his interpretation, by his perverse itch for himself discussing the argument expounded by Aristotle, for defending his opinions, and for refuting or reconciling those of others, he rather obscures than enlightens." At various times, also, some of the commentators, and especially those of the Alexandrian school, endeavoured to reconcile, or combined without reconciling, opposing doctrines of the great philosophers of the earlier times. Simplicius, for instance, and, indeed, a great number of the Alexandrian philosophers[7], as Alexander, Ammonius, and others, employed themselves in the futile task of reconciling the doctrines of the Pythagoreans, of the Eleatics, of Plato, and of the Stoics, with those of Aristotle. Boethius[8] entertained the design of translating into Latin the whole of Aristotle's and Plato's works, and of showing their agreement; a gigantic plan, which he never executed. Others employed themselves in disentangling the confusion which such attempts produced, as John the Grammarian, surnamed Philoponus, "the Labour-loving;" who, towards the end of the seventh century, maintained that Aristotle was entirely misunderstood by Porphyry and Proclus[9], who had pretended to incorporate his doctrines into those of the New Platonic school, or even to reconcile him with Plato

[6] Buhle, i. 288.
[8] Degerando, *Hist. des Syst.* iv. 100.
[7] Buhle, i. 311.
[9] Ib. iv. 155.

VOL. I.   U

himself on the subject of *ideas*.   Others, again,
wrote Epitomes, Compounds, Abstracts; and endeavoured to throw the works of the philosopher into
some simpler and more obviously regular form, as
John of Damascus, in the middle of the eighth
century, who made abstracts of some of Aristotle's
works, and introduced the study of the author into
theological education.   These two writers lived
under the patronage of the Arabs; the former was
favoured by Amrou, the conqueror of Egypt; the
latter was at first secretary to the Caliph, but afterwards withdrew to a monastery[10].

At this period the Arabians became the fosterers
and patrons of philosophy, rather than the Greeks.
Justinian had, by an edict, closed the school of
Athens, the last of the schools of heathen philosophy.   Leo, the Isaurian, who was a zealous Ico-
noclast, abolished also the schools where general
knowledge had been taught, in combination with
Christianity[11]; yet the line of the Aristotelian commentators was continued, though feebly, to the later
ages of the Greek empire.   Anna Comnena[12] mentions a Eustratus who employed himself upon the
dialectic and moral treatises, and whom she does
not hesitate to elevate above the Stoics and Platonists, for his talent in philosophical discussions.
Nicephorus Blemmydes wrote logical and physical
epitomes for the use of John Ducas; George Pachy-
meus composed an epitome of the philosophy of

[10] Deg. iv. 150.   [11] Ib. iv. 163.   [12] Ib. 167.

Aristotle, and a compend of his logic: Theodore Metochytes, who was famous in his time alike for his eloquence and his learning, has left a paraphrase of the books of Aristotle on Physics, on the Soul, the Heavens[13], &c. Fabricius states that this writer has a chapter, the object of which is to prove, that all philosophers, and Aristotle and Plato in particular, have disdained the authority of their predecessors. He could hardly help remarking in how different a spirit philosophy had been pursued since their time.

3. *Greek Commentators of Plato and others.*— I have spoken principally of the commentators of Aristotle, for he was the great subject of the commentators proper; and though the name of his rival, Plato, was graced by a list of attendants hardly less numerous, these, the Neoplatonists, as they are called, had introduced new elements into the doctrines of their nominal master, to such an extent that they must be placed in a different class. We may observe here however, how, in this school as in the Peripatetic, the race of commentators multiplied itself. Porphyry, who commented on Aristotle, was commented on by Ammonius; Plotinus's Enneads were commented on by Proclus and Dexippus. Psellus[14] the elder was a paraphrast of Aristotle; Psellus the younger, in the eleventh century, attempted to restore the New Platonic school. The former of these two writers had for his pupils two

[13] Deg. iv. 168.   [14] Ib. iv. 169.

men, the emperor Leo, surnamed the Philosopher, and Photius the patriarch, who exerted themselves to restore the study of literature at Constantinople. We still possess the Collection of Extracts of Photius, which, like that of Stobæus and others, shows the tendency of the age to compilations, abstracts, and epitomes,—the extinction of philosophical vitality.

4. *Arabian Commentators of Aristotle.*—The reader might perhaps have expected, that when the philosophy of the Greeks was carried among a new race of intellects, of a different national character and condition, the chain of this servile tradition would have been broken; that some new thoughts would have started forth; that some new direction, some new impulse, would have been given to the search for truth. It might have been anticipated that we should have had schools among the Arabians which should rival the Peripatetic, Academic and Stoic among the Greeks;—that they would pre-occupy the ground on which Copernicus and Galileo, Lavoisier and Linnæus, won their fame;—that they would make the next great steps in the progressive sciences. Nothing of this, however, happened. The Arabians cannot claim, in science or philosophy, any really great names; they produced no men and no discoveries which have materially influenced the course and destinies of human knowledge; they tamely adopted the intellectual servitude of the nation which they conquered by their arms; they

joined themselves at once to the string of slaves who were dragging the car of Aristotle and Plotinus. Nor, perhaps, on a little further reflection, shall we be surprized at this want of vigour and productive power, in this period of apparent national youth. The Arabians had not been duly prepared rightly to enjoy and use the treasures of which they became possessed. They had, like most uncivilized nations, been passionately fond of their indigenous poetry; their imagination had been awakened, but their rational powers and speculative tendencies were still torpid. They received the Greek philosophy without having passed through those gradations of ardent curiosity and keen research, of obscurity brightening into clearness, of doubt succeeded by the joy of discovery, by which the Greek mind had been enlarged and exercised. Nor had the Arabians ever enjoyed, as the Greeks had, the individual consciousness, the independent volition, the intellectual freedom, arising from the freedom of political institutions. They had not felt the contagious mental activity of a small city; the elation arising from the general sympathy in speculative pursuits diffused through an intelligent and acute audience; in short, they had not had a national education such as fitted the Greeks to be disciples of Plato and Hipparchus. Hence, their new literary wealth rather encumbered and enslaved, than enriched and strengthened them: in their want of taste for intellectual freedom, they were glad to give themselves up to the guidance of Aristotle and other dogmatists. Their military habits had accustomed them to look to a leader; their reverence for the book of their law had prepared them to accept a philosophical Koran also. Thus the Arabians, though they never translated the Greek poetry, translated, and merely translated, the Greek philosophy; they followed the Greek philosophers without deviation, or, at least, without any philosophical deviations. They became for the most part Aristotelians;—studied not only Aristotle, but the commentators of Aristotle; and themselves swelled the vast and unprofitable herd.

The philosophical works of Aristotle had, in some measure, made their way in the east, before the growth of the Saracen power. In the sixth century, a Syrian, Uranus[15], encouraged by the love of philosophy manifested by Cosroes, had translated some of the writings of the Stagirite; about the same time, Sergius had given some translations in Syriac. In the seventh century, Jacob of Edessa translated into this language the Dialectics, and added Notes to the work. Such labours became numerous; and the first Arabic translations of Aristotle were formed upon these Persian or Syriac texts. In this succession of transfusions, some mistakes must inevitably have been introduced.

The Arabian interpreters of Aristotle, like a large portion of the Alexandrian ones, gave to the

[15] Deg. iv. 196.

philosopher a tinge of opinions borrowed from another source, of which I shall have to speak under the head of *Mysticism*. But they are, for the most part, sufficiently strong examples of the peculiar spirit of commentation, to make it fitting to notice them here. At the head of them stands[16] Alkindi, who appears to have lived at the court of Almamon, and who wrote commentaries on the Organon of Aristotle. But Alfarabi was the glory of the school of Bagdad; his knowledge included mathematics, astronomy, medicine and philosophy. Born in an elevated rank, and possessed of a rich patrimony, he led an austere life, and devoted himself altogether to study and meditation. He employed himself particularly in unfolding the import of Aristotle's treatise On the Soul[17]. Avicenna (Ebn Sina) was at once the Hippocrates and the Aristotle of the Arabians; and certainly the most extraordinary man that the nation produced. In the course of an unfortunate and stormy life, occupied by politics and by pleasures, he produced works which were long revered as a sort of code of science. In particular, his writings on medicine, though they contain little besides a compilation of Hippocrates and Galen, took the place of both, even in the universities of Europe; and were studied as models at Paris and Montpellier, till the end of the seventeenth century, at which period they fell into an almost complete oblivion. Avicenna is conceived,

[16] Deg. iv. 187.　　　　[17] Ib. iv. 205.

by some modern writers[18], to have shown some power of original thinking in his representations of the Aristotelian Logic and Metaphysics. Averroes (Ebn Roshd) of Cordova, was the most illustrious of the Spanish Aristotelians, and became the guide of the schoolmen[19], being placed by them on a level with Aristotle himself, or above him. He translated Aristotle from the first Syriac version, not being able to read the Greek text. He aspired to, and retained for centuries, the title of the *Commentator;* and he deserves this title by the servility with which he maintains that Aristotle[20] carried the sciences to the highest possible degree, measured their whole extent, and fixed their ultimate and permanent boundaries; although his works are conceived to exhibit a trace of the New Platonism. Some of his writings are directed against an Arabian skeptic, of the name of Algazel, whom we have already noticed.

When the schoolmen had adopted the supremacy of Aristotle to the extent in which Averroes maintained it, their philosphy went further than a system of mere commentation, and became a system of dogmatism; we must, therefore, in another chapter, say a few words more of the Aristotelians in this point of view, before we proceed to the revival of science; but we must previously consider some other features in the character of the Stationary Period.

[18] Deg. iv. 206. [19] Ib. iv. 247. Averroes died A D. 1206.
[20] Deg. iv. 248.

CHAPTER III.

OF THE MYSTICISM OF THE MIDDLE AGES.

IT has been already several times hinted, that a new and peculiar element was introduced into the Greek philosophy which occupied the attention of the Alexandrian school; and that this element tinged a large portion of the speculations of succeeding ages. We may speak of this peculiar element as *Mysticism*; for, from the notion usually conveyed by this term, the reader will easily apprehend the general character of the tendency now spoken of; and especially when he sees its effect pointed out in various subjects. Thus, instead of referring the events of the external world to space and time, to sensible connexion and causation, men attempted to reduce such occurrences under spiritual and supersensual relations and dependencies; they referred them to superior intelligences, to theological conditions, to past and future events in the moral world, to states of mind and feelings, to the creatures of an imaginary mythology or demonology. And thus their physical Science became Magic, their Astronomy became Astrology, the study of the Composition of bodies became Alchemy, Mathematics became the contemplation of the Spiritual Relations of number and figure, and Philosophy became Theosophy.

The examination of this feature in the history of the human mind is important for us, in consequence of its influence upon the employments and the thoughts of the times now under our notice. This tendency materially affected both men's speculations and their labours in the pursuit of knowledge. By its direct operation, it gave rise to the newer Platonic philosophy among the Greeks, and to corresponding doctrines among the Arabians; and by calling into a prominent place astrology, alchemy, and magic, it long occupied most of the real observers of the material world. In this manner it delayed and impeded the progress of true science; for we shall see reason to believe that human knowledge lost more by the perversion of men's minds and the misdirection of their efforts, than it gained by any increase of zeal arising from the peculiar hopes and objects of the mystics.

It is not to our purpose to attempt any general view of the progress and fortunes of the various forms of Mystical Philosophy; but only to exhibit some of its characters, in so far as they illustrate those tendencies of thought which accompanied the retrogradation of inductive science. And of these, the leading feature which demands our notice is that already alluded to; namely, the practice of referring things and events, not to clear and distinct relations, obviously applicable to such cases;

—not to general rules capable of direct verification ; but to notions vague, distant, and vast, which we cannot bring into contact with facts, because they belong to a different region from the facts ; as when we connect natural events with moral or historical causes, or seek spiritual meanings in the properties of number and figure. Thus the character of Mysticism is, that it refers particulars, not to generalizations homogeneous and immediate, but to such as are heterogeneous and remote ; to which we must add, that the process of this reference is not a calm act of the intellect, but is accompanied with a glow of enthusiastic feeling.

1. *Neoplatonic Theosophy.*—The *Newer Platonism* is the first example of this Mystical Philosophy which I shall consider. The main points which here require our notice are, the doctrine of an Intellectual World resulting from the act of the Divine Mind, as the only reality ; and the aspiration after the union of the human soul with this Divine Mind, as the object of human existence. The "Ideas" of Plato were forms of our knowledge ; but among the Neoplatonists they became really existing, indeed the only really existing, objects ; and the inaccessible scheme of the universe which these ideas constitute, was offered as the great subject of philosophical contemplation. The desire of the human mind to approach towards its Creator and Preserver, and to obtain a spiritual access to Him, leads to an employment of the thoughts which

is well worth the notice of the religious philosopher; but such an effort, even when founded on
revelation and well regulated, is not a means of
advance in physics: and when it is the mere result
of natural enthusiasm, it may easily obtain such a
place in men's minds as to unfit them for the
successful prosecution of natural philosophy. The
temper, therefore, which introduces such supernatural communion into the general course of its
speculations, may be properly treated as mystical,
and as one of the causes of the decline of science
in the Stationary Period. The Neoplatonic philosophy requires our notice as one of the most remarkable forms of this Mysticism.

Though Ammonius Saccas, who flourished at the
end of the second century, is looked upon as the
beginner of the Neoplatonists, his disciple Plotinus is, in reality, the great founder of the school,
both by his works, which still remain to us, and by
the enthusiasm which his character and manners
inspired among his followers. He lived a life of
meditation, gentleness, and self-denial, and died in
the second year of the reign of Claudius (A.D. 270).
His disciple, Porphyry, has given us a Life of him,
from which we may see how well his habitual
manners were suited to make his doctrines impressive. "Plotinus, the philosopher of our time,"
Porphyry thus begins his biography, "appeared
like a person ashamed that he was in the body.
In consequence of this disposition, he could not

bear to talk concerning his family, or his parents, or his country. He would not allow himself to be represented by a painter or statuary; and once, when Aurelius entreated him to permit a likeness of him to be taken, he said, 'Is it not enough for us to carry this image in which nature has enclosed us, but we must also try to leave a more durable image of this image, as if it were so great a sight?' And he retained the same temper to the last. When he was dying, he said, 'I am trying to bring the divinity which is in us to the divinity which is in the universe.'" He was looked upon by his successors with extraordinary admiration and reverence; and his disciple Porphyry collected from his lips, or from fragmental notes, the six *Enneads* of his doctrines (that is, parts each consisting of *nine* Books,) which he arranged and annotated.

We have no difficulty in finding in this remarkable work examples of mystical speculation. The Intelligible World of realities or essences corresponds to the world of sense[1] in the classes of things which it includes. To the Intelligible World, man's mind ascends, by a triple road which Plotinus figuratively calls that of the Musician, the Lover, the Philosopher[2]. The activity of the human soul is identified by analogy with the motion of the heavens. "This activity is about a middle point, and thus it is circular; but a middle point

[1] vi. Ennead, iii. 1.   [2] ii. E. ii. 2.

is not the same in body and in the soul; in that, the middle point is local, in this, it is that on which the rest depends. There is, however, an analogy; for as in one case, so in the other, there must be a middle point, and as the sphere revolves about its center, the soul revolves about God through its affections."

The conclusion of the work is[3], as might be supposed, upon the approach to, union with, and fruition of God. The author refers again to the analogy between the movements of the soul and those of the heavens. " We move round him like a choral dance; even when we look from him we revolve about him; we do not always look at him, but when we do, we have satisfaction and rest, and the harmony which belongs to that divine movement. In this movement, the mind beholds the fountain of life, the fountain of mind, the origin of being, the cause of good, the root of the soul[4]." " There will be a time when this vision shall be continual; the mind being no more interrupted, nor suffering any perturbation from the body. Yet that which beholds is not that which is disturbed; and when this vision becomes dim, it does not obscure the knowledge which resides in demonstration, and faith, and reasoning; but the vision itself is not reason, but greater than reason, and before reason[5]."

The fifth book of the third Ennead, has for its

[3] vi. Enn. ix. 8.　　　[4] Ib. 9.　　　[5] Ib. 10.

subject the Dæmon which belongs to each man. It is entitled "Concerning Love;" and the doctrine appears to be, that the Love, or common source of the passions which is in each man's mind, is "the Dæmon which they say accompanies each man[6]." These dæmons were, however, (at least by later writers,) invested with a visible aspect and with a personal character, including a resemblance of human passions and motives. It is curious thus to see an untenable and visionary generalization falling back into the domain of the senses and the fancy, after a vain attempt to support itself in the region of the reason. This imagination soon produced pretensions to the power of making these dæmons or genii visible; and the Treatise on the Mysteries of the Egyptians, which is attributed to Iamblichus, gives an account of the secret ceremonies, the mysterious words, the sacrifices and expiations, by which this was to be done.

It is unnecessary for us to dwell on the progress of this school; to point out the growth of the Theurgy which thus arose; or to describe the attempts to claim a high antiquity for this system, and to make Orpheus, the poet, the first promulgator of its doctrines. The system, like all mystical systems, assumed the character rather of a religion than of a theory. The opinions of its disciples materially influenced their lives. It gave the world the spectacle of an austere morality, a devotional exaltation,

[6] Ficinus, Comm. in v. Enn. iii.

combined with the grossest superstitions of Paganism. The successors of Iamblichus appeared rather
to hold a priesthood, than the chair of a philosophical school[7]. They were persecuted by Constan-
tine and Constantius, as opponents of Christianity.
Sopater, a Syrian philosopher of this school, was
beheaded by the former emperor, on a charge that
he had bound the winds by the power of magic[8].
But Julian, who shortly after succeeded to the
purple, embraced with ardour the opinions of Iamblichus. Proclus (who died A.D. 487,) was one of
the greatest of the teachers of this school[9]; and
was, both in his life and doctrines, a worthy successor of Plotinus, Porphyry, and Iamblichus. We
possess a biography, or rather a panegyric of him,
by his disciple Marinus, in which he is exhibited
as a representation of the ideal perfection of the
philosophic character, according to the views of
the Neoplatonists. His virtues are arranged as
physical, moral, purificatory, theoretic, and theurgic.
Even in his boyhood, Apollo and Minerva visited
him in his dreams: he studied oratory at Alexandria, but it was at Athens that Plutarch and
Lysianus initiated him in the mysteries of the New
Platonists. He received a kind of consecration at
the hands of the daughter of Plutarch, the celebrated Asclepigenia, who introduced him to the
traditions of the Chaldeans, and the practices of
theurgy; he was also admitted to the mysteries

[7] Deg. iii. 407.   [8] Gibbon, iii. 352.   [9] Deg. iii 419.

of Eleusis. He became celebrated for his knowledge and eloquence; but especially for his skill in the supernatural arts which were connected with the doctrines of his sect. He appears before us rather as a hierophant than a philosopher. A large portion of his life was spent in evocations, purifications, fastings, prayers, hymns, intercourse with apparitions, and with the gods, and in the celebration of the festivals of Paganism, especially those which were held in honour of the Mother of the Gods. His religious admiration extended to all forms of mythology. The philosopher, said he, is not the priest of a single religion, but of all the religions in the world. Accordingly, he composed hymns in honour of all the divinities of Greece, Rome, Egypt, Arabia;—Christianity alone was excluded from his favour (M).

2. *Mystical Arithmetic.*—It is unnecessary further to exemplify, from Proclus, the general mystical character of the school and time to which he belonged; but we may notice more specially one of the forms of this mysticism, which very frequently offers itself to our notice, especially in him; and which we may call *Mystical Arithmetic.* Like all the kinds of Mysticism, this consists in the attempt to connect our conceptions of external objects by general and inappropriate notions of goodness, perfection, and relation to the divine essence and government; instead of referring such conceptions to those appropriate ideas, which, by

due attention, become perfectly distinct, and capable of being positively applied and verified. The subject which is thus dealt with, in the doctrines of which we now speak, is Number; a notion which tempts men into these visionary speculations more naturally than any other. For number is really applicable to moral notions,—to emotions and feelings, and to their objects,—as well as to the things of the material world. Moreover, by the discovery of the principle of musical concords, it had been found, probably most unexpectedly, that numerical relations were closely connected with sounds which could hardly be distinguished from the expression of thought and feeling; and a suspicion might easily arise, that the universe, both of matter and of thought, might contain many general and abstract truths of some analogous kind. The relations of number have so wide a bearing, that the ramifications of such a suspicion could not easily be exhausted, supposing men willing to follow them into darkness and vagueness; which it is precisely the mystical tendency to do. Accordingly, this kind of speculation appeared very early, and showed itself first among the Pythagoreans, as we might have expected, from the attention which they gave to the theory of harmony: and this, as well as some other of the doctrines of the Pythagorean philosophy, was adopted by the later Platonists, and, indeed, by Plato himself, whose speculations concerning number have decidedly a mystical character. The mere mathematical relations of numbers,—as odd and even,—perfect and imperfect, abundant and defective,—were, by a willing submission to an enthusiastic bias, connected with the notions of good and beauty, which were suggested by the terms expressing their relations; and principles resulting from such a connexion were woven into a wide and complex system. It is not necessary to dwell long on this subject; the mere titles of the works which treated of it show its nature. Archytas[10] is said to have written a treatise on the number *ten :* Telaugé, the daughter of Pythagoras, wrote on the number *four.* This number, indeed, which was known by the name of the *Tetractys*, was very celebrated in the school of Pythagoras. It is mentioned in the "Golden Verses," which are ascribed to him: the pupil is conjured to be virtuous,

Ναὶ μὰ τὸν ἀμετέρᾳ ψυχᾷ παραδόντα τετρακτὺν
Παγὰν ἀεννάου φύσεως . . . . .

> By him who stampt *The Four* upon the mind,
> *The Four*, the fount of nature's endless stream.

In Plato's works, we have evidence of a similar belief in religious relations of Number; and in the New Platonists, this doctrine was established as a system. Proclus, of whom we have been speaking, founds his philosophy, in a great measure, on the relation of Unity and Multiple; from this, he is led to represent the causality of the

[10] Mont. ii. 123.

X 2

Divine Mind by three Triads of abstractions; and in the developement of one part of this system, the number seven is introduced[11]. "The intelligible and intellectual gods produce all things triadically; for the monads in these latter are divided according to number; and what the monad was in the former, the number is in these latter. And the intellectual gods produce all things hebdomically; for they evolve the intelligible, and at the same time intellectual triads, into intellectual hebdomads, and expand their contracted powers into intellectual variety." Seven is what is called by arithmeticians a *prime* number, that is, it cannot be produced by the multiplication of other numbers. In the language of the New Platonists, the number seven is said to be a virgin, and without a mother, and it is therefore sacred to Minerva. The number six is a perfect number, and is consecrated to Venus.

The relations of space were dealt with in like manner, the geometrical properties being associated with such physical and metaphysical notions as vague thought and lively feeling could anyhow connect with them. We may consider, as an example of this[12], Plato's opinion concerning the particles of the four elements. He gave to each kind of particle one of the five regular solids, about which the geometrical speculations of himself and his pupils had been employed. The particles of

[11] Procl. v. 3, Taylor's Translation.   [12] Stanley, *Hist. Phil.*

fire were pyramids, because they are sharp, and tend upwards; those of earth are cubes, because they are stable, and fill space; the particles of air are octahedral, as most nearly resembling those of fire; those of water are icositetrahedron, as most nearly spherical. The dodecahedron is the figure of the element of the heavens, and shows its influence in other things, as in the twelve signs of the zodiac. In such examples we see how loosely space and number are combined or confounded by these mystical visionaries.

These numerical dreams of ancient philosphers have been imitated by modern writers; for instance, by Peter Bungo and Kircher, who have written De Mysteriis Numerorum. Bungo treats of the mystical properties of each of the numbers in order, at great length. And such speculations have influenced astronomical theories. In the first edition of the Alphonsine tables[13], the precession was represented by making the first point of Aries move, in a period of 7000 years, through a circle of which the radius was 18 degrees, while the circle moved round the ecliptic in 49,000 years; and these numbers, 7000 and 49,000, were chosen probably by Jewish calculators, or with reference to Judaical Sabbatarian notions.

3. *Astrology.*—Of all the forms which mysticism assumed, none was cultivated more assiduously than astrology. Although this art prevailed most

[13] Montucla, i. 511.

universally and powerfully during the stationary period, its existence, even as a detailed technical system, goes back to a very early age. It probably had its origin in the East; it is universally ascribed to the Babylonians and Chaldeans; the name Chaldean was, at Rome, synonymous with *mathematicus*, or astrologer; and we read repeatedly that this class of persons were expelled from Italy by a decree of the senate, both during the times of the republic and of the empire[14]. The recurrence of this act of legislation shows that it was not effectual; "It is a class of men," says Tacitus, "which, in our city, will always be prohibited, and will always exist." In Greece, it does not appear that the state showed any hostility to the professors of this art. They undertook, it would seem, then, as at a later period, to determine the course of a man's character and life from the configuration of the stars at the moment of his birth. We do not possess any of the speculations of the earlier astrologers; and we cannot therefore be certain that the notions which operated in men's minds when the art had its birth, agreed with the views on which it was afterwards defended, when it became a matter of controversy. But it appears probable, that, though it was at later periods supported by physical analogies, it was originally suggested by mythological belief. The Greeks spoke of the *influences* or *effluxes* (ἀπόρροιας) which

[14] Tacit. *Ann.* ii. 32. xii. 52. *Hist.* I. 22, II. 62.

proceeded from the stars; but the Chaldeans had probably thought rather of the powers which they exercised as *deities*. In whatever manner the sun, moon, and planets came to be identified with gods and goddesses, it is clear that the characters ascribed to these gods and goddesses regulate the virtues and powers of the stars which bear their names. This association, so manifestly visionary, was retained, amplified, and pursued, in an enthusiastic spirit, instead of being rejected for more distinct and substantial connexions; and a pretended science was thus formed, which bears the obvious stamp of mysticism.

That common sense of mankind which teaches them that theoretical opinions are to be calmly tried by their consequences and their accordance with facts, appears to have counteracted the prevalence of astrology in the better times of the human mind. Eudoxus, as we are informed by Cicero[15], rejected the pretensions of the Chaldeans; and Cicero himself reasons against them with arguments as sensible and intelligent as could be adduced by a writer of the present day; such as the different fortunes and characters of persons born at the same time; and the failure of the predictions, in the case of Pompey, Crassus, Cæsar, to whom the astrologers had foretold glorious old age and peaceful death. He also employs an argument which the reader would perhaps not expect from

[15] Cic. *de Div.* ii. 42.

him,—the very great remoteness of the planets, as compared with the distance of the moon. "What contagion can reach us," he asks, "from a distance almost infinite?"

Pliny argues on the same side, and with some of the same arguments[16]. "Homer," he says, "tells us that Hector and Polydamas were born the same night;—men of such different fortune. And every hour, in every part of the world, are born lords and slaves, kings and beggars."

The impression made by these arguments is marked in an anecdote told concerning Publius Nigidius Figulus, a Roman of the time of Julius Cæsar, whom Lucan mentions as a celebrated astrologer. It is said, that when an opponent of the art urged as an objection the different fates of persons born in two successive instants, Nigidius bade him make two contiguous marks on a potter's wheel, which was revolving rapidly near them. On stopping the wheel, the two marks were found to be really far removed from each other; and Nigidius is said to have received the name of Figulus (the potter), in remembrance of this story. His argument, says St. Augustine, who gives us the narrative, was as fragile as the ware which the wheel manufactured.

As the darkening times of the Roman empire advanced, even the stronger minds seem to have lost the clear energy which was requisite to throw

[16] *Hist. Nat.* vii. 49.

off this delusion. Seneca appears to take the influence of the planets for granted; and even Tacitus[17] seems to hesitate. "For my own part," says he, "I doubt; but certainly the majority of mankind cannot be weaned from the opinion, that, at the birth of each man, his future destiny is fixed; though some things may fall out differently from the predictions, by the ignorance of those who profess the art; and that thus the art is unjustly blamed, confirmed as it is by noted examples in all ages." The occasion which gives rise to these reflections of the historian is the mention of Thrasyllus, the favourite astrologer of the Emperor Tiberius, whose skill is exemplified in the following narrative. Those who were brought to Tiberius on any important matter, were admitted to an interview in an apartment situated on a lofty cliff in the island of Capreæ. They reached this place by a narrow path, accompanied by a single freedman of great bodily strength; and on their return, if the emperor had conceived any doubts of their trustworthiness, a single blow buried the secret and its victim in the ocean below. After Thrasyllus had, in this retreat, stated the results of his art as they concerned the emperor, Tiberius asked him whether he had calculated how long he himself had to live. The astrologer examined the aspect of the stars, and while he did this, as the narrative states, showed hesitation, alarm, increas-

[17] *Ann.* vi. 22.

ing terrour, and at last declared that, " the present hour was for him critical, perhaps fatal." Tiberius embraced him, and told him " he was right in supposing he had been in danger, but that he should escape it ;" and made him thenceforth his confidential counsellor.

The belief in the power of astrological prediction which thus obtained dominion over the minds of men of literary cultivation and practical energy, naturally had a more complete sway among the speculative but unstable minds of the later philosophical schools of Alexandria, Athens, and Rome. We have a treatise on astrology by Proclus, which will serve to exemplify the mystical principle in this form. It appears as a commentary on a work on the same subject called " Tetrabiblos," ascribed to Ptolemy; though we may reasonably doubt whether the author of the " Megale Syntaxis" was also the writer of the astrological work. A few notices of the commentary of Proclus will suffice[18]. The science is defended by urging how powerful we know the physical effects of the heavenly bodies to be. " The sun regulates all things on earth ;—the birth of animals, the growth of fruits, the flowing of waters, the change of health, according to the seasons ; he produces heat, moisture, dryness, cold, according to his approach to our zenith. The moon, which is the nearest of all bodies to the earth, gives out much *influence ;* and all things, animate and

[18] I. 2.

inanimate, sympathize with her; rivers increase and diminish according to her light; the advance of the sea, and its recess, are regulated by her rising and setting; and along with her, fruits and animals wax and wane, either wholly or in part." It is easy to see that by pursuing this train of associations (some real and some imaginary) very vaguely and very enthusiastically, the connexions which astrology supposes would receive a kind of countenance. Proclus then proceeds to state[19] the doctrines of the science. "The Sun," he says, "is productive of heat and dryness; this power is moderate in its nature, but is more perceived than that of the other luminaries, from his magnitude, and from the change of seasons. The nature of the Moon is for the most part moist; for being the nearest to the earth, she receives the vapours which rise from moist bodies, and thus she causes bodies to soften and rot. But by the illumination she receives from the sun, she partakes in a moderate degree of heat. Saturn is cold and dry, being most distant both from the heating power of the sun, and the moist vapours of the earth. His cold, however, is most prevalent, his dryness is more moderate. Both he and the rest receive additional powers from the configurations which they make with respect to the sun and moon." In the same manner it is remarked that Mars is dry and caustic, from his fiery nature, which, indeed, his colour shows. Jupiter is well

[19] I. 4.

compounded of warm and moist, as is Venus. Mercury is variable in his character. From these notions were derived others concerning the beneficial or hurtful effect of these stars. Heat and moisture are generative and creative elements; hence the ancients, says Proclus, deemed Jupiter, and Venus, and the Moon, to have a good power; Saturn and Mercury, on the other hand, had an evil nature.

Other distinctions of the character of the stars are enumerated, equally visionary, and suggested by the most fanciful connexions. Some are masculine, and some feminine: the Moon and Venus are of the latter kind. This appears to be merely a mythological or etymological association. Some are diurnal, some nocturnal; the Moon and Venus are of the latter kind, the Sun and Jupiter of the former; Saturn and Mars are both.

The fixed stars, also, and especially those of the zodiac, had especial influences and subjects assigned to them. In particular, each sign was supposed to preside over a particular part of the body; thus Aries had the head assigned to it, Taurus the neck, and so on.

The most important part of the sky in the astrologer's consideration, was that sign of the zodiac which rose at the moment of the child's birth; this was, properly speaking, the *horoscope*, the *ascendant*, or the *first house;* the whole circuit of the heavens being divided into twelve *houses*, in which life and death, marriage and children, riches and honours, friends and enemies, were distributed.

We need not attempt to trace the progress of this science. It prevailed extensively among the Arabians, as we might expect from the character of that nation. Albumasar, of Balkh in Khorasan, who flourished in the ninth century, who was one of their greatest astronomers, was also a great astrologer; and his work on the latter subject, " De Magnis Conjunctionibus, Annorum Revolutionibus ac eorum Perfectionibus," was long celebrated in Europe. Aboazen Haly (the writer of a treatise " De Judiciis Astrorum,") who lived in Spain in the thirteenth century, was one of the classical authors on this subject.

It will easily be supposed that when this *apotelesmatic* or *judicial* astrology obtained firm possession of men's minds, it would be pursued into innumerable subtle distinctions and extravagant conceits; and the more so, as experience could offer little or no check to such exercises of fancy and subtlety. For the correction of rules of astrological divination by comparison with known events, though pretended to by many professors of the art, was far too vague and fallible a guidance to be of any real advantage. Even in what has been called Natural Astrology, the dependence of the weather on the heavenly bodies, it is easy to see what a vast accumulation of well-observed facts is requisite to establish any true rule; and it is well known how long, in spite of facts, false and groundless rules (as the dependence of the weather on the moon) may keep their hold on men's minds. When the facts are such loose and many-sided things as human characters, passions, and happiness, it was hardly to be expected that even the most powerful minds should be able to find a footing sufficiently firm, to enable them to resist the impression of a theory constructed of sweeping and bold assertions, and filled out into a complete system of details. Accordingly, the connexion of the stars with human persons and actions was, for a long period, undisputed. The vague, obscure, and heterogeneous character of such a connexion, and its unfitness for any really scientific reasoning, could, of course, never be got rid of: and the bewildering feeling of earnestness and solemnity, with which the connexion of the heavens with man was contemplated, never died away. In other respects, however, the astrologers fell into a servile commentatorial spirit; and employed themselves in annotating and illustrating the works of their predecessors to a considerable extent, before the revival of true science.

It may be mentioned, that astrology has long been, and probably is, an art held in great esteem and admiration among other eastern nations besides the Mohammedans: for instance, the Jews, the Indians, the Siamese, and the Chinese. The prevalence of vague, visionary, and barren notions among these nations, cannot surprize us; for with

regard to them we have no evidence, as with regard to Europeans we have, that they are capable,
on subjects of physical speculation, of originating
sound and rational general principles. The Arts
may have had their birth in all parts of the globe;
but it is only Europe, at particular favoured
periods of its history, which has ever produced
Sciences.

We are, however, now speaking of a long
period, during which this productive energy was
interrupted and suspended. During this period
Europe descended, in intellectual character, to the
level at which the other parts of the world have
always stood. Her Science was then a mixture
of Art and Mysticism; we have considered several
forms of this Mysticism, but there are two others
which must not pass unnoticed, Alchemy and Magic.

We may observe, before we proceed, that the
deep and settled influence which Astrology had obtained among men, appears perhaps most strongly
in the circumstance, that the most vigorous and
clear-sighted minds which were concerned in the
revival of science, did not, for a long period, shake
off the persuasion, that there was, in this art, some
element of truth. Roger Bacon, Cardan, Kepler,
Tycho Brahe, Francis Bacon, are examples of this.
These, or most of them, rejected all the more obvious and extravagant absurdities with which the
subject had been loaded; but still conceived that
some real and valuable truth remained when all

these were removed. Thus Campanella[20], whom we shall have to speak of as one of the first opponents of Aristotle, wrote an "Astrology purified from all the Superstitions of the Jews and Arabians, and treated physiologically."

4. *Alchemy.*—Like other kinds of Mysticism, Alchemy seems to have grown out of the notions of moral, personal, and mythological qualities, which men associated with terms, of which the primary application was to physical properties. This is the form in which the subject is presented to us in the earliest writings which we possess on the subject of chemistry;—those of Geber[21] of Seville, who is supposed to have lived in the eighth or ninth century. The very titles of Geber's works show the notions on which this pretended science proceeds. They are, "Of the Search of Perfection;" "Of the Sum of Perfection, or of the Perfect Magistery;" "Of the Invention of Verity, or Perfection." The basis of this phraseology is the distinction of metals into more or less *perfect;* gold being the most perfect, as being the most valuable, most beautiful, most pure, most durable; silver the next; and so on. The "Search of Perfection," was, therefore, the attempt to convert other metals into gold; and doctrines were adopted which represented the metals as all compounded of the same elements, so that this was theoretically pos-

---

[20] Bacon, *De Aug.* iii. 4.
[21] Thomson's *Hist. of Chem.* i. 117.

sible. But the mystical trains of association were pursued much further than this; gold and silver were held to be the most noble of metals; gold was their King, and silver their Queen. Mythological associations were called in aid of these fancies, as had been done in astrology. Gold was Sol, the sun; silver was Luna, the moon; copper, iron, tin, lead, were assigned to Venus, Mars, Jupiter, Saturn. The processes of mixture and heat were spoken of as personal actions and relations, struggles and victories. Some elements were conquerors, some conquered; there existed preparations which possessed the power of changing the whole of a body into a substance of another kind: these were called *magisteries*[22]. When gold and quicksilver are combined, the king and the queen are married, to produce children of their own kind. It will easily be conceived, that when chemical operations were described in phraseology of this sort, the enthusiasm of the fancy would be added to that of the hopes, and observation would not be permitted to correct the delusion, or to suggest sounder and more rational views.

The exaggeration of the vague notion of perfection and power in the object of the alchemist's search, was carried further still. The same preparation which possessed the faculty of turning baser metals into gold, was imagined to be also a universal medicine, to have the gift of curing or pre-

[22] Boyle, Thomson's *Hist.* Ch. i. 25. Carolus Musitanus.

venting diseases, prolonging life, producing bodily strength and beauty: the *philosophers' stone* was finally invested with every desirable efficacy which the fancy of the "philosophers" could devise.

It has been usual to say that Alchemy was the mother of Chemistry; and that men would never have made the experiments on which the real science is founded, if they had not been animated by the hopes and the energy which the delusive art inspired. To judge whether this is truly said, we must be able to estimate the degree of interest which men feel in purely speculative truth, and in the real and substantial improvement of art to which it leads. Since the fall of Alchemy, and the progress of real Chemistry, these motives have been powerful enough to engage in the study of the science, a body far larger than the Alchemists ever were, and no less zealous. There is no apparent reason why the result should not have been the same, if the progress of true science had begun sooner. Astronomy was long cultivated without the bribe of Astrology. But, perhaps, we may justly say this;—that, in the stationary period, men's minds were so far enfeebled and degraded, that pure speculative truth had not its full effect upon them; and the mystical pursuits in which some dim and disfigured images of truth were sought with avidity, were among the provisions by which the human soul, even when sunk below its best condition, is perpetually directed to something

above the mere objects of sense and appetite;—
a contrivance of compensation, as it were, in the
intellectual and spiritual constitution of man.

5. *Magic.*—Magical Arts, so far as they were
believed in by those who professed to practise
them, and so far as they have a bearing in science,
stand on the same footing as astrology; and, indeed, a close alliance has generally been maintained between the two pursuits. Incapacity and
indisposition to perceive natural and philosophical
causation, an enthusiastic imagination, and such a
faith as can devise and maintain supernatural and
spiritual connexions, are the elements of this, as
of other forms of Mysticism. And thus that temper
which led men to aim at the magician's supposed
authority over the elements, is an additional exemplification of those habits of thought which
prevented the progress of real science, and the
acquisition of that command over nature which is
founded on science, during the interval now before
us.

But there is another aspect under which the
opinions connected with this pursuit may serve to
illustrate the mental character of the stationary
period.

The tendency, during the middle ages, to attribute the character of Magician to almost all
persons eminent for great speculative or practical
knowledge, is a feature of those times, which shows
how extensive and complete was the inability to

apprehend the nature of real science. In cultivated and enlightened periods, such as those of ancient Greece, or modern Europe, knowledge is wished for and admired, even by those who least possess it: but in dark and degraded periods, superior knowledge is a butt for hatred and fear. In the one case, men's eyes are open; their thoughts are clear; and, however high the philosopher may be raised above the multitude, they can catch glimpses of the intervening path, and see that it is free to all, and that elevation is the reward of energy and labour. In the other case, the crowd are not only ignorant, but spiritless; they have lost the pleasure in knowledge, the appetite for it, and the feeling of dignity which it gives: there is no sympathy which connects them with the learned man: they see him above them, but know not how he is raised or supported: he becomes an object of aversion and envy, of vague suspicion and terror; and these emotions are embodied and confirmed by association with the fancies and dogmas of superstition. To consider superior knowledge as Magic, and Magic as a detestable and criminal employment, was the form which these feelings of dislike assumed; and at one period in the history of Europe, almost every one who had gained any eminent literary fame, was spoken of as a magician. Naudæus, a learned Frenchman, in the seventeenth century, wrote "An Apology for all the Wise Men who have been unjustly reported Magicians, from the Creation to the present Age." The list of persons whom he thus thinks it necessary to protect, are of various classes and ages. Alkindi, Geber, Artephius, Thebit, Raymund Lully, Arnold de Villâ Novâ, Peter of Apono, and Paracelsus, had incurred the black suspicion as physicians or alchemists. Thomas Aquinas, Roger Bacon, Michael Scot, Picus of Mirandula, and Trithemius, had not escaped it, though ministers of religion. Even dignitaries, such as Robert Grosteste, bishop of Lincoln, Albertus Magnus, bishop of Ratisbon, Popes Sylvester the Second, and Gregory the Seventh, had been involved in the wide calumny. In the same way in which the vulgar confounded the eminent learning and knowledge which had appeared in recent times, with skill in dark and supernatural arts, they converted into wizards all the best-known names in the rolls of fame; as Aristotle, Solomon, Joseph, Pythagoras; and, finally, the poet Virgil was a powerful and skilful necromancer, and this fancy was exemplified by many strange stories of his achievements and practices.

The various results of the tendency of the human mind to mysticism, which we have here noticed, form prominent features in the intellectual character of the world, for a long course of centuries. The theosophy and theurgy of the Neoplatonists, the mystical arithmetic of the Pythagoreans and their successors, the predictions of the astrologers, the pretences of alchemy and magic, represent, not unfairly, the general character and disposition of men's thoughts, with reference to philosophy and science. That there were stronger minds, which threw off in a greater or less degree this train of delusive and unsubstantial ideas, is true; as, on the other hand, Mysticism, among the vulgar or the foolish, often went to an extent of extravagance and superstition, of which I have not attempted to convey any conception. The lesson which the preceding survey teaches us is, that during the stationary period, Mysticism, in its various forms, was a leading character, both of the common mind, and of the speculations of the most intelligent and profound reasoners; and that this Mysticism was the opposite of that habit of thought which we have stated Science to require; namely, clear Ideas, distinctly employed to connect well-ascertained Facts; inasmuch as the Ideas in which it dealt were vague and unstable, and the temper in which they were contemplated was an urgent and aspiring enthusiasm, which could not submit to a calm conference with experience upon even terms. The fervour of thought in some degree supplied the place of reason in producing belief; but opinions so obtained had no enduring value; they did not exhibit a permanent record of old truths, nor a firm foundation for new. Experience collected her stores in vain, or ceased to collect them, when she had only to pour them into the flimsy folds of the lap of Mysticism; who was, in truth, so much absorbed in looking for the treasures which were to fall from the skies, that she heeded little how scantily she obtained, or how loosely she held, such riches as might be found near her.

CHAPTER IV.

OF THE DOGMATISM OF THE STATIONARY PERIOD.

IN speaking of the character of the age of commentators, we noticed principally the ingenious servility which it displays;—the acuteness with which it finds ground for speculation in the expression of other men's thoughts;—the want of all vigour and fertility in acquiring any real and new truths. Such was the character of the reasoners of the stationary period from the first ; but, at a later day, this character, from various causes, was modified by new features. The servility which had yielded itself to the yoke, insisted upon forcing it on the necks of others ; the subtlety which found all the truth it needed in certain accredited writings, resolved that no one should find there, or in any other region, any other truths; speculative men became tyrants without ceasing to be slaves; to their character of commentators they added that of dogmatists.

1. *Origin of the Scholastic Philosophy.*—The causes of this change have been very happily analyzed and described by several modern writers[1].

---

[1] Dr. Hampden, in the Life of Thomas Aquinas. in the *Encyc. Metrop.* Degerando, *Hist. Comparée,* vol. iv. Also Tennemann, *Hist. of Phil.* vol. viii. Introduction.

The general nature of the process may be briefly stated to have been the following.

The tendencies of the later times of the Roman empire to a commenting literature, and a second-hand philosophy, have already been noticed. The loss of the dignity of political freedom, the want of the cheerfulness of advancing prosperity, and the substitution of the less philosophical structure of the Latin language for the delicate intellectual mechanism of the Greek; fixed and augmented the prevalent feebleness and barrenness of intellect. Men forgot, or feared, to consult nature, to seek for new truths, to do what the great discoverers of other times had done; they were content to consult libraries, to study and defend old opinions, to talk of what great geniuses had said. They sought their philosophy in accredited treatises, and dared not question such doctrines as they there found.

The character of the philosophy to which they were thus led, was determined by this want of courage and originality. There are various antagonist principles of opinion, which seem alike to have their root in the intellectual constitution of man, and which are maintained and developed by opposing sects, when the intellect is in vigorous action. Such principles are, for instance,—the claims of Authority and of Reason to our assent;—the source of our knowledge in Experience or in Ideas;—the superiority of a Mystical or of a Skeptical turn of thought. Such oppositions of doctrine were found in writers of the greatest fame; and two of those, who most occupied the attention of students, Plato and Aristotle, were, on several points of this nature, very diverse from each other in their tendency. The attempt to reconcile these philosophers by Boëthius and others, we have already noticed; and the attempt was so far successful, that it left on men's minds the belief in the possibility of a great philosophical system which should be based on both these writers, and have a claim to the assent of all sober speculators.

But, in the mean time, the Christian Religion had become the leading subject of men's thoughts; and divines had put forward its claims to be, not merely the guide of men's lives, and the means of reconciling them to their heavenly Master; but also to be a Philosophy in the widest sense in which the term had been used;—a consistent speculative view of man's condition and nature, and of the world in which he is placed.

These claims had been acknowledged; and, unfortunately, from the intellectual condition of the times, with no due apprehension of the necessary ministry of Observation, and Reason dealing with observation, by which alone such a system can be embodied. It was held, without any regulating principle, that the Philosophy which had been bequeathed to the world by the great geniuses of heathen antiquity, and the Philosophy which was deduced from, and implied by, the Revelations made by God to man, must be identical; and therefore, that Theology is the only true Philosophy. Indeed, the Neoplatonists had already arrived, by other roads, at the same conviction. John Scot Erigena, in the reign of Alfred, and consequently before the existence of the Scholastic Philosophy, properly so called, had reasserted this doctrine[2]. Anselm, in the eleventh century, again brought it forward[3]; and Bernard de Chartres, in the thirteenth[4].

This view was confirmed by the opinion which prevailed, concerning the nature of philosophical truth; a view supported by the theory of Plato, the practice of Aristotle, and the general propensities of the human mind: I mean the opinion that all science may be obtained by the use of reasoning alone;—that by analyzing and combining the notions which common language brings before us, we may learn all that we can know. Thus Logic came to include the whole of Science; and accordingly this Abelard expressly maintained[5]. I have already explained, in some measure, the fallacy of this belief, which consists, as has been well said[6], "in mistaking the universality of the theory of language for the generalization of facts." But on all accounts this opinion is readily accepted; and it led at once to the conclusion, that the Theological Philosophy which we have described, is complete as well as true.

[2] Deg. iv. 351.   [3] Ib. iv. 388.   [4] Ib. iv. 418.
[5] Ib. iv. 407.   [6] *Enc. Met.* 807.

Thus a Universal Science was established, with the authority of a Religious Creed. Its universality rested on erroneous views of the relation of words and truths; its pretensions as a science were admitted by the servile temper of men's intellects; and its religious authority was assigned it, by making all truth part of religion. And as Religion claimed assent within her own jurisdiction under the most solemn and imperative sanctions, Philosophy shared in her imperial power, and dissent from their doctrines was no longer blameless or allowable. Errour became wicked, dissent became heresy; to reject the received human doctrines, was nearly the same as to doubt the Divine declarations. The *Scholastic Philosophy* claimed the assent of all believers.

The external form, the details, and the text of this philosophy, were taken, in a great measure, from Aristotle; though, in the spirit, the general notions, and the style of interpretation, Plato and the Platonists had no inconsiderable share. Various causes contributed to the elevation of Aristotle to this distinction. His Logic had early been adopted as an instrument of theological disputation; and his spirit of systematization, of subtle distinction, and of analysis of words, as well as his disposition to argumentation, afforded the most natural and grateful employment to the commentating propensities. Those principles which we before noted as the leading points of his physical philosophy, were selected and adopted ; and these, presented in a most technical form, and applied in a systematic manner, constitute a large portion of the philosophy of which we now speak, so far as it pretends to deal with physics.

2. *Scholastic Dogmas.*—But before the complete ascendancy of Aristotle was thus established, when something of an intellectual waking took place after the darkness and sleep of the ninth and tenth centuries, the Platonic doctrines seem to have had, at first, a strong attraction for men's minds, as better falling in with the mystical speculations and contemplative piety which belonged to the times. John Scot Erigena[7] may be looked upon as the reviver of the New Platonism in the tenth century. Towards the end of the eleventh, Peter Damien[8], in Italy, reproduced, involved in a theological discussion, some Neoplatonic ideas. Godefroy[9] also, censor of St. Victor, has left a treatise, entitled *Microcosmus;* this is founded on a mystical analogy, often afterwards again brought forward, between Man and the Universe. "Philosophers and theologians," says the writer, "agree in considering man as a little world ; and as the world is composed of four elements, man is endowed with four faculties, the senses, the imagination, reason, and understanding." Bernard of Chartres[10], in his *Megascosmus* and *Microcosmus* took up the same notions. Hugo,

---

[7] Deg. iv. 35. [8] Ib. iv. 367. [9] Ib. iv. 413.
[10] Ib. iv. 419.

abbot of St. Victor, made a contemplative life the main point and crown of his philosophy; and is said to have been the first of the scholastic writers who made psychology his special study[11]. He says the faculties of the mind are "the senses, the imagination, the reason, the memory, the understanding, and the intelligence."

Physics does not originally and properly form any prominent part of the Scholastic Philosophy, which consists mainly of a series of questions and determinations upon the various points of a certain technical divinity. Of this kind is the *Book of Sentences* of Peter the Lombard (bishop of Paris), who is, on that account, usually called "Magister Sententiarum;" a work which was published in the twelfth century, and was long the text and standard of such discussions. The questions are decided by the authority of Scripture and of the Fathers of the Church; and are divided into four Books, of which the first contains questions concerning God and the doctrine of the Trinity in particular; the second is concerning the Creation; the third, concerning Christ and the Christian Religion; and the fourth treats of Religious and Moral Duties. In the second Book, as in many of the writers of this time, the nature of Angels is considered in detail, and the Orders of their Hierarchy, of which there were held to be nine. The physical discussions enter only as bearing upon the scriptural history of the crea-

[11] Deg. iv. 415.

tion, and cannot be taken as a specimen of the work; but I may observe, that in speaking of the division of the waters above the firmament, from the waters under the firmament, he gives one opinion, that of Bede, that the former waters are the solid crystalline heavens in which the stars are fixed[12], "for crystal, which is so hard and transparent, is made of water." But he mentions also the opinion of St. Augustine, that the waters above the heavens are there in a state of vapour (*vaporaliter*) and in minute drops; "if, then, water can, as we see in clouds, be so minutely divided that it may be thus supported as vapour on air, which is naturally lighter than water; why may we not believe that it floats above that lighter celestial element in still minuter drops and still lighter vapours? But in whatever manner the waters are there, we do not doubt that they are there."

The celebrated *Summa Theologiæ* of Thomas Aquinas is a work of the same kind; and anything which has a physical bearing forms an equally small part of it. Thus, of the 512 Questions of the *Summa*, there is only one (Part I., Quest. 115) "on Corporeal Action," or on any part of the material world; though there are several concerning the celestial Hierarchies, as "on the Act of Angels," "on the Speaking of Angels," "on the Subordination of Angels," "on Guardian Angels," and the like. This, of course, would not be remarkable in a

[12] Lib. ii. Distinct. xiv. *De opere secundæ diei.*

treatise on Theology, except this Theology were intended to constitute the whole of Philosophy.

We may observe, that in this work, though Plato, Avecibron, and many other heathen as well as Christian philosophers, are adduced as authority, Aristotle is referred to in a peculiar manner as "the philosopher." This is noticed by John of Salisbury, as attracting attention in his time; (he died A.D. 1182.) "The various masters of Dialectic," says he[13], "shine, each with his peculiar merit; but all are proud to worship the footsteps of Aristotle; so much so, indeed, that the name of *philosopher*, which belongs to them all, has been pre-eminently appropriated to him. He is called the philosopher *autonomatice*, that is, by excellence."

The Question concerning Corporeal Action, in Aquinas, is divided into six Articles; and the conclusion delivered upon the first, is[14], that "Body being compounded of power and act, is active as well as passive." Against this it is urged, that quantity is an attribute of body, and that quantity prevents action; that this appears in fact, since a larger body is more difficult to move. The author replies, that "quantity does not prevent corporeal form from action altogether, but prevents it from being a universal agent inasmuch as the form is individualized, which, in matter subject to quantity, it is. Moreover, the illustration deduced from the

[13] *Metalogicus*, lib. ii. cap. 16.　　　[14] *Summæ*, P. i. Q. 115. Art. 1.

ponderousness of bodies is not to the purpose; first, because the addition of quantity is not the cause of gravity, as is proved in the fourth book, De Cœlo and De Mundo" (we see that he quotes familiarly the physical treatises of Aristotle); "second, because it is false that ponderousness makes motion slower; on the contrary, in proportion as anything is heavier, the more does it move with its proper motion; thirdly, because action does not take place by local motion, as Democritus asserted; but by this, that something is drawn from power into act."

It does not belong to our purpose to consider either the theological or the metaphysical doctrines which form so large a portion of the treatises of the schoolmen. Perhaps it may hereafter appear, that some light is thrown on some of the questions which have occupied metaphysicians in all ages, by that examination of the history of the Progressive Sciences in which we are now engaged; but till we are able to analyze the leading controversies of this kind, it would be of little service to speak of them in detail. It may be noticed, however, that many of the most prominent of them refer to the great question,—"What is the relation between actual things and general terms?" Perhaps in modern times, the actual things would be more commonly taken as the point to start from; and men would begin by considering how classes and universals are obtained from individuals. But the schoolmen, founding their speculations on the received modes of considering such subjects, to which both Aristotle and Plato had contributed, travelled in the opposite direction, and endeavoured to discovĕr how individuals were deduced from genera and species;— what was "the Principle of Individuation." This was variously stated by different reasoners. Thus Bonaventura[15] solves the difficulty by the aid of the Aristotelian distinction of Matter and Form. ˏ The individual derives from the Form the property of *being something*, and from the Matter the property of being that *particular thing*. Duns Scotus[16], the great adversary of Thomas Aquinas in theology, placed the Principle of Individuation in "a certain positive determining entity," which his school called *Hæcceity*, or *thisness*. "Thus an individual man is Peter, because his *humanity* is combined with *Petreity*." The force of abstract terms is a curious question, and some remarkable experiments in their use had been made by the Latin Aristotelians before this time. In the same way in which we talk of the *quantity* and *quality* of a thing, they spoke of its *quiddity*[17].

We may consider the reign of mere disputation as fully established at the time of which we are now speaking; and the only kind of philosophy henceforth studied was one in which no sound physical science had or could have a place. The wavering abstractions, indistinct generalizations, and loose classifications of common language, which we have

[15] Deg. iv. 573.   [16]ˏ Ib. iv. 523.   [17] Ib. iv. 494.

already noted as the fountain of the physics of the Greek schools of philosophy, were also the only source from which the schoolmen of the middle ages drew their views, or rather their arguments: and though these notional and verbal relations were invested with a most complex and pedantic technicality, they did not, on that account, become at all more precise as notions, or most likely to lead to a single real truth. Instead of acquiring distinct ideas, they multiplied abstract terms; instead of real generalizations, they had recourse to verbal distinctions. The whole course of their employments tended to make them, not only ignorant of physical truth, but incapable of conceiving its nature.

Having thus taken upon themselves the task of raising and discussing questions by means of abstract terms, verbal distinctions, and logical rules alone, there was no tendency in their activity to come to an end, as there was no progress. The same questions, the same answers, the same difficulties, the same solutions, the same verbal subtleties,—sought for, admired, cavilled at, abandoned, reproduced, and again admired,—might recur without limit. John of Salisbury[18] observes of the Pa-

[18] He studied logic at Paris, at St. Geneviève, and then left them. " Duodecennium mihi elapsum est diversis studiis occupatum. Jucundum itaque visum est veteres quos reliqueram, et quos adhuc Dialectica detinebat in monte, (Sanctæ Genovefæ) revisere socios, conferre cum eis super ambiguitatibus pristinis; ut nostrûm invicem collatione mutuâ commetiremur profectum.

z 2　　　Inventi

risian teachers, that, after several years' absence he found them not a step advanced, and still employed in urging and parrying the same arguments; and this, as Mr. Hallam remarks[19], "was equally applicable to the period of centuries." The same knots were tied and untied; the same clouds were formed and dissipated. The poet's censure of "the Sons of Aristotle," is as just as happily expressed :—

> They stand
> Locked up together hand in hand;
> Every one leads as he is led,
> The same bare path they tread,
> And dance like Fairies a fantastic round,
> But neither change their motion nor their ground.

It will, therefore, be unnecessary to go into any detail respecting the history of the school philosophy of the thirteenth, fourteenth, and fifteenth centuries. We may suppose it to have been, during the intermediate time, such as it was at first and at last. An occasion to consider its later days will be brought before us by the course of our subject. But, even during the most entire ascendency of the scholastic doctrines, the elements of change were at work. While the doctors and the philosophers received all the ostensible homage of men, a doctrine and a philosophy of another kind were gradu-

Inventi sunt, qui fuerant, et ubi ; neque enim ad palmam visi sunt processisse ad quæstiones pristinas dirimendas, neque propositiunculam unam adjecerant. Quibus urgebant stimulis eisdem et ipsi urgebantur." &c. *Metalogicus*, lib. ii. cap. 10.

[19] *Middle Ages*, iii. 537.

ally forming: the practical instincts of man, their impatience of tyranny, the progress of the useful arts, the promises of alchemy, were all disposing men to reject the authority and deny the pretensions of the received philosophical creed. Two antagonist forms of opinion were in existence, which for some time went on detached, and almost independent of each other; but, finally, these came into conflict, at the time of Galileo; and the war speedily extended to every part of civilized Europe.

3. *Scholastic Physics.*—It is difficult to give briefly any appropriate examples of the nature of the Aristotelian physics which are to be found in the works of this time. As the gravity of bodies was one of the first subjects of dispute when the struggle of the rival methods began, we may notice the mode in which it was treated[20]. "Zabarella maintains that the proximate cause of the motion of elements is the *form*, in the Aristotelian sense of the term: but to this sentence we," says Keckerman, "cannot agree; for in all other things the *form* is the proximate cause, not of the *act*, but of the power or faculty from which the act flows. Thus in man, the rational soul is not the cause of the act of laughing, but of the risible faculty or power." Keckerman's system was at one time a work of considerable authority: it was published in 1614. By comparing and systematizing what he finds in Aristotle, he is led to state his results in the

[20] Keckermann, p. 1428.

form of definitions and theorems. Thus, "gravity is a motive quality, arising from cold, density, and bulk, by which the elements are carried downwards." "Water is the lower intermediate element, cold and moist." The first theorem concerning water is, "The moistness of water is controlled by its coldness, so that it is less than the moistness of the air; though, according to the sense of the vulgar, water appears to moisten more than air." It is obvious that the two properties of fluids, to have their parts easily moved, and to wet other bodies, are here confounded. I may, as a concluding specimen of this kind, mention those propositions or maxims concerning fluids, which were so firmly established, that, when Boyle propounded the true mechanical principles of fluid action, he was obliged to state his opinions as "hydrostatical *paradoxes*." These were,—that fluids do not gravitate *in proprio loco;* that is, that water has no gravity in or on water, since it is in its own place; —that air has no gravity on water, since it is above water, which is its proper place;—that earth in water tends to descend, since its place is below water;—that the water rises in a pump or siphon, because nature abhors a vacuum;—that some bodies have a positive levity in others, as oil in water; and the like.

4. *Authority of Aristotle among the Schoolmen.*—The authority of Aristotle, and the practice of making him the text and basis of the system,

especially as it regarded physics, prevailed during the period of which we speak. This authority was not, however, without its fluctuations. Launoy has traced one part of its history in a book *On the various Fortune of Aristotle in the University of Paris*. The most material turns of this fortune depend on the bearing which the works of Aristotle were supposed to have upon theology. Several of Aristotle's works, and more especially his metaphysical writings, had been translated into Latin, and were explained in the schools of the University of Paris, as early as the beginning of the thirteenth century[21]. At a council held at Paris in 1209, they were prohibited, as having given occasion to the heresy of Almeric (or Amauri), and because " they might give occasion to other heresies not yet invented." The Logic of Aristotle recovered its credit some years after this, and was publicly taught in the University of Paris, in the year 1215; but the Natural Philosophy and Metaphysics were prohibited by a decree of Gregory the Ninth, in 1231. The emperor, Frederic the Second, employed a number of learned men to translate into Latin, from the Greek and Arabic, certain books of Aristotle, and of other ancient sages; and we have a letter of Peter de Vineis, in which they are recommended to the attention of the University of Bologna: probably the same recommendation was addressed to other Universities. Both Albertus Magnus and

[21] Mosheim, iii. 157.

Thomas Aquinas wrote commentaries on Aristotle's works; and as this was done soon after the decree of Gregory the Ninth, Launoy is much perplexed to reconcile the fact with the orthodoxy of the two doctors. Campanella, who was one of the first to cast off the authority of Aristotle, says, " We are by no means to think that St. Thomas *aristotelized;* he only expounded Aristotle, that he might correct his errours; and I should conceive he did this with the license of the Pope." This statement, however, by no means gives a just view of the nature of Albertus's and Aquinas's commentaries. Both have followed their author with profound deference[22]. For instance, Aquinas[23] attempts to defend Aristotle's assertion, that if there were no resistance, a body would move through a space in no time; and the same defence is given by Scotus.

We may imagine the extent of authority and admiration which Aristotle would attain, when thus countenanced, both by the powerful and the learned. In universities, no degree could be taken without a knowledge of the philosopher. In 1452, Cardinal Totaril established this rule in the University of Paris[24]. When Ramus, in 1543, published an attack upon Aristotle, it was repelled by the power of the court, and the severity of the law. Francis the First published an edict, in which he states that he had appointed certain judges,

[22] Deg. N. 475.   [23] F. Piccolomini, ii. 835.
[24] Launoy, pp. 108, 128.

who had been of opinion[25], "que le dit Ramus avoit été téméraire arrogant et impudent; et que parcequ'en son livre des animadversions il reprenait Aristotle, estait évidemment connue et manifeste son ignorance." The books are then declared to be suppressed. It was often a complaint of pious men, that theology was corrupted by the influence of Aristotle and his commentators. Petrarch says[26], that one of the Italian learned men conversing with him, after expressing much contempt for the apostles and fathers, exclaimed, "Utinam tu Averroen pati posses, ut videres quanto ille tuis his nugatoribus major sit!"

When the revival of letters began to take place, and a number of men of ardent and elegant minds, susceptible to the impressions of beauty of style and dignity of thought, were brought in contact with Greek literature, Plato had naturally greater charms for them. A powerful school of Platonists (not Neoplatonists) was formed in Italy, including some of the principal scholars and men of genius of the time; as Picus of Mirandula in the middle, Marsilius Ficinus at the end, of the fifteenth century. At one time, it appeared as if the ascendancy of Aristotle was about to be overturned; but, in physics at least, his authority passed unshaken through this trial. It was not by disputation that Aristotle could be overthrown; and the Platonists were not persons whose doctrines led

[23] Launoy, p. 132.   [26] Hallam, *M. A.*, iii. 536.

them to use the only decisive method in such cases, the observation and unfettered interpretation of facts.

The history of their controversies, therefore, does not belong to our design. For like reasons we do not here speak of other authors, who opposed the scholastic philosophy on general theoretical grounds of various kinds. Such examples of insurrection against the dogmatism which we have been reviewing, are extremely interesting events in the history of the philosophy of science. But, in the present work, we are to confine ourselves to the history of science itself; in the hope that we may thus be able hereafter, to throw a steadier light upon that philosophy by which the succession of stationary and progressive periods which we are here tracing, may be in some measure explained. We are now to close our account of the stationary period, and to enter upon the great subject of the progress of physical science in modern times.

5. *Subjects omitted. Civil Law. Medicine.*— My object has been to make my way, as rapidly as possible, to this period of progress; and in doing this, I have had to pass over a long and barren tract, where almost all traces of the right road disappear. In exploring this region, it is not without some difficulty that he who is travelling with objects such as mine, continues a steady progress in the proper direction; for many curious and attractive subjects of research come in his way:

he crosses the track of many a controversy, which in its time divided the world of speculators, and of which the results may be traced, even now, in the conduct of moral, or political, or metaphysical discussions; or in the common associations of thought, and forms of language. The wars of the Nominalists and Realists; the disputes concerning the foundations of morals, and the motives of human actions; the controversies concerning predestination, free will, grace, and the many other points of metaphysical divinity; the influence of theology and metaphysics upon each other, and upon other subjects of human curiosity; the effects of opinion upon politics, and of political condition upon opinion; the influence of literature and philosophy upon each other, and upon society; and many other subjects;—might be well worth examination, if our hopes of success did not reside in pursuing, steadily and directly, those inquiries in which we can look for a definite and certain reply. We must even neglect two of the leading studies of those times, which occupied much of men's time and thoughts, and had a very great influence on society; the one dealing with Notions, the other with Things; the one employed about moral rules, the other about material causes, but both for practical ends; I mean, the study of the *Civil Law*, and of *Medicine*. The second of these studies will hereafter come before us, as one of the principal occasions which led to the cultivation of chemistry:

but, in itself, its progress is of too complex and indefinite a nature to be advantageously compared with that of the more exact sciences. The Roman Law is held, by its admirers, to be a system of deductive science, as exact as the mathematical sciences themselves; and it may, therefore, be useful to consider it, if we should, in the sequel, have to examine how far there can exist an analogy between moral and physical science. But, after a few more words on the middle ages, we must return to our task of tracing the progress of the latter.

CHAPTER V.

PROGRESS OF THE ARTS IN THE MIDDLE AGES.

1. *ART and Science.*—I shall, before I resume the history of science, say a few words on the subject described in the title of this chapter, both because I might otherwise be accused of doing injustice to the period now treated of; and also, because we shall by this means bring under our notice, some circumstances which were important as being the harbingers of the revival of progressive knowledge.

The accusation of injustice towards the state of science in the middle ages, if we were to terminate our survey of them with what has hitherto been said, might be urged from obvious topics. How do we recognize, it might be asked, in a picture of mere confusion and mysticism of thought, of servility and dogmatism of character, the powers and acquirements to which we owe so many of the most important inventions which we now enjoy? Parchment and paper, printing and engraving, improved glass and steel, gunpowder, clocks, telescopes, the mariner's compass, the reformed calendar, the decimal notation, algebra, trigonometry, chemistry, counterpoint, an invention equivalent to a new creation of music;—these are all possessions which we inherit from that which has been so disparagingly termed the Stationary Period. Above all, let us look at the monuments of architecture of this period ;—the admiration and the despair of modern architects, not only for their beauty, but for the skill disclosed in their construction. With all these evidences before us, how can we avoid allowing that the masters of the middle ages not only made some small progress in Astronomy, which has, grudgingly as it would seem, been admitted in a former Book ; but also that they were no small proficients in other sciences, in Optics, in Harmonics, in Physics, and, above all, in Mechanics ?

If, it may be added, we are allowed in the present day, to refer to the perfection of our Arts as evidence of the advanced state of our physical philosophy ;—if our steam-engines, our gas-illumination, our buildings, our navigation, our manufactures, are cited as triumphs of science ;—shall not prior inventions, made under far heavier disadvantages,—shall not greater works, produced in an earlier state of knowledge, also be admitted as witnesses that the middle ages had their share, and that not a small or doubtful one, of science ?

To these questions I answer, by distinguishing between Art, and Science in that sense of general Inductive Systematic Truth, which it bears in this work. To separate and compare, with precision, these two processes, belongs to the Philosophy of

Induction; and the attempt must be reserved for another place : but the leading differences are sufficiently obvious. Art is practical, Science is speculative : the former is seen in doing; the latter rests in the contemplation of what is known. The Art of the builder appears in his edifice, though he may never have meditated on the abstract propositions on which its stability and strength depends. The Science of the mathematical mechanician consists in his seeing that, under certain conditions, bodies must sustain each other's pressure, though he may never have applied his knowledge in a single case.

Now the remark which I have to make is this: —in all cases the Arts are prior to the related Sciences. Art is the parent, not the progeny, of Science; the realization of principles in practice forms part of the prelude, as well as of the sequel, of theoretical discovery. And thus the inventions of the middle ages, which have been above enumerated, though at the present day they may be portions of our sciences, are no evidence that the sciences then existed; but only that those powers of practical observation and practical skill were at work, which prepare the way for theoretical views and scientific discoveries.

It may be urged, that the great works of art do virtually take for granted principles of science; and that, therefore, it is unreasonable to deny science to great artists. It may be said, that the grand structures of Cologne, or Amiens, or Canterbury, could not have been erected without a profound knowledge of mechanical principles.

To this we reply, that *such* knowledge is manifestly not of the nature of that which we call *science*. If the beautiful and skilful structures of the middle ages prove that mechanics then existed as a science, mechanics must have existed as a science also among the builders of the Cyclopean walls of Greece and Italy, or of our own Stonehenge; for the masses which are there piled on each other, could not be raised without considerable mechanical skill. But we may go much further. The actions of every man who raises and balances weights, or walks along a pole, take for granted the laws of equilibrium; and even animals constantly avail themselves of such principles. Are these, then, acquainted with mechanics as a science? Again, if actions which are performed by taking advantage of mechanical properties prove a knowledge of the science of mechanics, they must also be allowed to prove a knowledge of the science of geometry, when they proceed on geometrical properties. But the most familiar actions of men and animals do this. The Epicureans held, as Proclus informs us, that even asses knew that two sides of a triangle are greater than the third. And they may truly be said to have a practical knowledge of this; but they have not, therefore, a science of geometry. And in like manner among men, if we consider the matter strictly, a practical assumption of a principle does not imply a speculative knowledge of it.

We may, in another way also, show how inadmissible are the works of the master Artists of the middle ages into the series of events which mark the advance of Science. The following maxim is applicable to a history, such as we are here endeavouring to write. We are employed in tracing the progress of such general principles as constitute each of the sciences which we are reviewing; and no facts or subordinate truths belong to our scheme, except so far as they lead to or are included in these higher principles; nor are they important to us, any further than as they prove such principles. Now with regard to processes of art like those which we have referred to, as the inventions of the middle ages, let us ask, *what* principle each of them illustrates? What chemical doctrine rests for its support on the phenomena of gunpowder, or glass, or steel? What new harmonical truth was illustrated in the Gregorian chant? What mechanical principle unknown to Archimedes was displayed in the printing-press? The practical value and use, the ingenuity and skill of these inventions is not questioned; but what is their place in the history of speculative knowledge? Even in those cases in which they enter into such a history, how minute a figure do they make! how great is the contrast between their practical and theoretical importance! They may in their operation have changed the face of the world; but in the history of the principles of the sciences to which they belong, they may be omitted without being missed.

As to that part of the objection which was stated by asking, why, if the arts of our age prove its scientific eminence, the arts of the middle ages should not be received as proof of theirs; we must reply to it, by giving up some of the pretensions which are often put forwards on behalf of the science of our times. The perfection of the mechanical and other arts among us proves the advanced condition of our sciences, only in so far as these arts have been perfected by the application of some great scientific truth, with a clear insight into its nature. The greatest improvement of the steam-engine was due to the steady apprehension of an atmological doctrine by Watt; but what distinct theoretical principle is illustrated by the beautiful manufactures of porcelain, or steel, or glass? A chemical view of these compounds, which would explain the conditions of success and failure in their manufacture, would be of great value in art; and it would also be a novelty in chemical theory; so little is the present condition of those processes a triumph of science, shedding intellectual glory on our age. And the same might be said of many, or of most, of the processes of the arts as now practised.

2. *Arabian Science.*—Having, I trust, established the view I have stated, respecting the relation of Art and Science, we shall be able very rapidly to dispose of a number of subjects which otherwise might seem to require a detailed notice. Though this distinction has been recognized by others, it has hardly been rigorously adhered to, in consequence of the indistinct notion of *science* which has commonly prevailed. Thus Gibbon, in speaking of the knowledge of the period now under our notice, says[1], "Much useful experience had been acquired in the practice of arts and manufactures; but the *science* of chemistry owes its origin and improvement to the industry of the Saracens. They," he adds, "first invented and named the alembic for the purposes of distillation, analyzed the substances of the three kingdoms of nature, tried the distinction and affinities of alcalis and acids, and converted the poisonous minerals into soft and salutary medicines." The formation and realization of the notions of *analysis* and of *affinity*, were important steps in chemical science, which, as I shall hereafter endeavour to show, it remained for the chemists of Europe to make at a much later period. If the Arabians had done this, they might with justice have been called the authors of the science of chemistry; but no doctrines can be adduced from their works which give them any title to this eminent· distinction. Their claims are dis-

[1] *Decline and Fall*, vol. x. p. 43.

A A 2

sipated at once by the application of the maxim above stated. *What* analysis of theirs tended to establish any received principle of chemistry? *What* true doctrine concerning the differences and affinities of acids and alkalis did they teach? We need not wonder if Gibbon, whose views of the boundaries of scientific chemistry were probably very wide and indistinct, could include the arts of the Arabians within its domain; but they cannot pass the frontier of science if philosophically defined, and steadily guarded.

The judgment which we are thus led to form respecting the chemical knowledge of the middle ages, and of the Arabians in particular, may serve to measure the condition of science in other departments; for chemistry has justly been considered one of their strongest points. In botany, anatomy, zoology, optics, acoustics, we have still the same observation to make, that the steps in science which, in the order of progress, next followed what the Greeks had done, were left for the Europeans of the sixteenth and seventeenth centuries. The merits and advances of the Arabian philosophers in astronomy and pure mathematics, we have already described.

3. *Experimextal Philosophy of the Arabians.*— The estimate to which we have thus been led, of the scientific merits of the learned men of the middle ages, is much less exalted than that which has been formed by many writers; and, among the

rest, by some of our own time. But I am persuaded that any attempt to answer the questions just asked, will expose the untenable nature of the higher claims which have been advanced in favour of the Arabians. We can deliver no just decision, except we will consent to use the terms of science in a strict and precise sense[2] : and if we do this, we shall find little, either in the particular · discoveries or general methods of the Arabians, which is important in the history of the Inductive Sciences.

The credit due to the Arabians for improvements in the general methods of philosophizing, is a more difficult question; and cannot be discussed at length by us, till we examine the history of such methods in the abstract, which, in the present work, it is not our intention to do. But we may observe, that we cannot agree with those who rank their

[2] If I might take the liberty of criticizing an author who has given a very interesting view of the period in question (*Mahometanism Unveiled*, by the Rev. Charles Forster, 1829), I would remark, that in his work this caution is perhaps too little observed. Thus, he says, in speaking of Alhazen (vol. ii. p. 270), "the theory of the telescope may be found in the work of this astronomer;" and of another, " the uses of magnifying glasses and telescopes, and the principle of their construction, are explained in the Great Work of (Roger) Bacon, with a truth and clearness which have commanded universal admiration." Such phrases would be much too strong, even if used respecting the optical doctrines of Kepler, which were yet incomparably more true and clear than those of Bacon. To employ such language, in such cases, is to deprive such terms as *theory* and *principles* of all meaning.

merits high in this respect. We have already seen, that their minds were completely devoured by the worst habits of the stationary period,—mysticism and commentation. They followed their Greek leaders, for the most part, with abject servility, and with only that kind of acuteness and independent speculation which the commentator's vocation implies. And in their choice of the standard subjects of their studies, they fixed upon those works, the Physics of Aristotle, which have never promoted the progress of science, except so far as they incited men to refute them; an effect which they never produced on the Arabians. That the Arabian astronomers made some advances beyond the Greeks, we have already stated: the two great instances are, the discovery of the Motion of the Sun's Apogee by Albategnius, and the discovery (recently brought to light) of the existence of the Moon's Second Inequality, by Aboul Wefa. But we cannot but observe in how different a manner they treated these discoveries, from that with which Hipparchus or Ptolemy would have done. The Variation of the moon, in particular, instead of being incorporated into the system by means of an Epicycle, as Ptolemy had done with the Evection, was allowed, almost immediately, so far as we can judge, to fall into neglect and oblivion: so little were the learned Arabians prepared to take their lessons from observation as well as books. That in many subjects they made experiments, may easily be allowed:

there never was a period of the earth's history, and least of all a period of commerce and manufactures, luxury and art, medicine and engineering, in which were not going on innumerable processes, which may be termed experiments; and, in addition to these, the Arabians adopted the pursuit of alchemy, and the love of exotic plants and animals. But so far from their being, as has been maintained[3], a people whose "experimental intellect" fitted them to form sciences which the "abstract intellect" of the Greeks failed in producing, it rather appears, that several of the sciences which the Greeks had founded, were never even comprehended by the Arabians. I do not know any evidence that these pupils ever attained to understand the real principles of mechanics, hydrostatics, and harmonics, which their masters had established. At any rate, when these sciences again came progressive, Europe had to start where Europe had stopped. There is no Arabian name which any one has thought of interposing between Archimedes the ancient, and Stevinus and Galileo the moderns.

4. *Roger Bacon.*—There is one writer of the middle ages, on whom much stress has been laid, and who was certainly a most remarkable person. Roger Bacon's works are not only so far beyond his age in the knowledge which they contain, but so different from the temper of the times, in his assertion of the supremacy of experiment, and in his

[3] *Mahometanism Unveiled,* ii. 271.

contemplation of the future progress of knowledge, that it is difficult to conceive how such a character could then exist. That he received much of his knowledge from Arabic writers, there can be no doubt; for they were in his time the repositories of all traditionary knowledge. But that he derived from them his disposition to shake off the authority of Aristotle, to maintain the importance of experiment, and to look upon knowledge as in its infancy, I cannot believe, because I have not myself hit upon, nor seen quoted by others, any passages in which Arabian writers express such a disposition. On the other hand, we do find in European writers, in the authors of Greece and Rome, the solid sense, the bold and hopeful spirit, which suggest such tendencies. We have already seen that Aristotle asserts, as distinctly as words can express, that all knowledge must depend on observation, and that science must be collected from facts by induction. We have seen, too, that the Roman writers, and Seneca in particular, speak with an enthusiastic confidence of the progress which science must make in the course of ages. When Roger Bacon holds similar language in the thirteenth century, the resemblance is probably rather a sympathy of character, than a matter of direct derivation; but I know of nothing which proves even so much as this sympathy with regard to Arabian philosophers.

A good deal has been said of late of the coincidences between his views, and those of his great

namesake in later times, Francis Bacon[4]. The resemblances consist mainly in such points as I have
just noticed; and we cannot but acknowledge, that
many of the expressions of the Franciscan friar
remind us of the large thoughts and lofty phrases
of the philosophical chancellor. How far the one
can be considered as having anticipated the method of the other, we shall examine more advantageously, when we come to consider what the
character and effect of Francis Bacon's works really
are (N).

5. *Architecture of the Middle Ages.*—But though
we are thus compelled to disallow several of the
claims which have been put forwards in support of
the scientific character of the middle ages, there are
two points in which we may, I conceive, really trace
the progress of scientific ideas among them; and
which, therefore, may be considered as the prelude
to the period of discovery. I mean their practical
architecture, and their architectural treatises.

In a previous chapter of this book, we have
endeavoured to explain how the indistinctness of
ideas, which attended the decline of the Roman empire, appears in the forms of their architecture;—
in the disregard, which the decorative construction
exhibits, of the necessary mechanical conditions of
support. The original scheme of Greek ornamental
architecture, had been horizontal masses resting on

---

[4] Hallam's *Middle Ages*, iii. 549. Forster's *Mahom. U.* ii.
313.

vertical columns: when the arch was introduced by the Romans, it was concealed, or kept in state of subordination: and the lateral support which it required was supplied latently, masked by some artifice. But the struggle between the *mechanical* and the *decorative construction*[5], ended in the complete disorganization of the classical style. The inconsistencies and extravagancies, of which we have noticed the occurrence, were results and indications of the fall of good architecture. The elements of the ancient system had lost all principle of connexion and regard to rule. Building became not only a mere art, but an art exercised by masters without skill, and without feeling for real beauty(o).

When, after this deep decline, architecture rose again, as it did in the twelfth and succeeding centuries, in the exquisitely beautiful and skilful forms of the Gothic style, what was the nature of the change which had taken place, so far as it bears upon the progress of science? It was this:—the idea of true mechanical relations in an edifice had been revived in men's minds, as far as was requisite for the purposes of art and beauty: and this, though a very different thing from the possession of the idea as an element of speculative science, was the proper preparation for that acquisition. The notion of support and stability again became conspicuous in the decorative construction, and universal in the

[5] See Mr. Willis's admirable *Remarks on the Architecture of the Middle Ages*, chap. ii.

forms of building. The eye which, looking for beauty in definite and significant relations of parts, is never satisfied except the weights appear to be duly supported[6], was again gratified. Architecture threw off its barbarous characters : a new decorative construction was matured, not thwarting and controlling, but assisting and harmonizing with the mechanical construction. All the ornamental parts were made to enter into the apparent construction. Every member, almost every moulding, became a sustainer of weight; and by the multiplicity of props assisting each other, and the consequent subdivision of weight, the eye was satisfied of the stability of the structure, notwithstanding the curiously-slender forms of the separate parts. The arch and the vault, no longer trammelled by an incompatible system of decoration, but favoured by more tractable forms, were only limited by the skill of the builders. Everything showed that, practically at least, men possessed and applied, with steadiness and pleasure, the idea of mechanical pressure and support.

The possession of this idea, as a principle of art, led, in the course of time, to its speculative developement as the foundation of a science; and thus architecture prepared the way for mechanics. But this advance required several centuries. The inter-

---

[6] Willis, pp. 15—21. I have throughout this description of the formation of the Gothic style availed myself of Mr. Willis's well-chosen expressions.

val between the admirable cathedrals of Salisbury, Amiens, Cologne, and the mechanical treatises of Stevinus, is not less than three hundred years. During this time, men were advancing towards science, but in the meantime, and perhaps from the very beginning of the time, art had begun to decline. The buildings of the fifteenth century, erected when the principles of mechanical support were just on the verge of being enunciated in general terms, exhibit those principles with a far less impressive simplicity and elegance than those of the thirteenth. We may hereafter inquire whether we find any other examples to countenance the belief, that the formation of Science is commonly accompanied by the decline of Art.

The leading principle of the style of the Gothic edifices was, not merely that the weights were supported, but that they were seen to be so; and that not only the mechanical relations of the larger masses, but of the smaller members also, were displayed. Hence we cannot admit as an origin or anticipation of the Gothic, a style in which this principle is not manifested. I do not see, in any of the representations of the early Arabic buildings, that distribution of weights to supports, and that mechanical consistency of parts, which elevates them above the character of barbarous architecture. Their masses are broken into innumerable members, without subordination or meaning, in a manner suggested apparently by caprice and the love of the marvellous. " In the construction of their mosques, it was a favourite artifice of the Arabs to sustain immense and ponderous masses of stone by the support of pillars so slender, that the incumbent weight seemed, as it were, suspended in the air by an invisible hand[7]." This pleasure in the contemplation of apparent impossibilities is a very general disposition among mankind; but it appears to belong to the infancy, rather than the maturity of intellect. On the other hand, the pleasure in the contemplation of what is clear, the craving for a thorough insight into the reasons of things, which marks the European mind, is the temper which leads to science.

6. *Treatises on Architecture.*—No one who has attended to the architecture which prevailed in England, France, and Germany, from the twelfth to the fifteenth century, so far as to comprehend its beauty, harmony, consistency, and uniformity, even in the minutest parts and most obscure relations, can look upon it otherwise than as a remarkably connected and definite artificial system. Nor can we doubt that it was exercised by a class of artists who formed themselves by laborious study and practice, and by communication with each other. There must have been bodies of masters and of scholars, discipline, traditions, precepts of art. How these associated artists diffused themselves over Europe, and whether history enables us to trace them in a distinct form, I shall not here discuss.

[7] *Mahometanism Unveiled,* ii. 255.

But the existence of a course of instruction, and of a body of rules of practice, is proved beyond dispute by the great series of European cathedrals and churches, so nearly identical in their general arrangements, and in their particular details. The question then occurs, have these rules and this system of instruction anywhere been committed to writing? Can we, by such evidence, trace the progress of the scientific idea, of which we see the working in these buildings?

We are not to be surprized, if, during the most flourishing and vigorous period of the art of the middle ages, we find none of its precepts in books. Art has, in all ages and countries, been taught and transmitted by practice and verbal tradition, not by writing. It is only in our own times, that the thought occurs as familiar, of committing to books all that we wish to preserve and convey. And, even in our own times, most of the Arts are learned far more by practice, and by intercourse with practitioners, than by reading. Such is the case, not only with Manufactures and Handicrafts, but with the Fine Arts, with Engineering, and even yet, with that art, Building, of which we are now speaking.

We are not, therefore, to wonder, if we have no treatises on Architecture belonging to the great period of the Gothic masters;—or if it appears to have required some other incitement and some other help, besides their own possession of their practical skill, to lead them to shape into a literary form the precepts of the art which they knew so well how to exercise :—or if, when they did write on such subjects, they seem, instead of delivering their own sound practical principles, to satisfy themselves with pursuing some of the frivolous notions and speculations which were then current in the world of letters.

Such appears to be the case. The earliest treatises on Architecture come before us under the form which the commentatorial spirit of the middle ages inspired. They are translations of Vitruvius, with annotations. In some of these, particularly that of Cesare Cesariano, published at Como, in 1521, we see, in a very curious manner, how the habit of assuming that, in every department of literature, the ancients must needs be their masters, led these writers to subordinate the members of their own architecture to the precepts of the Roman author. We have Gothic shafts, mouldings, and arrangements, given as parallelisms to others, which profess to represent the Roman style, but which are, in fact, examples of that mixed manner which is called the style of the *cinque cento* by the Italians, of the *renaissance* by the French, and which is commonly included in our *Elizabethan*. But in the early architectural works, besides the superstitions and mistaken erudition which thus choked the growth of real architectural doctrines, another of the peculiar elements of the middle ages comes into view ;—its mysticism. The dimensions and positions of the various parts of edifices and of their members, are determined by drawing triangles, squares, circles, and other figures, in such a manner as to bound them : and to these geometrical figures were assigned many abstruse significations. The plan and the front of the Cathedral at Milan are ·thus represented in Cesariano's work, bounded and subdivided by various equilateral triangles ; and it is easy to see, in the earnestness with which he points out these relations, the evidence of a fanciful and mystical turn of thought[8].

We thus find erudition and mysticism take the place of much of that developement of the architectural principles of the middle ages which would be so interesting to us. Still, however, these works are by no means without their value. Indeed many of the arts appear to flourish not at all the worse, for being treated in a manner somewhat mystical ; and it may easily be, that the relations of geometrical figures, for which fantastical reasons are given, may really involve principles of beauty or stability. But independently of this, we

[8] The plan which he has given, fol. 14, he has entitled " Ichnographia Fundamenti sacræ Ædis baricephalæ, Germanico more, à Trigono ac Pariquadrato perstructa, uti etiam ea quæ nunc Milani videtur."

The work of Cesariano was translated into German by Gualter Rivius, and published at Nuremberg, in 1548, under the title of *Vitruvius Teutsch,* with copies of the Italian diagrams. A few years ago, in an article in the *Wiener Jahrbücher,* (Oct.—Dec., 1821), the reviewer maintained, on the authority of the diagrams in Rivius's book, that Gothic architecture had its origin in Germany, and not in England.·

find, in the best works of the architects of all ages (including engineers), evidence that the true idea of mechanical pressure exists among them more distinctly than among men in general, although it may not be developed in a scientific form. This is true up to our own time, and the arts which such persons cultivate could not be successfully exercised if it were not so. Hence the writings of architects and engineers during the middle ages do really form a prelude to the works on scientific mechanics. Vitruvius, in his *Architecture*, and Julius Frontinus, who, under Vespasian, wrote *On Aqueducts*, of which he was superintendent, have transmitted to us the principal part of what we know respecting the practical mechanics and hydraulics of the Romans. In modern times the series is resumed. The early writers on architecture are also writers on engineering, and often on hydrostatics: for example, Leonardo da Vinci wrote on the equilibrium of water. And thus we are led up to Stevinus of Bruges, who was engineer to Prince Maurice of Nassau, and inspector of the dykes in Holland; and in whose work, on the processes of his art, is contained the first clear modern statement of the scientific principles of hydrostatics.

Having thus explained both the obstacles and the prospects which the middle ages offered to the progress of science, I now proceed to the history of the progress, when it was once again resumed.

NOTES TO BOOK IV.

(κ.) p. 268. Since the publication of my first edition, an account of Algazel or Algazzali and his works has been published under the title of *Essai sur les Ecoles Philosophiques chez les Arabes, et notamment sur la Doctrine d'Algazzali*, par August Schmölders. Paris. 1842. From this book it appears that Degerando's account of Algazzali is correct, when he says[1] that "his skepticism seems to have essentially for its object to destroy all systems of merely rational theology, in order to open an indefinite career, not only to faith guided by revelation, but also to the free exaltation of a mystical enthusiasm." It is remarked by Dr. Schmölders, following M. de Hammer-Purgstall, that the title of the work referred to in the text ought rather to be *Mutual Refutation of the Philosophers :* and that its object is to shew that Philosophy consists of a mass of systems, each of which overturns the others. The work of Algazzali which Dr. Schmölders has published, *On the Errours of Sects, &c.*, contains a kind of autographical account of the way in which the author was led to his views. He does not reject the truths of science, but he condemns the mental habits which are caused by laying too much stress upon science. Religious men, he says, are, by such a course, led to reject all science, even what relates to eclipses of the moon and sun ; and men of science are led to hate religion[2].

---

[1] *Hist. Comp.* iv. p. 227.   [2] *Essai*, p. 33.

(L.) p. 272. It appears however that scriptural arguments were found on the other side. St. Jerome says[3], speaking of the two cherubims with four faces, seen by the prophet, and the interpretation of the vision; "Alii vero qui philosophorum stultam sequunter sapientiam, duo hemispheria in duobus templi cherubim, nos et antipodes, quasi supinos et cadentes homines suspicantur."

(M.) p. 305. The reader will find an interesting view of the *School of Alexandria*, in M. Barthelemy Saint-Hilaire's *Rapport* on the *Memoires* sent to the Academy of Moral and Political Sciences at Paris, in consequence of its having, in 1841, proposed this as the subject of a prize, which was awarded in 1844. M. Saint-Hilaire has prefixed to this Rapport a dissertation on the Mysticism of that school. He, however, uses the term *Mysticism* in a wider sense than my purpose, which regarded mainly the bearing of the doctrines of this school upon the progress of the Inductive Sciences, led me to do. Although he finds much to admire in the Alexandrian philosophy, he declares that they were incapable of treating scientific questions. The extent to which this is true is well illustrated by the extract which he gives from Plotinus, on the question, "Why objects appear smaller in proportion as they are more distant." Plotinus denies that the reason of this is that the angles of vision become smaller. His reason for this denial is curious enough. If it were so, he says, how could the heaven appear smaller than it is, since it occupies the whole of the visual angle?

(N.) p. 361. In the *Philosophy of the Inductive Sciences*, I have given an account at considerable length

---

[3] *Comm. in Ezech.*, I. 6.

of Roger Bacon's mode of treating Arts and Sciences; and have also compared more fully his philosophy with that of Francis Bacon; and I have given a view of the bearing of this latter upon the progress of Science in modern times. *See Phil. Ind. Sc.* B. xii. chaps. 7 and 11.

(o.) p. 362. Since the publication of my first edition, Mr. Willis has shown that much of the "mason-craft" of the middle ages consisted in the geometrical methods by which the artists wrought out of the blocks the complex forms of their decorative system.

To the general indistinctness of speculative notions on mechanical subjects prevalent in the middle ages, there may have been some exceptions, and especially so long as there were readers of Archimedes. Boëtius had translated the mechanical works of Archimedes into Latin, as we learn from the enumeration of his works by his friend Cassiodorus (*Variar.* lib. i. cap. 45), "*Mechanicum* etiam Archimedem latialem siculis reddidisti." But *Mechanicus* was used in those times rather for one skilled in the art of constructing wonderful machines than in the speculative theory of them. The letter from which the quotation is taken is sent by King Theodoric to Boëtius, to urge him to send the king a water-clock.

BOOK V.

HISTORY

OF

FORMAL ASTRONOMY

AFTER THE STATIONARY PERIOD.

. . . Cyclopum educta caminis
Mænia conspicio, atque adverso fornice portas.
.   .   .   .   .

His demum exactis, perfecto munere Divæ,
Devenere locos lætos et amæna vireta
Fortunatorum nemorum sedesque beatas.
Largior hic campos æther et lumine vestit
Purpureo : solemque suum, sua sidera norunt.

VIRGIL, *Æn.* vi. 630.

They leave at length the nether gloom, and stand
Before the portals of a better land :
To happier plains they come, and fairer groves,
The seats of those whom heaven, benignant, loves ;
A brighter day, a bluer ether, spreads
Its lucid depths above their favoured heads ;
And, purged from mists that veil our earthly skies,
Shine suns and stars unseen by mortal eyes.

INTRODUCTION.

Of Formal and Physical Astronomy.

WE have thus rapidly traced the causes of the almost complete blank which the history of physical science offers, from the decline of the Roman empire, for a thousand years. Along with the breaking up of the ancient forms of society, were broken up the ancient energy of thinking, the clearness of idea, and steadiness of intellectual action. This mental declension produced a servile admiration for the genius of the better periods, and thus, the spirit of Commentation: Christianity established the claim of truth to govern the world; and this principle, misinterpreted and combined with the ignorance and servility of the times, gave rise to the Dogmatic System: and the love of speculation, finding no secure and permitted path on solid ground, went off into the regions of Mysticism.

The causes which produced the inertness and blindness of the stationary period of human knowledge, began at last to yield to the influence of the principles which tended to progression. The indistinctness of thought, which was the original feature in the decline of sound knowledge, was in a measure remedied by the steady cultivation of pure mathematics and astronomy, and by the progress of inventions in the arts, which call out and fix the distinctness of our conceptions of the relations of natural phenomena. As men's minds became clear, they became less servile: the perception of the nature of truth drew men away from controversies about mere opinion; when they saw distinctly the relations of *things*, they ceased to give their whole attention to what had been *said* concerning them; and thus, as science rose into view, the spirit of commentation lost its sway. And when men came to feel what it was to think for themselves on subjects of science, they soon rebelled against the right of others to impose opinions upon them. When they threw off their blind admiration for the ancients, they were disposed to cast away also their passive obedience to the ancient system of doctrines. When they were no longer inspired by the spirit of commentation, they were no longer submissive to the dogmatism of the schools. When they began to feel that they could discover truths, they felt also a persuasion of a right and a growing will so to do.

Thus the revived clearness of ideas, which made its appearance at the revival of letters, brought on a struggle with the authority, intellectual and civil, of the established schools of philosophy. This clearness of idea showed itself, in the first instance, in Astronomy, and was embodied in the system of Copernicus; but the contest did not come to a crisis till a century later, in the time of Galileo and other disciples of the new doctrine. It is our present business to trace the principles of this series of events in the history of philosophy.

I do not profess to write a history of Astronomy, any further than is necessary in order to exhibit the principles on which the progression of . science proceeds; and, therefore, I neglect subordinate persons and occurrences, in order to bring into view the leading features of great changes. Now in the introduction of the Copernican system into general acceptation, two leading views operated upon men's minds; the consideration of the system as exhibiting the apparent motions of the universe, and the consideration of this system with reference to its causes;—the *formal* and the *physical* aspect of the Theory;—the relations of Space and Time, and the relations of Force and Matter. These two divisions of the subject were at first not clearly separated; the second was long mixed, in a manner very dim and obscure, with the first, without appearing as a distinct subject of attention; but at last it was extricated and treated in a manner suitable to its nature. The views of Copernicus rested mainly on the formal condition of the universe, the relations of space and time; but Kepler, Galileo, and others, were led, by controversies and other causes, to give a gradually increasing attention to the physical relations of the heavenly bodies; an impulse was given to the study of Mechanics (the Doctrine of Motion,) which became very soon an important and extensive science; and in no long period, the discoveries of Kepler, suggested by a vague but intense belief in the physical connexion of the parts of the universe, led to the decisive and sublime generalizations of Newton.

The distinction of *formal* and *physical* Astronomy thus becomes necessary, in order to treat clearly of the discussions which the propounding of the Copernican theory occasioned. But it may be observed that, besides this great change, Astronomy made very great advances in the same path which we have already been tracing, namely, the determination of the quantities and laws of the celestial motions, in so far as they were exhibited by the ancient theories, or might be represented by obvious modifications of those theories. I speak of new Inequalities, new Phenomena, such as Copernicus, Galileo, and Tycho Brahe discovered. As, however, these were very soon referred to the Copernican rather than the Ptolemaic hypothesis, they may be considered as developements rather of the new than of the old Theory; and I shall, therefore, treat of them, agreeably to the plan of the former part, as the sequel of the Copernican Induction.

CHAPTER I.

PRELUDE TO THE INDUCTIVE EPOCH OF COPERNICUS.

THE Doctrine of Copernicus, that the Sun is the true center of the celestial motions, depends primarily upon the consideration that such a supposition explains very simply and completely all the obvious appearances of the heavens. In order to see that it does this, nothing more is requisite than a distinct conception of the nature of Relative Motion, and a knowledge of the principal Astronomical Phenomena. There was, therefore, no reason why such a doctrine might not be *discovered*, that is, suggested as a theory plausible at first sight, long before the time of Copernicus; or rather, it was impossible that this guess, among others, should not be propounded as a solution of the appearances of the heavens. We are not, therefore, to be surprized if we find, in the earliest times of astronomy, and at various succeeding periods, such a system spoken of by astronomers, and maintained by some as true, though rejected by the majority, and by the principal writers.

When we look back at such a difference of opinion, having in our minds, as we unavoidably have, the clear and irresistible considerations by which the Copernican Doctrine is established *for us*, it is difficult for us not to attribute superior sagacity and candour to those who held that side of the question, and to imagine those who clung to the Ptolemaic Hypothesis to have been blind and prejudiced;—incapable of seeing the beauty of simplicity and symmetry, or indisposed to resign established errours, and to accept novel and comprehensive truths. Yet in judging thus, we are probably ourselves influenced by prejudices arising from the knowledge and received opinions of our own times. For is it, in reality, clear that, before the time of Copernicus, the *Heliocentric* Theory (that which places the center of the celestial motions in the Sun,) had a claim to assent so decidedly superior to the Geocentric Theory, which places the Earth in the center? What is the basis of the heliocentric theory?—That the *relative* motions are *the same*, on that and on the other supposition. So far, therefore, the two hypotheses are exactly on the same footing. But, it is urged, on the heliocentric side we have the advantage of simplicity:—true; but we have, on the other side, the testimony of our senses; that is, the geocentric doctrine is the obvious and spontaneous interpretation of the appearances. Both these arguments, *simplicity* on the one side, and *obviousness* on the other, are vague, and we may venture to say, both indecisive. We cannot establish any strong preponderance of probability in favour of the former doctrine, without going much further into the arguments of the question.

Nor, when we speak of the superior *simplicity* of the Copernican theory, must we forget, that though this theory has undoubtedly, in this respect, a great advantage over the Ptolemaic, yet that the Copernican system itself is very complex, when it undertakes to account, as the Ptolemaic did, for the inequalities of the motions of the sun, moon, and planets; and that, in the hands of Copernicus, it retained a large share of the eccentrics and epicycles of its predecessor, and, in some parts, with increased machinery. The heliocentric theory, without these appendages, would not approach the Ptolemaic, in the accurate explanation of facts; and as those who had placed the sun in the center had never, till the time of Copernicus, shown how the inequalities were to be explained on that supposition, we may assert that after the promulgation of the theory of eccentrics and epicycles on the geocentric hypothesis, there was no *published* heliocentric theory which could bear a comparison with that hypothesis.

It is true, that all the contrivances of epicycles, and the like, by which the geocentric hypothesis was made to represent the phenomena, were susceptible of an easy adaptation to a heliocentric method, *when a good mathematician had once proposed to himself the problem;* and this was precisely what Copernicus undertook and executed.

But, till the appearance of his work, the heliocentric system had never come before the world except as a hasty and imperfect hypothesis; which bore a favourable comparison with the phenomena, so long as their general features only were known; but which had been completely thrown into the shade by the labour and intelligence bestowed upon the Hipparchian or Ptolemaic theories by a long series of great astronomers of all civilized countries.

But, though the astronomers who, before Copernicus, held the heliocentric opinion, cannot, on any good grounds, be considered as much more enlightened than their opponents, it is curious to trace the early and repeated manifestations of this view of the universe. The distinct assertion of the heliocentric theory among the Greeks is an evidence of the clearness of their thoughts, and the vigour of their minds; and it is a proof of the feebleness and servility of intellect in the stationary period, that, till the period of Copernicus, no one was found to try the fortune of this hypothesis, modified according to the improved astronomical knowledge of the time.

The most ancient of the Greek philosophers to whom the ancients ascribe the heliocentric doctrine, is Pythagoras; but Diogenes Laertius makes Philolaus, one of the followers of Pythagoras, the first author of this doctrine. We learn from Archimedes, that it was held by his contemporary, Aristarchus. " Aristarchus of Samos," says he[1], makes this supposition,—that the fixed stars and the sun remain at rest, and that the earth revolves round the sun in a circle." Plutarch[2] asserts that this, which was only a hypothesis in the hands of Aristarchus, was *proved* by Seleucus; but we may venture to say that, at that time, no such proof was possible. Aristotle had recognized the existence of this doctrine by arguing against it. "All things," says he[3], "tend to the center of the earth, and rest there, and therefore the whole mass of the earth cannot rest except there." Ptolemy had in like manner argued against the diurnal motion of the earth: such a revolution would, he urged, disperse into surrounding space all the loose parts of the earth. Yet he allowed that such a supposition would facilitate the explanation of some phenomena. Cicero appears to make Mercury and Venus revolve about the sun, as does Martianus Capella at a later period; and Seneca says[4], it is a worthy subject of contemplation, whether the earth be at rest or in motion: but at this period, as we may see from Seneca himself, that habit of intellect which was requisite for the solution of such a question, had been succeeded by indistinct views, and rhetorical forms of speech. If there were any good mathematicians and good observers at this period, they were employed in cultivating and verifying the Hipparchian theory.

[1] Archim. Arenarius. [2] *Quest. Plat.* Delamb. A. A. vi.
[3] Copernic. i. 7. [4] *Quest. Nat.* vii. 2.

Next to the Greeks, the Indians appear to have possessed that original vigour and clearness of thought, from which true science springs. It is remarkable that the Indians, also, had their heliocentric theorists. Aryabatta[5], (A.D. 1322), and other astronomers of that country, are said to have advocated the doctrine of the earth's revolution on its axis; which opinion, however, was rejected by subsequent philosophers among the Hindoos.

Some writers have thought that the heliocentric doctrine was *derived* by Pythagoras and other European philosophers, from some of the oriental nations. This opinion, however, will appear to have little weight, if we consider that the heliocentric hypothesis, in the only shape in which the ancients knew it, was too obvious to require much teaching; that it did not and could not, so far as we know, receive any additional strength from anything which the oriental nations could teach; and that each astronomer was induced to adopt or reject it, not by any information which a master could give him, but by his love of geometrical simplicity on the one hand, or the prejudices of sense on the other. Real science, depending on a clear view of the relation of phenomena to general theoretical ideas, cannot be communicated in the way of secret and exclusive traditions, like the mysteries of certain arts and crafts. If the philosopher do not *see* that the theory is true, he is little the better for

[5] Lib. U. K. *Hist. Ast.* p. 11.

having heard or read the words which assert its truth.

It is impossible, therefore, for us to assent to those views which would discover in the heliocentric doctrines of the ancients, traces of a more profound astronomy than any which they have transmitted to us. Those doctrines were merely the plausible conjectures of men with sound geometrical notions; but they were never extended so as to embrace the details of the existing astronomical knowledge; and perhaps we may say, that the analysis of the phenomena into the arrangements of the Ptolemaic system, was so much more obvious than any other, that it must necessarily come first, in order to form an introduction to the Copernican.

The true foundation of the heliocentric theory for the ancients, was, as we have intimated, its perfect geometrical consistency with the general features of the phenomena, and its simplicity. But it was unlikely that the human mind would be content to consider the subject under this strict and limited aspect alone. In its eagerness for wide speculative views, it naturally looked out for other and vaguer principles of connexion and relation. Thus, as it had been urged in favour of the geocentric doctrine, that the heaviest body must be in the center, it was maintained, as a leading recommendation of the opposite opinion, that it placed the Fire, the noblest element, in the Center of the Universe. The authority of mythological ideas was

C c

called in on both sides to support these views. Numa, as Plutarch[6] informs us, built a circular temple over the ever-burning Fire of Vesta; typifying, not the earth, but the Universe, which, according to the Pythagoreans, has the Fire seated at its Center. The same writer, in another of his works, makes one of his interlocutors say, "Only, my friend, do not bring me before a court of law on a charge of impiety; as Cleanthes said, that Aristarchus the Samian ought to be tried for impiety, because he removed that homestead of the universe." This, however, seems to have been intended as a pleasantry.

The prevalent physical views, and the opinions concerning the causes of the motions of the parts of the universe, were scarcely more definite than those concerning the relations of the four elements, till Galileo had founded the true doctrine of motion. Though, therefore, arguments on this part of the subject were the most important part of the controversy after Copernicus, the force of such arguments was at his time almost balanced. Even if more had been known on such subjects, the arguments would not have been conclusive: for instance, the vast mass of the heavens, which is commonly urged as a reason why the heavens do not move round the earth, would not make such a motion impossible; and, on the other hand, the motions of bodies at the earth's surface, which were alleged as inconsistent with its

---

[6] *De Facie in Orbe Lunæ*, 6.

motion, did not really disprove such an opinion. But according to the state of the science of motion before Copernicus, all reasonings from such principles were utterly vague and obscure.

We must not omit to mention a modern who preceded Copernicus, in the assertion at least of the heliocentric doctrine. This was Nicholas of Cusa, (a village near Treves,) a cardinal and bishop, who, in the first half of the fifteenth century, was very eminent as a divine and mathematician; and who in a work, *De Doctâ Ignorantiâ*, propounded the doctrine of the motion of the earth; more, however, as a paradox than as a reality. We cannot consider this as any distinct anticipation of a profound and consistent view of the truth.

᠂ We shall now examine further the promulgation of the Heliocentric System by Copernicus, and its consequences.

CHAPTER II.

INDUCTION OF COPERNICUS.—THE HELIOCENTRIC
THEORY·ASSERTED ON FORMAL GROUNDS.

IT will be recollected that the *formal* are opposed to the *physical* grounds of a theory; the former term indicating that it gives a satisfactory account of the relations of the phenomena in Space and Time, that is, of the Motions themselves; while the latter expression implies further that we include in our explanation the Causes of the motions, the laws of Force and Matter. The strongest of the considerations by which Copernicus was led to invent and adopt his system of the universe were of the former kind. He was dissatisfied, he says, in his Preface addressed to the Pope, with the want of symmetry in the Eccentric Theory, as it prevailed in his days; and weary of the uncertainty of the mathematical traditions. He then sought through all the works of philosophers, whether any had held opinions concerning the motions of the world, different from those received in the established mathematical schools. He found, in ancient authors, accounts of Philolaus and others, who had asserted the motion of the earth. "Then," he adds, " I, too, began to meditate concerning the motion of the earth : and though it appeared an absurd opinion, yet since I knew that, in previous times, others had been allowed the privilege of feigning what circles they chose, in order to explain the phenomena, I conceived that I also might take the liberty of trying whether, on the supposition of the earth's motion, it was possible to find better explanations than the ancient ones, of the revolutions of the celestial orbs.

"Having then assumed the motions of the earth, which are hereafter explained, by laborious and long observation I at length found, that if the motions of the other planets be compared with the revolution of the earth, not only their phenomena follow from the suppositions, but also that the several orbs, and the whole system, are so connected in order and magnitude, that no one part can be transposed without disturbing the rest, and introducing confusion into the whole universe."

Thus the satisfactory explanation of the apparent motions of the planets, and the simplicity and symmetry of the system, were the grounds on which Copernicus adopted his theory; as the craving for these qualities was the feeling which led him to seek for a new theory. It is manifest that in this, as in other cases of discovery, a clear and steady possession of abstract Ideas, and an aptitude in comprehending real Facts under these general conceptions, must have been leading characters in the discoverer's mind. He must have had a good geometrical head, and great astronomical know-

ledge.   He must have seen, with peculiar distinctness, the consequences which flowed from his suppositions as to the relations of space and time,—the
apparent motions which resulted from the assumed
real ones; and he must also have known well all
the irregularities of the apparent motions for which
he had to account.   We find indications of these
qualities in his expressions.   A steady and calm
contemplation of the theory is what he asks for, as
the main requisite to its reception.   If you suppose
the earth to revolve and the heaven to be at rest,
you will find, he says, "*si serio animadvertas*," if
you think steadily, that the apparent diurnal motion
will follow.   And after alleging his reasons for his
system, he says[1], "We are, therefore, not ashamed
to confess, that the whole of the space within the
orbit of the moon, along with the center of the
earth, moves round the sun in a year among the
other planets; the magnitude of the world being so
great, that the distance of the earth from the sun
has no apparent magnitude when compared with
the sphere of the fixed stars."   "All which things,
though they be difficult and almost inconceivable,
and against the opinion of the majority, yet, in the
sequel, by God's favour, we will make clearer than
the sun, at least to those who are not ignorant
of mathematics."

It will easily be understood, that since the ancient

[1] Nicolai Copernici Torinensis *de Revolutionibus Orbium
Cœlestium.*   Norimbergæ. M.D.XLIII. p. 9.

geocentric hypothesis ascribed to the planets those motions which were apparent only, and which really arose from the motion of the earth round the sun in the new hypothesis, the latter scheme must much simplify the planetary theory. Kepler[2] enumerates eleven motions of the Ptolemaic system, which are at once exterminated and rendered unnecessary by the new system. Still, as the real motions, both of the earth and the planets, are unequable, it was requisite to have some mode of representing their inequalities; and, accordingly, the ancient theory of eccentrics and epicycles was retained, so far as was requisite for this purpose. The planets revolved round the sun by means of a Deferent, and a great and small Epicycle; or else by means of an Eccentric and Epicycle, modified from Ptolemy's, for reasons which we shall shortly mention. This mode of representing the motions of the planets continued in use, till it was expelled by the discoveries of Kepler.

Besides the daily rotation of the earth on its axis, and its annual circuit about the sun, Copernicus attributed to the axis a "motion of declination," by which, during the whole annual revolution, the pole was constantly directed towards the same part of the heavens. This constancy in the absolute direction of the axis, or its moving parallel to itself, may be more correctly viewed as not indicating any separate motion. The axis continues in

---

[2] *Myst. Cosm.* cap. 1.

the same direction, because there is nothing to make it change its direction; just as a straw, lying on the surface of a cup of water, continues to point nearly in the same direction when the cup is carried round a room. And this was noticed by Copernicus's adherent, Rothman[3], a few years after the publication of the work *De Revolutionibus*. "There is no occasion," he says, in a letter to Tycho Brahe, "for the triple motion of the earth: the annual and diurnal motions suffice." This errour of Copernicus, if it be looked upon as an errour, arose from his referring the position of the axis to a limited space, which he conceived to be carried round the sun along with the earth, instead of referring it to fixed or absolute space. When, in a Planetarium, the earth is carried round the sun by being fastened to a material radius, it is requisite to give a motion to the axis by *additional* machinery, in order to enable it to *preserve* its parallelism. A similar confusion of geometrical conception, produced by a double reference to absolute space and to the center of revolution, often leads persons to dispute whether the moon, which revolves about the earth, always turning to it the same face, revolves about her axis or no.

It is also to be noticed that the precession of the equinoxes made it necessary to suppose the axis of the earth to be not exactly parallel to itself, but to deviate from that position by a slight annual

[3] Tycho. Epist. i. p. 184, A. D. 1590.

difference. Copernicus erroneously supposes the precession to be unequable; and his method of explaining this change, which is simpler than that of the ancients, becomes more simple still, when applied to the true state of the facts.

The tendencies of our speculative nature, which carry us onwards in pursuit of symmetry and rule, and which thus produced the theory of Copernicus, as they produce all theories, perpetually show their vigour by overshooting their mark. They obtain something by aiming at much more. They detect the order and connexion which exist, by imagining relations of order and connexion which have no existence.. Real discoveries are thus mixed with baseless assumptions; profound sagacity is combined with fanciful conjecture; not rarely, or in peculiar instances, but commonly, and in most cases; probably in all, if we could read the thoughts of the discoverers as we read the books of Kepler. To try wrong guesses is apparently the only way to hit upon right ones. The character of the true philosopher is, not that he never conjectures hazardously, but that his conjectures are clearly conceived and brought into rigid contact with facts. He sees and compares distinctly the ideas and the things,— the relations of his notions to each other and to phenomena. Under these conditions it is not only excusable, but necessary for him, to snatch at every semblance of general rule;—to try all promising forms of simplicity and symmetry.

Copernicus is not exempt from giving us, in his work, an example of this character of the inventive spirit.   The axiom that the celestial motions must be circular and uniform, appeared to him to have strong claims to acceptation; and his theory of the inequalities of the planetary motions is fashioned upon it.   His great desire was to apply it more rigidly than Ptolemy had done.   The time did not come for rejecting the axiom, till the observations of Tycho Brahe and the calculations of Kepler had been made.

I shall not attempt to explain, in detail, Copernicus's system of the planetary inequalities.   He retained epicycles and eccentrics, altering their centers of motion; that is, he retained what was *true* in the old system, *translating* it into his own. The peculiarities of his method consisted in making such a combination of epicycles as to supply the place of the *equant*[4], and to make all the motions equable about the centers of motion.   This device was admired for a time, till Kepler's elliptic theory expelled it, with all other forms of the theory of epicycles: but we must observe that Copernicus was aware of some of the discrepancies which belonged to that theory as it had, up to that time, been propounded.   In the case of Mercury's orbit, which is more eccentric than that of the other planets, he makes suppositions which are complex indeed, but which show his perception of the im-

[4] See p. 235.

perfection of the common theory; and he proposes a new theory of the moon, for the very reason which did at last overturn the doctrine of epicycles, namely, that the ratio of their distances from the earth at different times was inconsistent with the circular hypothesis[5].

It is obvious, that, along with his mathematical clearness of view, and his astronomical knowledge, Copernicus must have had great intellectual boldness and vigour, to conceive and fully develope a theory so different as his was, from all received doctrines. His pupil and expositor, Rheticus, says to Schener, "I beg you to have this opinion concerning that learned man, my Preceptor; that he was an ardent admirer and follower of Ptolemy; but when he was compelled by phenomena and demonstration, he thought he did well to aim at the same mark at which Ptolemy had aimed, though with a bow and shafts of a very different material from his. We must recollect what Ptolemy says, Δεῖ δ᾽ ἐλευθέρον εἶναι τῇ γνώμῃ τὸν μέλλοντα φιλοσοφεῖν. 'He who is to follow philosophy must be a freeman in mind.'" Rheticus then goes on to defend his master from the charge of disrespect to the ancients: "That temper," he says, "is alien from the disposition of every good man, and most especially from the spirit of philosophy, and from no one more utterly than from my Preceptor. He

[5] *De Rev.* iv. c. 2.

was very far from rashly rejecting the opinions of ancient philosophers, except for weighty reasons and irresistible facts, through any love of novelty. His years, his gravity of character, his excellent learning, his magnanimity and nobleness of spirit, are very far from having any liability to such a temper, which belongs either to youth, or to ardent and light tempers, or to those τῶν μέγα φρονούντων ἐπὶ θεωρίᾳ μικρῇ, 'who think much of themselves and know little,' as Aristotle says." Undoubtedly this deference for the great men of the past, joined with the talent of seizing the spirit of their methods when the letter of their theories is no longer tenable, is the true mental constitution of discoverers.

Besides the intellectual energy which was requisite in order to construct a system of doctrines so novel as those of Copernicus, some courage was necessary to the publication of such opinions; certain, as they were, to be met, to a great extent, by rejection and dispute, and perhaps by charges of heresy and mischievous tendency. This last danger, however, must not be judged so great as we might infer from the angry controversies and acts of authority which occurred in Galileo's time. The Dogmatism of the stationary period, which identified the cause of philosophical and religious truth, had not yet distinctly felt itself attacked by the advance of physical knowledge; and therefore had not begun to look with alarm on such movements. Still, the claims of Scripture and of ecclesiastical authority were asserted as paramount on all subjects; and it was obvious that many persons would be disquieted or offended, with the new interpretation of many scriptural expressions, which the true theory would make necessary. This evil Copernicus appears to have foreseen; and this and other causes long withheld him from publication. He was himself an ecclesiastic; and, perhaps by the patronage of his maternal uncle, was prebendary of the church of St. John at Thorn, and a canon of the church of Frawenburg, in the diocese of Ermeland[6]. He was a student at Bologna, a professor of mathematics at Rome in the year 1500, and afterwards pursued his studies and observations at Fruemburg, at the mouth of the Vistula[7]. His discovery of his system must have occurred before 1507, for in 1543 he informs Pope Paulus the Third, in his dedication, that he had kept his book by him for four times the nine years recommended by Horace, and then only published it at the earnest entreaty of his friend Cardinal Schomberg, whose letter is prefixed to the work. "Though I know," he says, "that the thoughts of a philosopher do not depend on the judgment of the many, his study being to seek out truth in all things as far as that is permitted by God to human reason: yet when I considered," he adds, "how

[6] Rheticus, *Nar.* p. 94.   [7] Riccioli.

absurd my doctrine would appear, I long hesitated whether I should publish my book, or whether it were not better to follow the example of the Pythagoreans and others, who delivered their doctrines only by tradition and to friends." It will be observed that he speaks here of the opposition of the established school of Astronomers, not of Divines. The latter, indeed, he appears to consider as a less formidable danger. "If perchance," he says at the end of his preface, "there be μα-ταιολόγοι, vain babblers, who knowing nothing of mathematics, yet assume the right of judging on account of some place of Scripture perversely wrested to their purpose, and who blame and attack my undertaking; I heed them not, and look upon their judgments as rash and contemptible." He then goes on to show that the globular figure of the earth (which was, of course, at that time, an undisputed point among astronomers,) had been opposed on similar grounds by Lactantius, who, though a writer of credit in other respects, had spoken very childishly in that matter. In another epistle prefixed to the work (apparently from another hand, and asserted by Kepler[s] to be by Andreas Osiander), the reader is reminded that the hypotheses of astronomers are not necessarily asserted to be true, by those who propose them, but only to be a way of *representing* facts. We may ob-

---

[s] See the motto to Kepler's *De Stellâ Martis*.

serve that, in the time of Copernicus, when the motion of the earth had not been connected with the physical laws of matter and motion, it could not be considered so distinctly real as it necessarily was held to be in after times.

The delay of the publication of Copernicus's work brought it to the end of his life: he died in the year 1543, in which it was published. His system was, however, to a certain extent, promulgated, and his fame diffused before that time. Cardinal Schomberg, in his letter of 1536, which has been already mentioned says, "Some years ago, when I heard tidings of your merit by the constant report of all persons, my affection for you was augmented, and I congratulated the men of our time, among whom you flourish in so much honour. For I had understood that you were not only acquainted with the discoveries of ancient mathematicians, but also had formed a new system of the world, in which you teach that the earth moves, the sun occupies the lowest, and consequently, the middle place, the sphere of the fixed stars remains immoveable and fixed." He then proceeds to entreat him earnestly to publish his work. The book appears to have been written in 1539[9], and is stated to have been sent in 1540 by Achilles P. Gessarus of Feldkirch to Dr. Vogelinus of Constance, as a Palingenesia, or New Birth of Astronomy. At the end of the *De Revolutioni-*

[9] Mæstlin.

bus is the *Narratio* of Rheticus, already quoted. Rheticus, it appears, went to Copernicus for the purpose of studying his theory, and speaks of his "Preceptor" with strong admiration, as we have seen. "He appears to me," says he, "more to resemble Ptolemy than any other astronomer." This, it must be recollected, was selecting the highest known subject of comparison.

CHAPTER III.

SEQUEL TO COPERNICUS.—THE RECEPTION AND DE-
VELOPMENT OF THE COPERNICAN THEORY.

Sect. 1.—*First Reception of the Copernican Theory.*

THE theories of Copernicus made their way among astronomers, in the manner in which true astronomical theories always obtain the assent of competent judges. They led to the construction of Tables of the motion of the sun, moon, and planets, as the theories of Hipparchus and Ptolemy had done; and the verification of the doctrines was to be looked for, from the agreement of these Tables with observation, through a sufficient course of time. The work *De Revolutionibus* contains such Tables. In 1551 Reinhold improved and repub-lished Tables founded on the principles of Coper-nicus. "We owe," he says in his preface, "great obligations to Copernicus, both for his laborious observations, and for restoring the doctrine of the Motions. But though his geometry is perfect, the good old man appears to have been, at times, care-less in his numerical calculations. I have, there-fore, recalculated the whole, from a comparison of his observations with those of Ptolemy and others,

following nothing but the general plan of Copernicus's demonstrations." These Prutenic Tables were
republished in 1571 and 1585, and continued in
repute for some time; till superseded by the Rudolphine Tables of Kepler in 1627. The name
Prutenic, or Prussian, may be considered as a
tribute to the fame of Copernicus, for it shows that
his discoveries had inspired his countrymen with
the ambition of claiming a place in the literary
community of Europe. In something of the same
spirit, Rheticus wrote an *Encomium Borussiæ*
which was published along with his *Narratio*.

The Tables founded upon the Copernican system were, at first, much more generally adopted
than the heliocentric doctrine on which they were
founded. Thus Magin published at Venice, in 1587,
*New Theories of the Celestial Orbits, agreeing
with the Observations of Nicholas Copernicus.* But
in the preface, after praising Copernicus, he says,
" Since, however, he, either for the sake of showing his talents, or induced by his own reasons, has
revived the opinion of Nicetas, Aristarchus, and
others, concerning the motion of the earth, and
has disturbed the established constitution of the
world, which was a reason why many rejected, or
received with dislike, his hypotheses, I have thought
it worth while, that, rejecting the suppositions of
Copernicus, I should accommodate other causes to
his observations, and to the Prutenic tables."

· This doctrine, however, was, as we have shown,

received with favour by many persons, even before its general publication (p). We have already seen the enthusiasm with which Rheticus, who was Copernicus's pupil in the latter years of his life, speaks of him. "Thus," says he, "God has given to my excellent preceptor a reign without end; which may He vouchsafe to guide, govern, and increase, to the restoration of astronomical truth. Amen."

Of the immediate converts of the Copernican system, who adopted it before the controversy on the subject had attracted attention, I shall only add Mæstlin, and his pupil, Kepler. Mæstlin published in 1588 an *Epitome Astronomiæ*, in which the immobility of the earth is asserted; but in 1596 he edited Kepler's *Mysterium Cosmographicum*, and the *Narratio* of Rheticus; and in an epistle of his own, which he inserts, he defends the Copernican system by those physical reasonings which we shall shortly have to mention, as the usual arguments in this dispute. Kepler himself, in the outset of the work just named, says, "When I was at Tübigen, attending to Michael Mæstlin, being disturbed by the manifold inconveniences of the usual opinion concerning the world, I was so delighted with Copernicus, of whom he made great mention in his lectures, that I not only defended his opinions in our disputations of the candidates, but wrote a thesis concerning the First Motion which is produced by the revolution of the earth." This must have been in 1590.

The differences of opinion respecting the Copernican system, of which we thus see traces, led to a controversy of some length and extent. This controversy turned principally upon physical considerations, which were much more distinctly dealt with by Kepler, and others of the followers of Copernicus, than they had been by the discoverer himself. I shall, therefore, give a separate consideration to this part of the subject. It may be proper, however, in the first place, to make a few observations on the progress of the doctrine, independently of these physical speculations.

Sect. 2.—Diffusion of the Copernican Theory.

THE diffusion of the Copernican opinions in the world did not take place rapidly at first. Indeed, it was necessarily some time before the progress of observation, and of theoretical mechanics, gave the heliocentric doctrine that superiority in argument, which now makes us wonder that men should have hesitated when it was presented to them. Yet there were some speculators of this kind, who were attracted at once by the enlarged views of the universe which it opened to them. Among these was the unfortunate Giordano Bruno of Nola, who was burnt as a heretic at Rome in 1600. The heresies which led to his unhappy fate were, however, not his astronomical opinions, but a work which he published in England, and dedicated to Sir Philip

Sydney, under the title of *Spaccio della Bestia Trionfante*, and which is understood to contain a bitter satire of the Catholic religion and the papal government. Montucla conceives that, by his rashness in visiting Italy after putting forth such a work, he compelled the government to act against him. Bruno embraced the Copernican opinions at an early period, and connected with them the belief in innumerable worlds besides that which we inhabit; as also certain metaphysical or theological doctrines, which he called the Nolan Philosophy. In 1591 he published *De innumerabilibus Mundis et infigurabili, seu de Universo et Mundis*, in which he maintains that each star is a sun, about which revolve planets like our earth; but this opinion is mixed up with a large mass of baseless verbal speculations.

Giordano Bruno is a disciple of Copernicus on whom we may look with peculiar interest, since he probably had a considerable share in introducing the new opinions into England[1]. He visited this country in the reign of Queen Elizabeth, and speaks of her and of her councillors in terms of praise, which appear to show that his book was intended for English readers; though he describes the mob which was usually to be met with in the streets of London, with expressions of great disgust: " Una plebe la quale in essere irrespettevole, incivile,

[1] See Burton's *Anat. Mel.*, Pref. " Some prodigious tenet or paradox of the earth's motion," &c. " Bruno," &c.

rozza, rustica, selvatica, et male allevata, non cede ad altra che pascer possa la terra nel suo seno[2]." The work to which I refer is *La Cena de le Cenere*, and narrates what took place at a supper held on the evening of Ash Wednesday (about 1583, see p. 145 of the book), at the house of Sir Fulk Greville, in order to give " Il Nolano" an opportunity of defending his peculiar opinions. His principal antagonists are two " Dottori d' Oxonia," whom Bruno calls Nundinio and Torquato. The subject is not treated in any very masterly manner on either side; but the author makes himself have greatly the advantage not only in argument, but in temper and courtesy : and in support of his representations of " pedantesca, ostinatissima ignoranza et presunzione, mista con una rustica incivilità, che farebbe prevaricar la pazienza di Giobbe," in his opponents, he refers to a public disputation which he had held at Oxford with these doctors of theology, in presence of Prince Alasco, and many of the English nobility[3].

Among the evidences of the difficulties which still lay in the way of the reception of the Copernican system, we may notice Bacon, who, as is well known, constantly refused his assent to it. It is to be observed, however, that he does not reject the opinion of the earth's motion in so peremptory and dogmatical a manner as he is sometimes accused of doing : thus in the *Thema Cœli*

[2] *Opere di Giordano Bruno,* vol. i. p. 146.   [3] vol. i. p. 179.

he says, "The earth, then, being supposed to be at rest (for that now appears to us the *more true* opinion)." And in his tract *On the Cause of the Tides*, he says, "If the tide of the sea be the extreme and diminished limit of the diurnal motion of the heavens, it will follow that the earth is immovable; or at least that it moves with a much slower motion than the water." In the *Descriptio Globi Intellectualis* he gives his reasons for not accepting the heliocentric theory. "In the system of Copernicus there are many and grave difficulties: for the threefold motion with which he encumbers the earth is a serious inconvenience; and the separation of the sun from the planets, with which he has so many affections in common, is likewise a harsh step: and the introduction of so many immovable bodies into nature, as when he makes the sun and the stars immovable, the bodies which are peculiarly lucid and radiant; and his making the moon adhere to the earth in a sort of epicycle; and some other things which he assumes, are proceedings which mark a man who thinks nothing of introducing fictions of any kind into nature, provided his calculations turn out well." We have already explained that, in attributing *three* motions of the earth, Copernicus had presented his system encumbered with a complexity not really belonging to it. But it will be seen shortly, that Bacon's fundamental objection to this system was his wish for a system which could be supported by sound physical considerations; and it must be allowed, that at the period of which we are speaking, this had not yet been done in favour of the Copernican hypothesis. We may add, however, that it is not quite clear that Bacon was in full possession of the details of the astronomical systems which that of Copernicus was intended to supersede; and that thus he, perhaps, did not see how much less harsh were these fictions, as .he called them, than those which were the inevitable alternatives. Perhaps he might even be liable to a little of that indistinctness, with respect to strictly geometrical conceptions, which we have remarked in Aristotle. We can hardly otherwise account for his not seeing any use in resolving the apparently irregular motion of a planet into separate regular motions. Yet he speaks slightingly of this important step[4]. "The motion of planets, which is constantly talked of as the motion of regression, or renitency, from west to east, and which is ascribed to the planets as a proper motion, is not true; but only arises from appearance, from the greater advance of the starry heavens towards the west, by which the planets are left behind to the east." Undoubtedly those who spoke of such a motion of regression, were aware of this; but they saw how the motion was simplified by this way of conceiving it, which Bacon seems not to have seen. Though, therefore, we may admire Bacon for the

[4] *Thema Cœli*, p. 246.

stedfastness with which he looked forwards to physical astronomy as the great and proper object of philosophical interest, we cannot give him credit for seeing the full value and meaning of what had been done, up to his time, in Formal Astronomy.

Bacon's contemporary, Gilbert, whom he frequently praises as a philosopher, was much more disposed to adopt the Copernican opinions, though even he does not appear to have made up his mind to assent to the whole of the system. In his work, *De Magnete*, (printed 1600,) he gives the principal arguments in favour of the Copernican system, and decides that the earth revolves on its axis[5]. He connects this opinion with his magnetic doctrines; and especially endeavours by that means to account for the precession of the equinoxes. But he does not seem to have been equally confident of its annual motion. In a posthumous work, published in 1651, (*De Mundo Nostro Sublunari Philosophia Nova*) he appears to hesitate between the systems of Tycho and Copernicus[6]. Indeed, it is probable that at this period many persons were in a state of doubt on such subjects. Milton, at a period somewhat later, appears to have been still undecided. In the opening of the eighth book of the Paradise Lost, he makes Adam state the difficulties of the Ptolemaic hypothesis, to which the archangel Raphael opposes the usual answers; but

[5] Lib. vi. capp. 3, 4.   [6] Lib. ii. cap. 20.

afterwards suggests to his pupil the newer system :

> . . . . What if seventh to these
> The planet earth, so stedfast though she seem,
> Insensibly three different motions move?
>
> *Par. Lost*, B. viii.

Milton's leaning however, seems to have been for the new system; we can hardly believe that he would otherwise have conceived so distinctly, and described with such obvious pleasure, the motion of the earth :

> Or she from west her silent course advance
> With inoffensive pace, that spinning sleeps
> On her soft axle, while she paces even,
> And bears thee soft with the smooth air along.
>
> *Par. Lost*, B. viii.

Perhaps the works of the celebrated Bishop Wilkins tended more than any others to the diffusion of the Copernican system in England, since even their extravagancies drew a stronger attention to them. In 1638, when he was only twenty-four years old, he published a book entitled *The Discovery of a New World; or, a Discourse tending to prove that it is probable there may be another habitable World in the Moon; with a Discourse concerning* the possibility of a passage thither. The latter part of his subject was, of course, an obvious mark for the sneers and witticisms of critics. Two years afterwards, in 1640, appeared his *Discourse concerning a new Planet; tending to prove that it is probable our Earth is one of the Planets:* in which he urged the reasons in favour of the heliocentric system; and explained away the opposite arguments, especially those drawn from the supposed declarations of Scripture. Probably a good deal was done for the establishment of those opinions by Thomas Salusbury, who was a warm admirer of Galileo, and published, in 1661, a translation of several of his works bearing upon this subject. The mathematicians of this country, in the seventeenth century, as Napier and Briggs, Horrox and Crabtree, Oughtred and Ward, Wallis and Wren, were probably all decided Copernicans. Kepler dedicates one of his works to Napier, and Ward invented an approximate method of solving Kepler's problem, still known as "the simple elliptical hypothesis." Horrox wrote, and wrote well, in defence of the Copernican opinion, in his *Keplerian Astronomy defended and promoted*, composed (in Latin) probably about 1635, but not published till 1673, the author having died at the age of twenty-two, and his papers having been lost. But Salusbury's work was calculated for another circle of readers. "The book," he says in the introductory address, "being, for subject and design, intended chiefly for gentlemen, I have been as careless of using a studied pedantry in my style, as careful in contriving a pleasant and beautiful impression." In order, however, to judge of the advantage under which the Copernican system now came forwards, we must consider the additional evidence for it which was brought to light by Galileo's astronomical discoveries.

Sect. 3.—*The Heliocentric Theory confirmed by Facts.—Galileo's Astronomical Discoveries.*

THE long interval which elapsed between the last great discoveries made by the ancients and the first made by the moderns, had afforded ample time for the developement of all the important consequences of the ancient doctrines. But when the human mind had been thoroughly roused again into activity, this was no longer the course of events. Discoveries crowded on each other; one wide field of speculation was only just opened, when a richer promise tempted the labourers away into another quarter. Hence the history of this period contains the beginnings of many sciences, but exhibits none fully worked out into a complete or final form. Thus the science of statics, soon after its revival, was eclipsed and overlaid by that of dynamics; and the Copernican system, considered merely with reference to the views of its author, was absorbed in the commanding interest of physical astronomy.

Still, advances were made which had an important bearing on the heliocentric theory, in other ways than by throwing light upon its physical principles. I speak of the new views of the heavens which the Telescope gave: the visible inequalities of the moon's surface; the moon-like phases of the planet Venus; the discovery of the satellites of Jupiter, and of the ring of Saturn. These discoveries excited at the time the strongest interest; both from the novelty and beauty of the objects they presented to the sense; from the way in which they seemed to gratify man's curiosity with regard to the remote parts of the universe; and also from that of which we have here to speak, their bearing upon the conflict of the old and the new philosophy, the heliocentric and geocentric theories. It may be true, as Lagrange and Montucla say, that the laws which Galileo discovered in mechanics implied a profounder genius than the novelties he detected in the sky: but the latter naturally attracted the greater share of the attention of the world, and were matter of keener discussion.

It is not to our purpose to speak here of the details and of the occasion of the invention of the Telescope; it is well known that Galileo constructed his about 1609, and proceeded immediately to apply it to the heavens. The discovery of the Satellites of Jupiter was almost immediately the reward of this activity: and these were announced in his *Nuncius Sidereus*, published at Venice in 1610. The title of this work will best convey an idea of the claim it made to public notice: "The *Sidereal Messenger*, announcing great and very wonderful spectacles, and offering them to the consideration of every one, but especially of philosophers and astronomers; which have been observed by *Galileo Galilei*, &c. &c., by the assistance of a perspective glass lately invented by him; namely, in the face of the moon, in innumerable fixed stars in the milky-way, in nebulous stars, but especially in four planets which revolve round Jupiter at different intervals and periods with a wonderful celerity; which, hitherto not known to any one, the author has recently been the first to detect, and has decreed to call the *Medicean stars*."

The interest this discovery excited was intense: and men were at this period so little habituated to accommodate their convictions on matters of science to newly-observed facts, that several of "the paper-philosophers," as Galileo termed them, appear to have thought they could get rid of these new objects by writing books against them. The effect which the discovery had upon the reception of the Copernican system was immediately very considerable. It showed that the real universe was very different from that which ancient philosophers had imagined, and suggested at once the thought that it contained mechanism more various and more vast than had yet been conjectured. And when the system of the planet Jupiter thus offered to the bodily eye a model or image of the solar system according to the views of Copernicus, it supported the belief of such an arrangement of the planets, by an analogy all but irresistible. It thus, as a writer[7] of

[7] Sir J. Herschel.

our own times has said, "gave the *holding turn* to the opinions of mankind respecting the Copernican system." We may trace this effect in Bacon, even though he does not assent to the motion of the earth. "We affirm," he says[8], "the *sun-following arrangement* (solisequium) of Venus and Mercury; since it has been found by Galileo that Jupiter also has attendants."

The *Nuncius Sidereus* contained other discoveries which had the same tendency in other ways. The examination of the moon showed, or at least seemed to show, that she was a solid body, with a surface extremely rugged and irregular. This, though perhaps not bearing directly upon the question of the heliocentric theory, was yet a blow to the Aristotelians, who had, in their philosophy, made the moon a body of a kind altogether different from this, and had given an abundant quantity of reasons for the visible marks on her surface, all proceeding on these preconceived views. Others of his discoveries produced the same effect; for instance, the new stars invisible to the naked eye, and those extraordinary appearances called nebulæ.

But before the end of the year, Galileo had new information to communicate, bearing more decidedly on the Copernican controversy. This intelligence was indeed decisive with regard to the motion of Venus about the sun; for he found that that planet, in the course of her revolution, assumes the

[8] *Thema Cœli*, ix. p. 253.

same succession of phases which the moon exhibits in the course of a month.   This he expressed by a Latin verse :

Cynthiæ figuras æmulatur mater amorum :
The queen of love like Cynthia shapes her forms :

transposing the letters of this line in the published account, according to the practice of the age; which thus showed the ancient love for combining verbal puzzles with scientific discoveries, while it betrayed the newer feeling, of jealousy respecting the priority of discovery of physical facts.

It had always been a formidable objection to the Copernican theory that this appearance of the planets had not been observed.   The author of that theory had endeavoured to account for this, by supposing that the rays of the sun passed freely through the body of the planet; and Galileo takes occasion to praise him for not being deterred from adopting the system which, on the whole, appeared to agree best with the phenomena, by meeting with some appearances which it did not enable him to explain[9].   Yet while the fate of the theory was yet undecided, this could not but be looked upon as a weak point in its defences.

The objection, in another form also, was embarrassing alike to the Ptolemaic and Copernican systems.   Why, it was asked, did not Venus appear four times as large when near her perigee, as when near her apogee ?   The author of the epistle pre-

[9] L. U. K. *Life of Galileo*, p. 35.

fixed to Copernicus's work had taken refuge in this argument from the danger of being supposed to believe in the reality of the system ; and Bruno had attempted to answer it by saying, that luminous bodies were not governed by the same laws of perspective as opaque ones. But a more satisfactory answer now readily offered itself. Venus does not appear four times as large when she is four times as near, because her *bright part* is *not* four times as large, though her visible diameter is ; and as she is too small for us to see her shape with the naked eye, we judge of her size only by the quantity of light.

The other great discoveries made in the heavens by means of telescopes, as that of Saturn's ring and his satellites, the spots in the sun, and others, belong to the further progress of astronomy. But we may here observe, that this doctrine of the motion of Mercury and Venus about the sun was further confirmed by Kepler's observation of the transit of the former planet over the sun in 1631. Our countryman Horrox was the first person who, in 1639, had the satisfaction of seeing a transit of Venus.

These events are a remarkable instance of the way in which a discovery in art, (for at this period, the making of telescopes must be mainly so considered,) may influence the progress of science. We shall soon have to notice a still more remarkable example of the way in which two sciences (Astronomy and Mechanics) may influence and promote the progress of each other.

E E

Sect. 4.—The Copernican System opposed on Theological Grounds.

THE doctrine of the Earth's motion round the Sun, when it was asserted and promulgated by Copernicus, soon after 1500, excited no visible alarm among the theologians of his own time. Indeed, it was received with favour by the most intelligent ecclesiastics; and lectures in support of the heliocentric doctrine were delivered in the ecclesiastical colleges. But the assertion and confirmation of this doctrine by Galileo, about a century later, excited a storm of controversy, and was visited with severe condemnation. Galileo's own behaviour appears to have provoked the interference of the ecclesiastical authorities; but there must have been a great change in the temper of the times to make it possible for his adversaries to bring down the sentence of the Inquisition upon opinions which had been so long current without giving any serious offense (Q).

The heliocentric doctrine had for a century been making its way into the minds of thoughtful men, on the general ground of its simplicity and symmetry. Galileo appears to have thought that now, when these original recommendations of the system had been reinforced by his own discoveries and reasonings, it ought to be universally acknowledged as a truth and a reality. And when arguments against the fixity of the sun and the motion of the earth were adduced from the expressions of scripture, he could not be satisfied without maintaining his favourite opinion to be conformable to scripture as well as to philosophy; and he was very eager in his attempts to obtain from authority a declaration to this effect. The ecclesiastical authorities were naturally averse to express themselves in favour of a novel opinion, startling to the common mind, and contrary to the most obvious meaning of the words of the Bible ; and when they were compelled to pronounce, they decided against Galileo and his doctrines. He was accused before the Inquisition in 1615 ; but at that period the result was that he was merely recommended to confine himself to the mathematical reasonings upon the system, and to abstain from meddling with the scripture. Galileo's zeal for his opinions soon led him again to bring the question under the notice of the Pope, and the result was a declaration of the Inquisition that the doctrine of the earth's motion appeared to be contrary to the sacred scripture. Galileo was prohibited from defending and teaching this doctrine in any manner, and promised obedience to this injunction. But in 1632 he published his *Dialogo delli due Massimi Sistemi del Mondo, Tolemaico e Copernicano:*" and in this, he defended the heliocentric system by all the strongest arguments which its admirers used. Not only so, but he introduced into this *Dialogue* a character under the name of Simplicius, in whose mouth was put the defence of all the ancient dogmas, and who was represented as defeated at all points in the discussion ; and he prefixed to the *Dialogue* a notice, *To the Discreet Reader*, in which, in a vein of transparent irony, he assigned his reasons for the publication. " Some years ago," he says, " a wholesome edict was promulgated at Rome, which, in order to check the perilous scandals of the present age, imposed silence upon the Pythagorean opinion of the motion of the earth. There was not wanting," he adds, " persons who rashly asserted that this decree was the result, not of a judicious inquiry, but of a passion ill-informed ; and complaints were heard that counsellors, utterly unacquainted with astronomical observations, ought not to be allowed, with their undue prohibitions, to clip the wings of speculative intellects. At the hearing of rash lamentations like these, my zeal could not keep silence." And he then goes on to say that he wishes, by the publication of his *Dialogue*, to show that the subject had been fully examined at Rome. The result of this was that Galileo was condemned for his infraction of the injunction laid upon him in 1616 ; his *Dialogue* was prohibited ; he himself was commanded to abjure on his knees the doctrine which he had taught ; and this abjuration he performed (R).

This celebrated event must be looked upon rather as a question of decorum than a struggle in which the interests of truth and free inquiry were deeply concerned. The general acceptance of the Copernican System was no longer. a matter of doubt. Several persons in the highest positions, including the Pope himself, looked upon the doctrine with favourable eyes; and had shown their interest in Galileo and his discoveries. They had tried to prevent his involving himself in trouble by discussing the question on scriptural grounds. It is probable that his knowledge of those favourable dispositions towards himself and his opinions led him to suppose that the slightest colour of professed submission to the church in his belief would enable his arguments in favour of the system to pass unvisited: the notice which I have quoted, in which the irony is quite transparent and the sarcasm glaringly obvious, was deemed too flimsy a veil for the purpose of decency, and indeed must have aggravated the offense. But it is not to be supposed that the inquisitors believed Galileo's abjuration to be sincere, or even that they wished it to be so. It is stated that when Galileo had made his renunciation of the earth's motion, he rose from his knees, and stamping on the earth with his foot, said, *E pur si muove*—" and yet it *does* move." This is sometimes represented as the heroic soliloquy of a mind cherishing its conviction of the truth in spite of persecution: I think we may more naturally conceive it uttered as a playful epigram in the ear of a cardinal's secretary, with a full knowledge that it would be immediately repeated to his master.

The ecclesiastical authorities having once declared the doctrine of the earth's motion to be contrary to scripture and heretical, long adhered in form to this declaration, and did not allow the Copernican system to be taught in any other way than as a "hypothesis." The Padua edition of Galileo's works, published in 1744, contains the *Dialogue* which now, the editors say, "Esce finalmente alla luce colle debite license;" but they add, " quanto allo Quistione principale del moto della terra, anche noi ci conformiamo alla ritrazione et protesta dell' autore dichiarando nella piu solenne forma, che non però nè dee ammetersi se non come pura Ipotesi Mathematice, che serve a spiegare piu agevolamento certi fenomeni." And in the edition of Newton's *Principia*, published in 1760, by Le Sueur and Jacquier, of the Order of Minims, the editors prefix to the Third Book their *Declaratio*, that though Newton assumes the hypothesis of the motion of the earth, and therefore they had used similar language, they were, in doing this, assuming a character which did not belong to them. " Hinc alienam coacti sumus gerere personam." They add, " Cæterum latis a summis Pontificibus contra telluris motum Decretis, nos obsequi profitemur."

By thus making decrees against a doctrine which in the course of time was established as an indisputable scientific truth, the See of Rome was guilty of an unwise and unfortunate stretch of ecclesiastical authority. But though we do not hesitate to pronounce such a judgment on this case, we may add that there is a question of no small real difficulty, which the progress of science often brings into notice, as it did then. The Revelation on which our religion is founded, seems to declare, or to take for granted, opinions on points on which Science also gives her decision; and we then come to this dilemma,—that doctrines, established by a scientific use of reason, may seem to contradict the declarations of revelation, according to our view of its meaning;—and yet, that we cannot, in consistency with our religious views, make reason a judge of the truth of revealed doctrines. In the case of Astronomy, on which Galileo was called in question, the general sense of cultivated and sober-minded men has long ago drawn that distinction between religious and physical tenets, which is necessary to resolve this dilemma. On this point, it is reasonably held, that the phrases which are employed in Scripture respecting astronomical facts, are not to be made use of to guide our scientific opinions; they may be supposed to answer their end if they fall in with common notions, and are thus effectually subservient to the moral and religious import of revelation. But the establishment of this distinction was not accomplished without long and distressing controversies.

Nor, if we wish to include all cases in which the same dilemma may again come into play, is it easy to lay down an adequate canon for the purpose. For we can hardly foresee, beforehand, what part of the past history of the universe may eventually be found to come within the domain of science ; or what bearing the tenets, which science esta-blishes, may have upon our view of the provi-dential and revealed government of the world. But without attempting here to generalize on this sub-ject, there are two reflections which may be worth our notice : they are supported by what took place in reference to Astronomy on the occasion of which we are speaking; and may, at other periods, be applicable to other sciences.

In the first place, the meaning which any gene-ration puts upon the phrases of Scripture, depends, more than is at first sight supposed, upon the received philosophy of the time.   Hence, while men imagine that they are contending for Reve-lation, they are, in fact, contending for their own interpretation of Revelation, unconsciously adapted to what they believe to be rationally probable. And the new interpretation, which the new phi-losophy requires, and which appears to the older school to be a fatal violence done to the authority of religion, is accepted by their successors without the dangerous results which were apprehended. When the language of Scripture, invested with its new meaning, has become familiar to men, it is found that the ideas which it calls up, are quite as reconcileable as the former ones were, with the soundest religious views. And the world then looks back with surprize at the errour of those who thought that the essence of Revelation was involved in their own arbitrary version of some collateral circumstance. At the present day we can hardly conceive how reasonable men should have imagined that religious reflections on the stability of the earth, and the beauty and use of the luminaries which revolve round it, would be interfered with by its being acknowledged that this rest and motion are apparent only.

In the next place, we may observe that those who thus adhere tenaciously to the traditionary or arbitrary mode of understanding Scriptural expressions of physical events, are always strongly condemned by succeeding generations. They are looked upon with contempt by the world at large, who cannot enter into the obsolete difficulties with which they encumbered themselves; and with pity by the more considerate and serious, who know how much sagacity and right-mindedness are requisite for the conduct of philosophers and religious men on such occasions; but who know also how weak and vain is the attempt to get rid of the difficulty by merely denouncing the new tenets as inconsistent with religious belief, and by visiting the promulgators of them with severity such as the state of opinions and institutions may allow. The

prosecutors of Galileo are still held up to the scorn
and aversion of mankind; although, as we have
seen, they did not act till it seemed that their
position compelled them to do so, and then proceeded with all the gentleness and moderation
which were compatible with judicial forms.

*Sect. 5.—The Heliocentric Theory confirmed on
Physical considerations.—(Prelude to Kepler's
Astronomical Discoveries.)*

BY physical views, I mean, as I have already said,
those which depend on the causes of the motions
of matter, as, for instance, the consideration of the
nature and laws of the force by which bodies fall
downwards.   Such considerations were necessarily
and immediately brought under notice by the examination of the Copernican theory; but the loose
and inaccurate notions which prevailed respecting
the nature and laws of force, prevented, for some
time, all distinct reasoning on this subject, and
gave truth little advantage over errour.   The formation of a new Science, the Science of Motion
and its Causes, was requisite, before the heliocentric system could have justice done it with regard
to this part of the subject.

    This discussion was at first carried on, as was
to be expected, in terms of the received, that is,
the Aristotelian doctrines.   Thus, Copernicus says
that terrestrial things appear to be at rest when
they have a motion according to nature, that is,

a circular motion; and ascend or descend when they have, in addition to this, a rectilinear motion by which they endeavour to get into their own place. But his disciples soon began to question the Aristotelian dogmas, and to seek for sounder views by the use of their own reason. "The great argument against this system," says Mæstlin, "is that heavy bodies are said to move to the center of the universe, and light bodies from the center. But I would ask, where do we get this experience of heavy and light bodies? and how is our knowledge on these subjects extended so far that we can reason with certainty concerning the center of the whole universe? Is not the only residence and home of all the things which are heavy and light to us, the earth and the air which surrounds it? and what is the earth and the ambient air with respect to the immensity of the universe? It is a point, a punctule, or something, if there be anything, still less. As our light and heavy bodies tend to the center of our earth, it is credible that the sun, the moon, and the other lights, have a similar affection, by which they remain round as we see them, but none of these centers is necessarily the center of the universe."

The most obvious and important physical difficulty attendant upon the supposition of the motion of the earth was thus stated. If the earth move, how is it that a stone, dropped from the top of a high tower, falls exactly at the foot of the tower? since the tower being carried from west to east by the diurnal revolution of the earth, the stone must be left behind to the west of the place from which it was let fall. The proper answer to this was, that the motion which the falling body received from its tendency downwards was *compounded* with the motion which, before it fell, it had in virtue of the earth's rotation : but this answer could not be clearly made or apprehended, till Galileo and his pupils had established the laws of such compositions of motion arising from different forces. Rothman, Kepler, and other defenders of the Copernican system, gave their reply somewhat at a venture, when they asserted that the motion of the earth was communicated to bodies at its surface. Still, the facts which indicate and establish this truth are obvious, when the subject is steadily considered ; and the Copernicans soon found that they had the superiority of argument on this point as well as others. The attacks upon the Copernican system by Durret, Morin, Riccioli, and the defence of it by Galileo, Lansberg, Gassendi[10], left on all candid reasoners a clear impression in favour of the system. Morin attempted to stop the motion of the earth, which he called breaking its wings ; his *Alæ Terræ Fractæ* was published in 1643, and answered by Gassendi. And Riccioli, as late as 1653, in his *Almagestum Novum*, enumerated fifty-seven Copernican argu-

---

[10] *Del. A. M.* vol. i. p. 594.

ments, and pretended to refute them all : but such reasonings˙ now made no converts ; and by this time the mechanical objections to the motion of the earth were generally seen to be baseless, as we shall relate when we come to speak of the progress of mechanics as a distinct science. In the mean time, the beauty and simplicity of the heliocentric theory were perpetually winning the admiration even of those who, from one cause or other, refused their assent to it. Thus Riccioli, the last of its considerable opponents, allows its superiority in these respects ; and acknowledges (in 1653) that the Copernican belief appears rather to increase than diminish under the condemnation of the decrees of the Cardinals. He applies to it the lines of Horace[11] :

> Per damna per cædes, ab ipso
> Sumit opes animumque ferro.

> Untamed its pride, unchecked its course,
> From foes and wounds it gathers force.

We have spoken of the influence of the motion of the earth on the motions of bodies at its surface ; but the notion of a physical connexion among the parts of the universe was taken up by Kepler in another point of view, which would probably have been considered as highly fantastical, if the result had not been, that it led to by far the most magnificent and most certain train of truths which the whole expanse of human knowledge can show. I

[11] *Almag. Nov.* p. 102.

speak of the persuasion of the existence of numerical and geometrical laws connecting the distances, times, and forces of the bodies which revolve about the central sun That steady and intense conviction of this governing principle, which made its developement and verification the leading employment of Kepler's most active and busy life, cannot be considered otherwise than as an example of profound sagacity. That it was connected, though dimly and obscurely, with the notion of a central agency or influence of some sort, emanating from the sun, cannot be doubted. Kepler, in his first essay of this kind, the *Mysterium Cosmographicum*, says, " The motion of the earth, which Copernicus had proved by *mathematical* reasons, I wanted to prove by *physical*, or, if you prefer it, metaphysical." In the twentieth chapter of that work, he endeavours to make out some relation between the distances of the planets from the sun and their velocities. The inveterate yet vague notions of forces which preside in this attempt, may be judged of by such passages as the following :—" We must suppose one of two things : either that the moving spirits, in proportion as they are more removed from the sun, are more feeble ; or that there is one moving spirit in the center of all the orbits, namely, in the sun, which urges each body the more vehemently in proportion as it is nearer ; but in more distant spaces languishes in consequence of the remoteness and attenuation of its virtue."

We must not forget, in reading such passages, that they were written under a belief that force was requisite to keep up, as well as to change the motion of each planet; and that a body, moving in a circle, would *stop* when the force of the central point ceased, instead of moving off in a tangent to the circle, as we now know it would do. The force which Kepler supposes is a tangential force, in the direction of the body's motion, and nearly perpendicular to the radius; the force which modern philosophy has established, is in the direction of the radius, and nearly perpendicular to the body's path. Kepler was right no further than in his suspicion of a connexion between the cause of motion and the distance from the center; not only was his knowledge imperfect in all particulars, but his most general conception of the mode of action of a cause of motion was erroneous.

With these general convictions and these physical notions in his mind, Kepler endeavoured to detect numerical and geometrical relations among the parts of the solar system. After extraordinary labour, perseverance, and ingenuity, he was eminently successful in discovering such relations; but the glory and merit of interpreting them according to their physical meaning, was reserved for his greater successor, Newton.

CHAPTER IV.

INDUCTIVE EPOCH OF KEPLER.

Sect. 1.—*Intellectual Character of Kepler.*

SEVERAL persons[1], especially in recent times, who have taken a view of the discoveries of Kepler, appear to have been surprized and somewhat discontented that conjectures, apparently so fanciful and arbitrary as his, should have led to important discoveries. They seem to have been alarmed at the *Moral* that their readers might draw, from the tale of a Quest of Knowledge, in which the Hero, though fantastical and self-willed, and violating in his conduct, as they conceived, all right rule and sound philosophy, is rewarded with

---

[1] Laplace, *Précis. de l'Hist. d'Ast.* p. 94. " Il est affligeant pour l'esprit humain de voir ce grand homme, même dans ses dernières ouvrages, se complaire avec délices dans ses chimériques spéculations, et les regarder comme l'âme et la vie de l'astronomie.'
Hist. of Ast., L. U. K., p. 53. " This success [of Kepler] may well inspire with dismay those who are accustomed to consider experiment and rigorous induction as the only means to interrogate nature with success."
Life of Kepler, L. U. K., p. 14, " Bad philosophy." P. 15, " Kepler's miraculous good fortune in seizing truths across the wildest and most absurd theories." P. 54, " The danger of attempting to follow his method in the pursuit of truth."

the most signal triumphs. Perhaps one or two reflections may in some measure reconcile us to this result.

In the first place, we may observe that the leading thought which suggested and animated all Kepler's attempts was true, and we may add, sagacious and philosophical; namely, that there must be *some* numerical or geometrical relations among the times, distances, and velocities of the revolving bodies. of the solar system. This settled and constant conviction of an important truth regulated all the conjectures, apparently so capricious and fanciful, which he made and examined, respecting particular relations in the system.

In the next place, we may venture to say, that advances in knowledge are not commonly made without the previous exercise of some boldness and license in guessing. The discovery of new truths requires, undoubtedly, minds careful and scrupulous in examining what is suggested; but it requires, no less, such as are quick and fertile in suggesting. What is Invention, except the talent of rapidly calling before us many possibilities, and selecting the appropriate one? It is true, that when we have rejected all the inadmissible suppositions, they are quickly forgotten by most persons; and few think it necessary to dwell on these discarded hypotheses, and on the process by which they were condemned, as Kepler has done. But all who discover truths must have reasoned upon many errors, to obtain each truth; every accepted doctrine must have been one selected out of many candidates. In making many conjectures, which on trial proved erroneous, Kepler was no more fanciful or unphilosophical than other discoverers have been. Discovery is not a " cautious" or "rigorous" process, in the sense of abstaining from such suppositions. But there are great differences in different cases, in the facility with which guesses are proved to be errours, and in the degree of attention with which the errour and the proof are afterwards dwelt on. Kepler certainly was remarkable for the labour which he gave to such self-refutations, and for the candour and copiousness with which he narrated them; his works are in this way extremely curious and amusing; and are a very instructive exhibition of the mental process of discovery. But in this respect, I venture to believe, they exhibit to us the usual process (somewhat caricatured) of inventive minds: they rather exemplify the *rule* of genius than (as has generally been hitherto taught,) the *exception*. We may add, that if many of Kepler's guesses now appear fanciful and absurd, because time and observation have refuted them, others, which were at the time equally gratuitous, have been confirmed by succeeding discoveries in a manner which makes them appear marvellously sagacious; as, for instance, his assertion of the rotation of the sun on his axis, before the invention of the telescope, and his opinion that the obliquity of the

ecliptic was decreasing, but would, after a long-continued diminution, stop, and then increase again[2].
Nothing can be more just, as well as more poetically
happy, than Kepler's picture of the philosopher's
pursuit of scientific truth, conveyed by means of an
allusion to Virgil's shepherd and shepherdess :—

> Malo me Galatea petit, lasciva puella
> Et fugit ad salices et se cupit ante videri.
>
> Coy yet inviting, Galatea loves
> To sport in sight, then plunge into the groves ;
> The challenge given, she darts along the green,
> Will not be caught, yet would not run unseen.

We may notice as another peculiarity of Kepler's reasonings, the length and laboriousness of the
processes by which he discovered the errours of his
first guesses. One of the most important talents
requisite for a discoverer, is the ingenuity and skill
which devises means for rapidly testing false suppositions as they offer themselves. This talent
Kepler did not possess : he was not even a good
arithmetical calculator, often making mistakes,
some of which he detected and laments, while
others escaped him to the last. But his defects in
this respect were compensated by his courage and
perseverance in undertaking and executing such
tasks ; and, what was still more admirable, he never
allowed the labour he had spent upon any conjecture to produce any reluctance in abandoning
the hypothesis, as soon as he had evidence of its

[2] Bailly, *A. M.* iii. 175.

inaccuracy. The only way in which he rewarded himself for his trouble, was by describing to the world, in his lively manner, his schemes, exertions, and feelings.

The *mystical* parts of Kepler's opinions, as his belief in astrology, his persuasion that the earth was an animal, and many of the loose moral and spiritual as well as sensible analyses by which he represented to himself the powers which he supposed to prevail in the universe, do not appear to have interfered with his discovery, but rather to have stimulated his invention, and animated his exertions. Indeed, where there are clear scientific ideas on one subject in the mind, it does not appear that mysticism on others is at all unfavourable to the successful prosecution of research.

I conceive, then, that we may consider Kepler's character as containing the general features of the character of a scientific discoverer, though some of the features are exaggerated, and some too feebly marked. His spirit of invention was undoubtedly very fertile and ready, and this and his perseverance served to remedy his deficiency in mathematical artifice and method. But the peculiar physiognomy is given to his intellectual aspect by his dwelling in a most prominent manner on those erroneous trains of thought which other persons conceal from the world, and often themselves forget, because they find means of stopping them at the outset. In the beginning of his book (*Argumenta Capitum*) he says, "if Christopher Columbus, if Magellan, if the Portuguese when they narrate their wanderings, are not only excused, but if we do not wish these passages omitted, and should lose much pleasure if they were, let no one blame me for doing the same." Kepler's talents were a kindly and fertile soil, which he cultivated with abundant toil and vigour; but with great scantiness of agricultural skill and implements. Weeds and the grain throve and flourished side by side almost undistinguished; and he gave a peculiar appearance to his harvest, by gathering and preserving the one class of plants with as much care and diligence as the other.

Sect. 2.—Kepler's Discovery of his Third Law.

I SHALL now give some account of Kepler's speculations and discoveries. The first discovery which he attempted, the relation among the successive distances of the planets from the sun, was a failure; his doctrine being without any solid foundation, although propounded by him with great triumph, in a work which he called *Mysterium Cosmographicum*, and which was published in 1596. The account which he gives of the train of his thoughts on this subject, namely, the various suppositions assumed, examined, and rejected, is curious and instructive, for the reasons just stated; but we shall not dwell upon these essays, since they led only to an opinion now entirely abandoned. The doctrine which professed to give the true relation of the orbits of the different planets, was thus delivered[3] "The orbit of the earth is a circle; round the sphere to which this circle belong describe a dodecahedron; the sphere including this will give the orbit of Mars. Round Mars describe a tetrahedron; the circle including this will be the orbit of Jupiter. Describe a cube round Jupiter's orbit; the circle including this will be the orbit of Saturn. Now inscribe in the Earth's orbit an icosahedron; the circle inscribed in it will be the orbit of Venus.' Inscribe an octahedron in the orbit of Venus; the circle inscribed in it will be Mercury's orbit. This is the reason of the number of the planets." The five kinds of polyhedral bodies here mentioned are the only "regular solids."

But though this part of the *Mysterium Cosmographicum* was a failure, the same researches continued to occupy Kepler's mind; and twenty-two years later led him to one of the important rules known to us as "Kepler's laws;" namely, to the rule connecting the mean distances of the planets from the sun with the times of their revolutions. This rule is expressed in mathematical terms by saying that the squares of the periodic times are in the same proportion as the cubes of the distances; and was of great importance to Newton in leading him to the law of the sun's attractive force. We may properly consider this discovery as the sequel

[3] L. U. K. Kepler, 6.

of the train of thought already noticed. In the beginning of the *Mysterium*, Kepler had said, "In the year 1595, I brooded with the whole energy of my mind on the subject of the Copernican system. There were three things in particular of which I pertinaciously sought the causes why they are not other than they are; the number, the size, and the motion of the orbits." We have seen the nature of his attempt to account for the two first of these points. He had also made some essays to connect the motions of the planets with their distances, but with his success in this respect he was not himself completely satisfied. But in the fifth book of the *Harmonice Mundi*, published in 1619, he says, "What I prophesied two-and-twenty years ago as soon as I had discovered the five solids among the heavenly bodies; what I firmly believed before I had seen the *Harmonics* of Ptolemy; what I promised my friends in the title of this book (*On the most perfect Harmony of the Celestial Motions*), which I named before I was sure of my discovery; what sixteen years ago I regarded as a thing to be sought; that for which I joined Tycho Brahe, for which I settled in Prague, for which I have devoted the best part of my life to astronomical contemplations; at length I have brought to light, and have recognized its truth beyond my most sanguine expectations."

The rule thus referred to is stated in the third chapter of this fifth book. "It is," he says, "a most certain and exact thing that the proportion which exists between the periodic times of any two planets is precisely the sesquiplicate of the proportion of their mean distances; that is, of the radii of the orbits. Thus, the period of the earth is one year, that of Saturn thirty years; if any one trisect the proportion, that is, take the cube root of it, and double the proportion so found, that is, square it, he will find the exact proportion of the distances of the earth and of Saturn from the sun. For the cube root of 1 is 1, and the square of this is 1; and the cube root of 30 is greater than 3, and therefore the square of it is greater than 9. And Saturn at his mean distance from the sun is at a little more than 9 times the mean distance of the earth."

When we now look back at the time and exertions which the establishment of this law cost Kepler, we are tempted to imagine that he was strangely blind in not seeing it sooner. His object, we might reason, was to discover a law connecting the distances and the periodic times. What law of connexion could be more simple and obvious, we might say, than that one of these quantities should vary as some *power* of the other, or as some *root*, or as some combination of the two, which in a more general view, may still be called a *power?* And if the problem had been viewed in this way, the question must have occurred, to *what* power of the periodic times are the distances proportional? And the answer must have been, that they are proportional to the square of the cube root. This *ex-post-facto* obviousness of discoveries is a delusion to which we are liable with regard to many of the most important principles. In the case of Kepler, we may observe, that the process of connecting two classes of quantities by comparing their *powers,* is obvious only to those who are familiar with general algebraical views; and that in Kepler's time, algebra had not taken the place of geometry, as the most usual vehicle of mathematical reasoning. It may be added, also, that Kepler always sought his *formal* laws by means of *physical* reasonings; and these, though vague or erroneous, determined the nature of the mathematical connexion which he assumed. Thus in the *Mysterium* he had been led by his notions of moving virtue of the sun to this conjecture, among others, that, in the planets, the increase of the periods will be double of the difference of the distances; which supposition he found to give him an approach to the actual proportion of the distances, but one not sufficiently close to satisfy him.

The greater part of the fifth Book of the *Harmonics of the Universe* consists in attempts to explain various relations among the distances, times, and eccentricities of the planets, by means of the ratios which belong to certain concords and discords. This portion of the work is so complex and laborious, that probably few modern readers have

had courage to go through it.   Delambre[4] acknowledges that his patience often failed him during the
task; and subscribes to the judgment of Bailly;
"After this sublime effort, Kepler replunges himself
in the relations of music to the motions, the distance, and the eccentricities of the planets.   In all
these harmonic ratios there is not one true relation; in a crowd of ideas there is not one truth : he
becomes a man after being a spirit of light."   Certainly these speculations are of no value, but we
may look on them with toleration, when we recollect that Newton has sought for analogies between
the spaces occupied by the prismatic colours and
the notes of the gamut[5].   The numerical relations
of concords are so peculiar that we can easily suppose them to have other bearings than those which
first offer themselves.

It does not belong to my present purpose to
speak at length of the speculations concerning the
forces producing the celestial motions by which
Kepler was led to this celebrated law, or of those
which he deduced from it, and which are found in
the *Epitome Astronomiæ Copernicanæ*, published
1622.   In that work also (p. 554), he extended this
law, though in a loose manner, to the satellites of
Jupiter.   These *physical* speculations were only a
vague and distant prelude to Newton's discoveries;
and the law, as a *formal* rule, was complete in
itself.   We must now attend to the history of

[4] *A. M.* a. 358.   [5] *Opticks*, B. 2. p. iv. Obs. 5.

the other two laws with which Kepler's name is associated.

Sect. 3.—Kepler's Discovery of his First and Second Laws.—Elliptical Theory of the Planets.

THE propositions designated as Kepler's first and second laws are these: that the orbits of the planets are elliptical; and that the areas described, or *swept*, by lines drawn from the sun to the planet are proportional to the times employed in the motion.

The occasion of the discovery of these laws was the attempt to reconcile the theory of Mars to the theory of eccentrics and epicycles; the event of it was the complete overthrow of that theory, and the establishment, in its stead, of the Elliptical Theory of the planets. Astronomy was now ripe for such a change. As soon as Copernicus had taught men that the orbits of the planets were to be referred to the sun, it obviously became a question, what was the true form of these orbits, and the rule of motion of each planet in its own orbit. Copernicus represented the motions in longitude by means of eccentrics and epicycles, as we have already said; and the motions in latitude by certain *librations*, or alternate elevations and depressions of epicycles. If a mathematician had obtained a collection of true positions of a planet, the form of the orbit, and the motion of the star would have been determined with reference to the sun as well as to the earth; but this was not possible, for though the *geocentric* position, or the direction in which the planet was seen, could be observed, its distance from the earth was not known.   Hence, when Kepler attempted to determine the orbit of a planet, he combined the observed geocentric places with successive modifications of the theory of epicycles, till at last he was led, by one step after another, to change the epicyclical into the elliptical theory.   We may observe, moreover, that at every step he endeavoured to support his new suppositions by what he called, in his fanciful phraseology, " sending into the field a reserve of new physical reasonings on the rout and dispersion of the veterans (s) :" that is, by connecting his astronomical hypotheses with new imaginations, when the old ones became untenable.   We find, indeed, that this is the spirit in which the pursuit of knowledge is generally carried on with success : those men arrive at truth who eagerly endeavour to connect remote points of their knowledge, not those who stop cautiously at each point till something compels them to go beyond it.

Kepler joined Tycho Brahe at Prague in 1600, and found him and Longomontanus busily employed in correcting the theory of Mars; and he also then entered upon that train of researches which he published in 1609 in his extraordinary work *On the Motions of Mars*.   In this work, as ·in others, he gives an account, not only of his success, but of his failures, explaining, at length, the various suppositions which he had made, the notions by which he had been led to invent or to entertain them, the processes by which he had proved their falsehood, and the alternations of hope and sorrow, of vexation and triumph, through which he had gone.   It will not be necessary for us to cite many passages of these kinds, curious and amusing as they are.

One of the most important truths contained in the motions of Mars is the discovery that the plane of the orbit of the planet should be considered with reference to the sun itself, instead of referring it to any of the other centers of motion which the eccentric hypothesis introduced; and that, when so considered, it had none of the librations which Ptolemy and Copernicus had attributed to it.   The fourteenth chapter of the second part asserts, "'Plana eccentricorum esse ἀτάλαντα;'" that the planes are *unlibrating;* retaining always the same inclination to the ecliptic, and the same *line of nodes.*   With this step Kepler appears to have been justly delighted.   His reflections on it are very philosophical.   "Copernicus," he says, "not knowing the value of what he possessed (his system), undertook to represent Ptolemy, rather than Nature, to which, however, he had approached more nearly than any other person.   For being rejoiced that the quantity of the latitude of each planet was increased by the approach of the earth to the planet, according to his theory, he did not venture to reject the rest of Ptolemy's increase of latitude, but in order to express it, devised librations of the planes of the eccentric, depending not upon its own eccentric, but (most improbably) upon the orbit of the earth, which has nothing to do with it. I always fought against this impertinent tying to- gether of two orbits, even before I saw the obser- vations of Tycho ; and I therefore rejoice much that in this, as in others of my preconceived opinions, the observations were found to be on my side." Kepler established his point by a fair and laborious calculation of the results of observations of Mars made by himself and Tycho Brahe; and had a right to exult when the result of these cal- culations confirmed his views of the symmetry and simplicity of nature.

We may judge of the difficulty of casting off the theory of eccentrics and epicycles, by recollect- ing that Copernicus did not do it at all, and that Kepler only did it after repeated struggles; the history of which occupies thirty-nine chapters of his book. At the end of them he says, " This prolix disputation was necessary, in order to pre- pare the way to the natural form of the equations, of which I am now to treat[6]. My first errour was, that the path of a planet is a perfect circle ;—an opinion which was a more mischievous thief of my time, in proportion as it was supported by the authority of all philosophers, and apparently agree-

[6] *De Stellâ Martis*, iii. 40.

able to metaphysics." But before he attempts to correct this erroneous part of his hypothesis he sets about discovering the law according to which the different. parts of the orbit are described in the case of the earth, in which case the eccentricity is so small that the effect of the oval form is insensible. The result of this inquiry was[7] the Rule, that the time of describing any arc of the orbit is proportional to the area intercepted between the curve and two lines drawn to the extremities of the arc. It is to be observed that this rule, at first, though it had the recommendation of being selected after the unavoidable abandonment of many, which were suggested by the notions of those times, was far from being adopted upon any very rigid or cautious grounds. A rule had been proved at the apsides of the orbit, by calculation from observations, and had then been extended by conjecture to other parts of the orbit; and the rule of the areas was only an approximate and inaccurate mode of representing this rule, employed for the purpose of brevity and convenience, in consequence of the difficulty of applying, geometrically, that which Kepler now conceived to be the true rule, and which required him to find the sum of the lines drawn from the sun to *every* point of the orbit. When he proceeded to apply this rule to Mars, in whose orbit the oval form is

[7] Ibid. p. 194.

*

much more marked, additional difficulties came in his way; and here again the true supposition, that the *oval* is of that special kind called *ellipse*, was adopted at first only in order to simplify calculation[8], and the deviation from exactness in the result was attributed to the inaccuracy of those approximate processes. The supposition of the oval had already been forced upon Purbach in the case of Mercury, and upon Reinhold in the case of the Moon. The center of the epicycle was made to describe an egg-shaped figure in the former case, and a lenticular figure in the latter[9].

It may serve to show the kind of labour by which Kepler was led to his result, if we here enumerate, as he does in his forty-seventh chapter[10], six hypotheses, on which he calculated the longitudes of Mars, in order to see which best agreed with observation.

1.   The simple eccentricity.

2.   The bisection of the eccentricity, and the duplication of the superior part of the equation.

3.   The bisection of the eccentricity and a stationary point of equations, after the manner of Ptolemy.

4.   The vicarious hypothesis by a free section of the eccentricity made to agree as nearly as possible with the truth.

[8] *De Stellâ Martis*, iv. c. 47.   [9] L. U. K. Kepler, p. 30.

[10] *De Stellâ Martis*, p. 228.

5. The physical hypothesis on the supposition of a perfect circle.

6. The physical hypothesis on the supposition of a perfect ellipse.

By the physical hypothesis, he meant the doctrine that the time of a planet's describing any part of its orbit is proportional to the distance of the planet from the sun, for which supposition, as we have said, he conceived that he had assigned physical reasons.

The two last hypotheses came the nearest to the truth, and differed from it only by about eight minutes, the one in excess and the other in defect. And, after being much perplexed by this remaining error, it at last occurred to him[11] that he might take another ellipsis, exactly intermediate between the former one and the circle, and that this must give the path and the motion of the planet. Making this assumption, and taking the areas to represent the times, he now saw[12] that both the longitude and the distances of Mars would agree with observation to the requisite degree of accuracy. The rectification of the former hypothesis, when thus stated, may, perhaps, appear obvious. And Kepler informs us that he had nearly been anticipated in this step. (c. 55.) "David Fabricius, to whom I had communicated my hypothesis of cap. 45, was able, by his observations, to show that it erred in

[11] *De Stellâ Martis*, c. 58.   [12] Ibid. p. 235.

making the distances too short at mean longitudes;
of which he informed me by letter while I was
labouring, by repeated efforts, to discover the true
hypothesis. So nearly did he get the start of me
in detecting the truth." But this was less easy
than it might seem. When Kepler's first hypothesis
was enveloped in the complex construction requisite in order to apply it to each point of the
orbit, it was far more difficult to see where the
errour lay, and Kepler hit upon it only by noticing
the coincidences of certain numbers, which, as he
says, raised him as if from sleep, and gave him
a new light. We may observe, also, that he was
perplexed to reconcile this new view, according to
which the planet described an exact ellipse, with
his former opinion, which represented the motion
by means of libration in an epicycle. "This," he
says, "was my greatest trouble, that, though I
considered and reflected till I was almost mad, I
could not find why the planet to which, with so
much probability, and with such an exact accordance of the distances, the libration in the diameter
of the epicycle was attributed, should, according
to the indication of the equations, go in an elliptical path. What an absurdity on my part! as if
libration in the diameter might not be a way to
the ellipse!"

Another scruple respecting this theory arose.
from the impossibility of solving, by any geome-

trical construction, the problem to which Kepler was thus led, namely, " to divide the area of a semi-circle in a given ratio, by a line drawn from any point of the diameter." This is still termed " Kepler's Problem," and is, in fact, incapable of exact geometrical solution. As, however, the calculation can be performed, and, indeed, was performed by Kepler himself, with a sufficient degree of accuracy to show that the elliptical hypothesis is true, the insolubility of this problem is a mere mathematical difficulty in the deductive process, to which Kepler's inductions gave rise.

Of Kepler's physical reasonings we shall speak more at length on another occasion. His numerous and fanciful hypotheses had discharged their office, when they had suggested to him his many lines of laborious calculation, and encouraged him under the exertions and disappointments to which these led. The result of this work was the formal laws of the motion of Mars, established by a clear in-duction, since they represented, with sufficient ac-curacy, the best observations. And we may allow that Kepler was entitled to the praise which he claims in the motto on his first leaf. Ramus had said that if any one would construct an astronomy without hypothesis he would be ready to resign to him his professorship in the University of Paris. Kepler quotes this passage, and adds, "it is well, Ramus, that you have run from this pledge, by

quitting life and your professorship[13]; if you held
it still, I should, with justice, claim it." This was
not saying too much, since he had entirely overturned the hypothesis of eccentrics and epicycles,
and had obtained a theory which was a mere representation of the motions and distances as they
were observed.

[13] Ramus perished in the Massacre of St. Bartholomew.

CHAPTER V.

SEQUEL TO THE EPOCH OF KEPLER. RECEPTION, VERIFICATION, AND EXTENSION OF THE ELLIPTICAL THEORY.

Sect. 1.—*Application of the Elliptical Theory to the Planets.*

THE extension of Kepler's discoveries concerning the orbit of Mars to the other planets, obviously offered itself as a strong probability, and was confirmed by trial. This was made in the first place upon the orbit of Mercury; which planet, in consequence of the largeness of its eccentricity, exhibits more clearly than the others the circumstances of the elliptical motion. These and various other supplementary portions of the views to which Kepler's discoveries had led, appeared in the latter part of his *Epitome Astronomiæ Copernicanæ*, published in 1622.

The real verification of the new doctrine concerning the orbits and motions of the heavenly bodies was, of course, to be found in the construction of tables of those motions, and in the continued comparison of such tables with observation. Kepler's discoveries had been founded, as we have

seen, principally on Tycho's observations.   Longomontanus (so called as being a native of Langberg
in Denmark,) published in 1621 in his *Astronomia
Danica*, tables founded upon the theories as well
as the observations of his countryman.   Kepler[1] in
1627 published his tables of the planets, which he
called *Rudolphine Tables*, the result and application of his own theory.   In 1633, Lansberg, a Bel-
gian, published also *Tabulæ Perpetuæ*, a work which
was ushered into the world with considerable pomp
and pretension, and in which the author cavils very
keenly at Kepler and Brahe.   We may judge of the
impression made upon the astronomical world in
general by these rival works, from the account
which our countryman Jeremy Horrox has given of
their effect on him.   He had been seduced by the
magnificent promises of Lansberg, and the praises
of his admirers, which are prefixed to the work,
and was persuaded that the common opinion which
preferred Tycho and Kepler to him was a prejudice.
In 1636, however, he became acquainted with Crabtree, another young astronomer, who lived in the
same part of Lancashire.   By him Horrox was
warned that Lansberg was not to be depended on;
that his hypotheses were vicious, and his observations falsified or forced into agreement with his
theories.   He then read the works and adopted the
opinions of Kepler; and after some hesitation which
he felt at the thought of attacking the object of his

[1] *Rheticus, Narratio*, p. 98.

former idolatry, he wrote a dissertation on the points of difference between them. It appears that, at one time, he intended to have offered himself as the umpire who was to adjudge the prize of excellence among the three rival theories of Longomontanus, Kepler and Lansberg; and, in allusion to the story of ancient mythology, his work was to have been called *Paris Astronomicus;* we easily see that he would have given the golden apple to the Keplerian goddess. Succeeding observations confirmed his judgment: and the *Rudolphine Tables*, thus published seventy-six years after the Prutenic, which were founded on the doctrines of Copernicus, were for a long time those universally used.

Sect. 2.—*Application of the Elliptical Theory to the Moon.*

THE reduction of the moon's motions to rule was a harder task than the formation of planetary tables, if accuracy was required; for the moon's motion is affected by an incredible number of different and complex inequalities, which, till their law is detected, appear to defy all theory. Still, however, progress was made in this work. The most important advances were due to Tycho Brahe. In addition to the first and second inequalities of the moon (the *Equation of the Center*, known very early, and the *Evection* which Ptolemy had discovered), Tycho proved that there was another inequality, which he termed the *Variation*[2], which depended on the moon's position with respect to the sun, and which at its maximum was forty minutes and a half, about a quarter of the evection. He also perceived, though not very distinctly, the necessity of another correction of the moon's place depending on the sun's longitude, which has since been termed the *Annual Equation*.

These steps concerned the Longitude of the Moon; Tycho also made important advances in the knowledge of the Latitude. The Inclination of the Orbit had hitherto been assumed to be the same at all times; and the motion of the Node had been supposed uniform. He found that the inclination increased and diminished by twenty minutes, according to the position of the line of nodes; and that the nodes, though they regress upon the whole, sometimes go forwards and sometimes go backwards.

Tycho's discoveries concerning the moon are given in his *Progymnasmata*, which was published in 1603, two years after the author's death. He represents the moon's motion in longitude by means of certain combinations of epicycles and eccentrics. But after Kepler had shown that such devices are to be banished from the planetary system, it was

---

[2] We have seen (Chap. III), that Aboul-Wefa, in the tenth century, had already noticed this inequality; but his discovery had been entirely forgotten long before the time of Tycho, and has only recently been brought again into notice.

impossible not to think of extending the elliptical theory to the moon. Horrox succeeded in doing this; and in 1638 sent this essay to his friend Crabtree. It was published in 1673, with the numerical elements requisite for its application added by Flamsteed. Flamsteed had also (in 1671 and 2) compared this theory with observation, and found that it agreed far more nearly than the *Philolaic Tables* of Bullialdus, or the *Carolinian Tables* of Street (*Epilogus ad Tabulas*). Moreover Horrox, by making the center of the ellipse revolve in an epicycle, gave an explanation of the evection, as well as of the equation of the center (T).

Modern astronomers, by calculating the effects of the perturbing forces of the solar system, and comparing their calculations with observation, have added many new corrections or equations to those known at the time of Horrox; and since the motions of the heavenly bodies were even then affected by these variations as yet undetected, it is clear that the tables of that time must have shown some errours when compared with observation. These errours much perplexed astronomers, and naturally gave rise to the question whether the motions of the heavenly bodies really were exactly regular, or whether they were not affected by accidents as little reducible to rule as wind and weather. Kepler had held the opinion of the *casualty* of such errours; but Horrox, far more philosophically, argues against this opinion, though he allows that he is much

embarrassed by the deviations.   His arguments
show a singularly clear and strong apprehension of
the features of the case, and their real import.   He
says[3], " these errours of the tables are alternately in
excess and defect; how could this constant compensation happen if they were casual?   Moreover,
the alternation from excess to defect is most rapid
in the moon, most slow in Jupiter and Saturn, in
which planets the errour continues sometimes for
years.   If the errours were casual, why should they
not last as long in the moon as in Saturn?   But if
we suppose the tables to be right in the mean
motions, but wrong in the equations, these facts are
just what must happen; since Saturn's inequalities
are of long period, while those of the moon are
numerous, and rapidly changing."   It would be
impossible, at the present moment, to reason better
on this subject; and the doctrine, that all the apparent irregularities of the celestial motions are really
regular, was one of great consequence to establish
at this period of the science.

Sect. 3.—Causes of the further Progress of Astronomy.

WE are now arrived at the time when theory and
observation sprang forwards with emulous energy.
The physical theories of Kepler, and the reasónings
of other defenders of the Copernican theory, led

[3] *Astron. Kepler.* Proleg. p. 17.

inevitably, after some vagueness and perplexity, to a sound science of mechanics; and this science in time gave a new face to astronomy. But in the mean time, while mechanical mathematicians were generalizing from the astronomy already established, astronomers were accumulating new facts, which pointed the way to new theories and new generalizations. Copernicus, while he had established the permanent length of the year, had confirmed the motion of the sun's apogee, and had shown that the eccentricity of the earth's orbit, and the obliquity of the ecliptic, were gradually, though slowly, diminishing. Tycho had accumulated a store of excellent observations. These, as well as the laws of the motions of the moon and planets already explained, were materials on which the Mechanics of the Universe was afterwards to employ its most matured powers. In the mean time, the telescope had opened other new subjects of notice and speculation; not only confirming the Copernican doctrine by the phases of Venus, and the analogical examples of Jupiter and Saturn, which with their satellites appeared like models of the solar system; but disclosing unexpected objects, as the ring of Saturn, and the spots of the sun. The art of observing made rapid advances, both by the use of the telescope, and by the sounder notions of the construction of instruments which Tycho introduced. Copernicus had laughed at Rheticus, when he was disturbed about single minutes; and declared that if he could be sure to

ten minutes of space, he should be as much delighted as Pythagoras was when he discovered the
property of the right-angled triangle.   But Kepler
founded the revolution which he introduced on a
quantity less than this. "Since," he says[4], " the divine
goodness has given us in Tycho an observer so exact
that this errour of eight minutes is impossible, we
must be thankful to God for this, and turn it to
account.   And these eight minutes, which we must
not neglect, will, of themselves, enable us to recon-
struct the whole of astronomy."   In addition to
other improvements, the art of numerical calculation made an inestimable advance by means of
Napier's invention of Logarithms; and the progress
of other parts of pure mathematics was proportional to the calls which astronomy and physics
made upon them.

The exactness which observation had attained
enabled astronomers both to verify and improve the
existing theories, and to study the yet unsystema-
tized facts. The science was, therefore, forced along
by a strong impulse on all sides.   We now proceed
to speak of the new path into which this pressure
forced it; but, in order to this, we must first trace
the rise and progress of the Science of Mechanics.

[4] *De Stellâ Martis*, c. 19.

NOTES TO BOOK V.

(P.) p. 403. THE doctrine of the motion of the earth was first publicly maintained at Rome by Wilmanstadt, who professed to have received it from Copernicus. See Venturi, *Essai sur les Ouvrages Physico-Mathematiques de Leonard da Vinci, avec des Fragmens tirés de ses Manuscrits apportes d'Italie.* Paris, 1797: and, as there quoted, *Marini Archiatri Pontificii*, Tom. II. p. 251.

Leonardo da Vinci himself, about 1510, explained how a body by describing a kind of spiral, might descend towards a revolving globe, so that its apparent motion relative to a point in the surface of the globe, might be in a straight line leading to the center. He thus showed that he had entertained in his thoughts the hypothesis of the earth's rotation, and was employed in removing the difficulties which accompanied this supposition, by means of the consideration of the composition of motions.

Regiomontanus (who died in 1476) is said to have been inclined to this hypothesis, but to have combated it *ex professo*[5].

(Q.) p. 418. It appears to me that the different degree of toleration accorded to the heliocentric theory in the time of Copernicus and of Galileo, must be ascribed in a great measure to the controversies and alarms which had in the mean time arisen out of the Reformation in

---

[5] Schoneri *Opera*, Part II. Art. 127.

religion, and which had rendered the Romish Church more jealous of innovations in received opinions than it had previously been. It appears too that the discussion of such novel doctrines was, at that time at least, less freely tolerated in Italy than in other countries. In 1597, Kepler writes to Galileo thus : " Confide Galilæe et progredere. Si bene conjecto, pauci de præcipuis Europæ Mathematicis a nobis secedere volent ; tanta vis est veritatis. Si tibi Italia minus est idonea ad publicationem et si aliqua habitures es impedimenta, forsan Germania nobis hanc libertatem concedet." *Venturi, Mem. di Galileo.* Vol. I. p. 19.

I would not however be understood to assert the condemnation of new doctrines in science to be either a general or a characteristic practice of the Romish Church. Certainly the intelligent and cultivated minds of Italy, and many of the most eminent of her ecclesiastics among them, have always been the foremost in promoting and welcoming the progress of science : and, as I have stated, there were found, among the Italian ecclesiastics of Galileo's time many of the earliest and most enlightened adherents of the Copernican system. The condemnation of the doctrine of the earth's motion, is, so far as I am aware, the only instance in which the Papal authority has pronounced a decree upon a point of science. And the most candid of the adherents of the Romish Church condemn the assumption of authority in such matters, which in this one instance, at least, was made by the ecclesiastical tribunals. The author of the *Ages of Faith* (Book VIII. p. 248) says, " A congregation, it is to be lamented, declared the new system to be opposed to Scripture, and therefore heretical." In more recent times, as I have elsewhere remarked[6] the Church of Authority and the Church of Private Judgment have each its peculiar temptations and dangers, when there appears to be a discrepance between Scripture and Philosophy.

But though we may acquit the popes and cardinals in Galileo's time of stupidity and perverseness in rejecting manifest scientific truths, I do not see how we can acquit them of dissimulation and duplicity. Those persons appear to me to defend in a very strange manner the conduct of the ecclesiastical authorities of that period, who boast of the liberality with which Copernican professors were placed by them in important offices, at the very time when the motion of the earth had been declared by the same authorities contrary to Scripture. Such merits cannot make us approve of their conduct in demanding from Galileo a public recantation of the system which they thus favoured in other ways, and which they had repeatedly told Galileo he might hold as much as he pleased. Nor can any one, reading the plain language of the sentence passed upon Galileo, and of the abjuration forced from him, find any value in the plea which has been urged, that the opinion was denominated *a heresy* only in a wide, improper, and technical sense.

But if we are thus unable to excuse the conduct of Galileo's judges, I do not see how we can give our unconditional admiration to the philosopher himself. Perhaps the conventional decorum which, as we have seen, was required in treating of the Copernican system, may excuse or explain the furtive mode of insinuating his doctrines which he often employs, and which some of his

[6] *Phil. Ind. Sci.* Book x. Chap. 4.

historians admire as subtle irony, while others blame it as insincerity. But I do not see with what propriety Galileo can be looked upon as a "martyr of science." Undoubtedly he was very desirous of promoting what he conceived to be the cause of philosophical truth; but it would seem that, while he was restless and eager in urging his opinions, he was always ready to make such submissions as the spiritual tribunals required. He would really have acted as a martyr, if he had uttered his " e pur si muove," in the place of his abjuration, not after it. But in this case he would have been a martyr to a cause of which the merit was of a mingled character; for his own special and favourite share in the reasonings by which the Copernican system was supported, was the argument drawn from the flux and reflux of the sea, which argument is altogether false. He considered this as supplying a mechanical ground of belief, without which the mere astronomical reasons were quite insufficient; but in this case he was deserted by the mechanical sagacity which appeared in his other speculations.

(R.) p. 400. Throughout the course of the proceedings against him, Galileo was treated with great courtesy and indulgence. He was condemned to a nominal imprisonment. " Te damnamus ad formalem carcerem hujus S. officii ad tempus arbitrio nostro limitandum; et titulo poenitentia salutaris praecipimus ut tribus annis futuris recites semel in hebdomada septem psalmos penitentiales." But this confinement was reduced to his being placed under some slight restrictions, first at the house of Nicolini, the ambassador of his own sovereign, and afterwards at the country seat of Archbishop Piccolomini, one of his own warmest friends.

It has sometimes been asserted or insinuated that Galileo was subjected to bodily torture. An argument has been drawn from the expressions used in his sentence: " Cum vero nobis videretur non esse a te integram veritatem pronunciatam circa tuam intentionem; judicavimus necesse esse venire ad rigorosum examen tui, in quo respondisti catholicè." It has been argued by M. Libri (*Hist. des Sciences Mathematiques en Italie*, vol. iv. p. 259,) and M. Quinet (*L'Ultramontanisme*, iv. Leçon, p. 104,) that the *rigorosum examen* necessarily implies bodily torture, notwithstanding that no such thing is mentioned by Galileo and his contemporaries, and notwithstanding the consideration with which he was treated in all other respects: but M. Biot more justly remarks, (*Biogr. Univ.* Art. *Galileo*,) that such a procedure is incredible.

To the opinion of M. Biot, we may add that of Delambre, who rejects the notion of Galileo's having been put to the torture, as inconsistent with the general conduct of the authorities towards him, and as irreconcilable with the accounts of the trial given by Galileo himself, and by a servant of his, who never quitted him for an instant. He adds also, that it is inconsistent with the words of his sentence, "ne tuus iste gravis et perniciosus error ac transgressio remaneat *omnino impunitus;*" for the errour would have been already very far from impunity, if Galileo had been previously subjected to the rack. He adds, very reasonably, " il ne faut noircir personne sans preuve, pas même l'inquisition."

(s.) p. 444. I will insert this passage, as a specimen of Kepler's fanciful mode of narrating the defeats which he received in the war which he carried on with Mars.

" Dum in hunc modum de Martis motibus triumpho, eique ut planè devicto tabularum carceres et equationum compedes necto, diversis nuntiatur locis, futilem victoriam ut bellum totâ mole recrudescere. Nam domi quidem hostis ut captivus contemptus, rupit omnia equationum vincula, carceresque tabularum effregit. Foris speculatores profligerunt meas causarum physicarum arcessitas copias earumque jugum excusserunt resumtâ libertate. Jamque parum abfuit quia hostis fugitivus sese cum rebellibus suis conjungeret meque in desperationem adigeret : nisi raptim, nova rationum physicarum subsidia, fusis et palantibus veteribus, submisissem, et qua·se captivus proripuisset, omni diligentia, edoctus vestgiis ipsius nullâ morâ interpositâ inhæsisserem."

(T.) p. 457. ·Horrox (*Horrockes* as he himself spelt his name) gave a first sketch of his theory in letters to his friend Crabtree in 1638: in which the variation of the excentricity is not alluded to. But in Crabtree's letter to Gascoigne in·1642, he gives Horrox's rule concerning it ; and Flamsteed in his *Epilogue* to the Tables, published by Wallis along with Horrox's works in 1673, gave an explanation of the theory which made it amount very nearly to a revolution of the center of the ellipse in an epicycle. Halley afterwards made a slight alteration ; but hardly, I think, enough to justify Newton's assertion ; (*Princip.* Lib. iii. Prop. 35. Schol.) " Halleius centrum ellipseos in epicyclo locavit." See Baily's *Flamsteed*, p. 683.

END OF VOL. I.

ImTheStory.com

Lightning Source UK Ltd.
Milton Keynes UK
UKHW021103200720
366842UK00011B/2846